More Bucket List Adventures

next chapter travel

Australia to Europe by Sea, Greece, Türkiye & India by Rail

Emma Scattergood

What happens when you plan it, pack it... and just go.

Copyright © 2025 by Emma Scattergood

All rights reserved. No part of this publication may be reproduced, stored in a retrieval system, or transmitted in any form or by any means, electronic, mechanical, photocopying, recording, or otherwise, without prior written permission from the copyright holder.

The information in this book is true and complete to the best of the author's knowledge. It is intended for informational and entertainment purposes only. The author and publisher make no representations or warranties regarding the accuracy or applicability of the content and disclaim any liability for any loss or damage resulting from its use.

Cover design and interior formatting by 100Covers

Paperback ISBN 978-0-6453070-6-1

Ebook ISBN 978-0-6453070-7-8

Contents

Preface: (It's Not Always Easy Planning a Holiday) ix
Chapter 1: Catching a Train in Australia 1
Chapter 2: Sailing from Sydney to Perth 6
Chapter 3: Eight Days to Reach Mauritius 13
Chapter 4: Home of the Dodo 20
Chapter 5: On Safari in Africa 26
Chapter 6: On Top of the Table in Cape Town 34
Chapter 7: The Namibian Desert 42
Chapter 8: Santa Cruz de Tenerife 51
Chapter 9: Disappointed by Casablanca 57
Chapter 10: Discovering Gaudi in Barcelona 65
Chapter 11: Our Return to Malta 72
Chapter 12: What Santorini is Really Like 78
Chapter 13: We Made it to Athens 86
Chapter 14: Revisiting the Parthenon 92
Chapter 15: The Oracle of Delphi 100
Chapter 16: Nafplio and the Peloponnese Region of Greece 107
Chapter 17: Loutraki and the Corinth Canal 113
Chapter 18: Thessaloniki, Pella, Edessa and Naoussa 120
Chapter 19: The Bus to Bulgaria 130
Chapter 20: Wandering Sofia and Plovdiv 136
Chapter 21: The Overnight Train to Türkiye 141
Chapter 22: Exploring Incredible Istanbul 148
Chapter 23: Catching a Train to Ankara 157
Chapter 24: Not Ballooning in Cappadocia 165
Chapter 25: Traversing the Konya Plains 173

Chapter 26: The Overnight Train to Izmir 181
Chapter 27: Touring Ancient Ephesus 188
Chapter 28: From Pamukkale to Istanbul 193
Chapter 29: Farewell Türkiye 199
Chapter 30: Hello, Crazy India 205
Chapter 31: Exploring Delhi 210
Chapter 32: Journeying to Jaipur 218
Chapter 33: Having Fun in Rajasthan 223
Chapter 34: The Train to Ranthambore 230
Chapter 35: Searching for (Elusive) Tigers 237
Chapter 36: Agra and the Stunning Taj Mahal 243
Chapter 37: Surviving the Overnight Train to Varanasi 251
Chapter 38: Life Near the Ganges 257
Chapter 39: Back in Delhi 263
Chapter 40: Homeward Bound 269

Author's Note 273
Previous Books by Emma Scattergood 275
About the Author 279

Also By Emma Scattergood

Bucket Lists and Walking Sticks
Itchy Feet & Bucket Lists
My Breast Cancer Adventure

You do not find yourself.
You make yourself.
Step by step.
Choice by choice.

PREFACE

(It's Not Always Easy Planning a Holiday)

October 2023

Determined to reclaim a life breast cancer has prematurely tried to extinguish, I find myself once again sitting at a computer.

A little over twelve months ago, I had booked a one-way cruise to Greece for my walking stick-wielding husband and myself. Departing in late March 2024, we would be sailing on one of Richard Branson's elegant new Virgin Voyages ships, travelling via Asia and the Suez Canal. I made this booking shortly after finishing chemotherapy, while still undergoing radiation treatment. It was my desperate attempt to return to a life pre-cancer, pre-treatment, pre-after effects. To recover a way of living I loved.

In the months since, the itinerary had grown to include a second, short cruise to Italy and Türkiye, as well as a tour of Israel, a country I had longed to visit. I had not yet worked out how we would be returning home to Australia, but I had named the adventure Itinerary One, and it lived in an Excel spreadsheet. A beautiful, meticulously detailed Excel spreadsheet.

Given that we do not like group tours and try to avoid travel agents, I am often asked how we organise our adventures. Well, Excel is the answer. Lovely, dependable Excel.

Right now, Itinerary One shows countries, transits and dates – or, more specifically, when, how and where we will be. It is also tracking hotel bookings, visa requirements, currency fluctuations, immunisations, transport links, SIM cards and costs – everything required to plan an independent journey.

It is fortunate everything is so well organised, website addresses saved, Booking.com so adaptable – because last week, Hamas attacked Israel, and it is looking increasingly unlikely that a visit there will be possible. Changes are needed, which is why I am back at the computer and about to birth Itinerary Two.

January 2024

Itinerary Two is looking plumper than a Christmas turkey. It now spans three months. We will still sail from Australia in late March, which is in just over two months' time, and arrive in Greece in early May. But the second cruise and Israel are gone.

Instead, after two weeks exploring the Greek mainland, we will bus to Bulgaria, train to Türkiye, then fly to Egypt. Inspired by the TV show, *Joanna Lumley's Silk Road Adventure*, captivated by Turkish baths, the history of Constantinople, and morning skies filled with hot-air balloons, Türkiye has long been on my wish list. I am looking forward to exploring its various regions before heading to Egypt. I do not think I need to explain why we are going there – doesn't everyone want to visit Egypt?

But despite the excitement and planning, things are not as straightforward as I would like. Hostilities in the Middle East are escalating, and travel along the Red Sea and through the Suez Canal is starting to look dangerous. Even visiting Egypt is becoming a concern. Today, Smartraveller, the Australian government's travel advisory website, raised Egypt's travel risk from Level 2, 'Exercise a high level of caution', to Level 3, 'Reconsider your need to travel'.

Given this warning, it feels prudent to make changes. It looks like it's back to the computer and time for a new itinerary.

Early February 2024

With just seven weeks to go, Itinerary Three is looking great. Dropping Egypt was a tremendous disappointment and the replacement country needed to be something remarkable to soften the blow. Somehow, India, a place both of us had always wanted to visit, though admittedly we are a little apprehensive, slipped its way into our thoughts and, eventually, found its way onto the spreadsheet.

Richard's cruise via the Suez Canal, along with our plans to explore Greece, Bulgaria and Türkiye, remain intact. India will now be the exciting stopover on our long journey home.

We have been fortunate with cancellations. I only ever use Booking.com when securing accommodation and always make sure there are no cancellation fees until the day before arrival. Cancelling our Egypt hotels was easy, and since we had not yet booked any flights or transport, there was nothing to lose there.

However, I am still uneasy. Events in the Middle East are not improving, only escalating. A Yemen-based Islamist group, the Houthis, are attacking ships in the Red Sea. Many cargo ships, and most passenger vessels, are now forgoing the Suez Canal and, instead, diverting around Africa.

It does not feel right, or safe, to be embarking on a cruise that will take us through a battle hotspot – yet that is what we are about to do. There are also our physical limitations to consider. Though only in our fifties, we are not exactly spry – not quite up for war zones. Darryl, my husband, still lives with life-altering injuries from a motorbike accident in 2011 that left him hospitalised for five months. I am still undergoing treatment following a 2022 Stage 3 breast cancer diagnosis.

Pushing aside concerns of unpredictable health and the threat of missiles overhead, many of the planning items on our spreadsheet are complete, or close to it.

We have booked most of our cruise shore excursions, learnt about eSIMs, downloaded Busbud to book our Greece-to-Bulgaria bus, and used the website The Man in Seat Sixty-One to research sleeper trains into Türkiye – though that is proving trickier than expected.

I am researching currencies and will buy them before we leave. I have a rough idea of where we will be visiting in Bulgaria, I am working with a local in Türkiye, and I am communicating with a tour operator in India. While we prefer not to use agencies, independent, in-country operators are sometime a necessary exception.

We are even on top of our immunisations, though this was not without drama. One hour after receiving two injections covering diphtheria, tetanus, whooping cough, hepatitis, influenza and COVID-19, Darryl was dizzy, nauseous and knocked flat with a pounding headache.

My medications also need attention. Alongside a host of self-prescribed supplements and letrozole, a hormone-blocking medication used to fight estrogen-positive breast cancer, I am also on abemaciclib (brand name Verzenio). While not yet fully approved for use in Australia, I am fortunate to be part of a special program open to just three hundred patients fighting advanced or metastatic breast cancer. This means I receive the medication for free and it arrives in the post every thirty days.

Given that we will be away for three months or more, I am trying to convince the company that supplies this medication to send me enough in advance. It has been a bit of a battle convincing them and, along with trimming down my supplements to manageable, transportable quantities, is something I am still working on.

Mid-February 2024

Six weeks to go. An email arrives. Richard has changed his mind. Sending a ship with over two thousand civilians and eight hundred staff through a conflict zone? Perhaps not the wisest move, it's potentially messy and possibly litigious.

He has cancelled the itinerary completely and offered us a new one. This version has us sailing south of Australia, north of Antarctica, under Africa, and up into the Mediterranean via the Strait of Gibraltar. There will be fewer port stops and more sea days, but it will still get us to Athens, on schedule, allowing our plans from there to continue unchanged.

Stunned by the late notice, but excited, because the new itinerary includes Mauritius, South Africa, Namibia, Tenerife and Morocco, all places we have yet to visit, there is nothing for it but to open my laptop, pull up a new sheet and allow Itinerary Four to spring into existence.

With much of our journey already in place or falling into place, initially, Itinerary Four focuses on checking visas, cancelling defunct tours and scrambling for new ones. Due to the last-minute schedule change, Virgin Voyages are struggling to provide adequate shore excursions, so it is better we find our own. We are part of a Facebook group created solely for this one cruise, and through it we find new port options and discover many passengers have opted out of the cruise altogether.

As departure day draws near, Itinerary Four starts to solidify. I tweak our Greece trip, finalise our three-day visit to Bulgaria and expand on Türkiye. Train tickets are earmarked for purchasing when they become available (most global train operators only release tickets thirty to ninety days in advance). I consult Viator and GetYourGuide and approach tour guide companies.

The India leg still needs some work, but it is starting to look good. Itinerary Four also now boasts a tick next to my medication – meaning I have wrestled my supplements into manageable quantities and received a four-month supply of Verzenio from the company running the program. I have also bought train tickets to Sydney and an insurance policy, downloaded an eSIM, secured foreign currency and obtained visas for India and Türkiye.

This morning, Singapore Airlines announced a sale on flights, so we have even ticked off our flights home.

25 March 2024

One day to go. The travel cubes are packed, ready to be squeezed into suitcases. The cutlery and plastic plates we always travel with are stowed. Currencies, tickets and passports are safely hidden, toiletries sorted. The house has been prepared for our absence, the fridge emptied and family farewelled.

Turning off the printer, I grab the double-sided A4 document it has just spat out and give it one last look over. Itinerary Four, you fought hard for your existence. Now, show us what you've got for two slightly battered, next-chapter Australians (who also happen to be vegetarian).

CHAPTER 1

Catching a Train in Australia

'**Why did you bring them?** Why didn't you just throw them away?' I cry, exasperated.

'Because I thought they'd make a good snack for the train,' Darryl replies, juggling his walking stick and suitcase in one hand, and an umbrella and a large plastic bag filled with plump grapes in the other.

'But grapes? They're not the easiest food to travel with,' I say – just as Darryl loses his grip on the bag and it drops to the ground with a squelch.

'See? And besides, we can get a coffee and croissant from the stand outside the station when we get there.'

'Well, I wasn't going to just throw perfectly good grapes away,' Darryl says, awkwardly retrieving the now-damp bag of slightly bruised fruit.

It is 6am on a very wet Tuesday morning, and we are standing at our local bus stop in our home town of Brunswick Heads, on the north coast of NSW, waiting for the coach that will take us to the nearest operating train station. It is dark and cold and, when it finally arrives, it's a relief to stow our bags, dump our dripping umbrellas and board our chariot. With only a few sleepy bodies onboard, we both take a double seat, grapes perched carefully on the one next to Darryl.

For the next ninety minutes, as the sun fights its battle against the night and the torrential rain, I sit back and let the sensation of being on the move again wash over me. It is a pleasure only fellow travellers can understand, an excitement that, once tasted, is never forgotten.

It almost feels unbelievable that we are travelling again. That it has been more than four years since we returned from circumnavigating the globe by train and ship. Four years since the world was thrown into chaos by a pandemic. Two years since I was forever changed by cancer.

Twenty-four months ago, deep in the throes of chemotherapy, recovering from a double mastectomy, learning to eliminate estrogen-positive food and damaging toxins from my lifestyle and becoming a vegetarian, I thought I would never feel this excitement again. Diagnosed with not only high-risk breast cancer but also a brain tumour, there was a real possibility I wouldn't.

A good doctor, a great oncologist and an amazing – albeit resigned – husband are the reasons I am sitting on this bus today.

The rain has vanished, but the day is still cold and grey when we pull up at the station.

'We were told we could get coffee and croissants from a vendor here?' I ask one of the station porters. 'But I can't see anyone.'

'Coffee,' he replies, looking slightly confused. 'Croissants? Nah. Haven't seen anyone selling those for years. Not since Covid.'

'We've been travelling for two hours now. Is there anywhere we can get a drink or something to eat?'

'Nah. Sorry, love. You'll have to wait for the train. Get a coffee there.'

It is a poor reflection on the Australian train travel network and supports the scepticism displayed by our daughter, Paige, in a recent conversation.

'Your cruise to Athens leaves from Sydney and you're catching the train there? Not flying? It takes hours. I did it once. Never again.'

'That's right. Fifteen hours, actually. We felt that if we were going to spend a good majority of the next few months catching trains around Bulgaria, Türkiye and India, then we should be prepared to catch them in Australia as well.'

Despite Paige's scepticism and the train's tortoise-like pace, the journey goes remarkably well. The carriage is warm, the seats are comfortable and the toilets reasonably clean, although they do make me worry about the Indian ones ahead. A small buffet car, staffed by friendly attendants, serves something they call coffee, and the dahl for lunch and curry for dinner are surprisingly tasty. Even Darryl's battered grapes make a decent snack as we alternate between reading and gazing at the passing landscape.

As we edge closer to Australia's biggest city, the scattered eucalypts, lush farmland and grazing cattle give way to small rural towns, quiet stations and, eventually, dense urban sprawl. It is a real cross-section of regional New South Wales, and I am glad to have done it.

From Central Station, it's a short underground train ride to Town Hall, followed by a short walk. By 11pm, we are tucked into our comfortable bed in an upgraded room at the Grace Hotel. Despite the long travel day and late hour, that glow of excitement, of expectation, still floods my body.

The following morning gives us the opportunity to inspect our hotel by daylight as we go in search of breakfast. Built in the 1920s, the Art Deco Grace Hotel was once the headquarters of the Grace Brothers department store. It is a beautiful, grand and well-located old building, and we pledge to adopt it for any future visits to Sydney.

'What time do we need to be at Circular Quay?' Darryl asks some time later, wiping the remnants of his avocado-on-toast breakfast from his mouth.

'Three o'clock,' I reply. 'But the Banksy exhibition opens at ten.'

We were initially disappointed with our late embarkation time, but any frustration at having to while away hours before boarding our cruise ship disappeared when we discovered the city was hosting a Banksy exhibition. We are both fans of the anonymous street artist, known for using publicly visible spaces and a distinctive stencilling technique to convey powerful messages. Housed within Sydney's beautiful sandstone, heritage-listed Town Hall, the exhibition is highly memorable.

'What exhibit did you like best?'

'I'm probably being predictable, but I liked the stencil of *Girl with Balloon*,' I answer Darryl. 'It is meant to remind us to hold on to hope, even if it feels out of reach. How about you? Did you have a favourite?'

'Not really. The rats and policemen were good. The location was great. I liked your choice – not sure about your bag.'

Exiting the exhibition, we had passed through the obligatory gift store. Calico tote bags depicting various Banksy images had caught my eye. Thinking one might come in handy during our travels, I had bought one. Little did I realise at the time, but my *Girl with Balloon* tote bag would be the first of a few more souvenir purchases.

Richard Branson's *Resilient Lady*, a Virgin Voyages cruise ship, looks incredibly striking when, at 2pm, we find ourselves at the Overseas Passenger Terminal at Circular Quay. Seventeen decks high and weighing 110,000 tons, she dominates this part of Sydney Harbour. Her paintwork is also distinctive. Expecting her to be painted a vibrant red in line with the Virgin brand, I am surprised to find her a sleek navy-grey, with only small touches of scarlet. When I overhear someone nearby say she looks like a warship, I find myself agreeing.

We have arrived an hour early and are content to wait, but when we hand our bags over to baggage control, we are advised to make our way straight to check-in. Whether it is Darryl's walking stick that has prompted this, or Virgin is simply ahead of schedule, we do not know. Either way, we are happy to show our booking details, receive our bracelets, which will act as both our onboard payment method and our cabin key – and step on board.

CHAPTER 2

Sailing from Sydney to Perth

'**We must have arrived at** our first port. The ship's not moving,' Darryl informs me the following morning.

I reach for my watch, which is charging on the odd-shaped bedside table beside me, note the early time – 5am – and snuggle further back under my doona.

Once, an early wake-up call like this would have seen me leap out of bed, run through my morning yoga or stretching routine, then head outside for a three-kilometre walk. But post-cancer diagnosis, and now living with the side effects of my medications, those early starts are fewer and further between. I still stretch and walk, just slightly later in the morning. Verzenio, a drug that stops cancer cells from growing by blocking certain enzymes, comes with some very unpleasant and debilitating side effects. Since I began taking it seventeen months ago, there has not been a single day without nausea, diarrhoea or chronic fatigue. Add in letrozole, the hormone-blocking medication, which brings aching muscles, sore joints and brain fog, and I do not mind rewarding myself with an extra hour in bed each day.

Besides, this morning's slumber gives me space to reflect on yesterday's arrival, last night's explorations and the ship itself.

For all the hype, I am not yet overly awed with Richard's *Resilient Lady*. Only ten months old and packed with innovative ideas, her arrival into Sydney had sparked a flood of media attention. While I love the free wi-fi, our bracelets instead of key cards, and the twenty small food outlets in lieu of a main dining room and buffet, I am not impressed with her design.

Our wandering yesterday revealed a ship with far fewer open areas than I had expected. Inside, the winding layout reminds me of a rabbit warren, and there is no lounge with a view towards the bow. Outside, seating is limited and much of it faces inward. The one exterior entertainment area that *does* face seaward, the Dock House bar, was overflowing when we visited last night, and I suspect it will stay that way for the duration of the cruise.

'I don't mind our room, though,' I call out to Darryl a little later as I press a button on an electronic tablet to open the room's blackout curtains, then another to turn off the lights.

'It is definitely the biggest we have ever had on a cruise ship, and I like the fresh decor – and our red balcony hammock.'

'But what about the bathroom?' Darryl replies. 'Some people might have a bit of trouble actually getting into it. It's tiny.'

Closeting myself in the bathroom cubicle a short while later, I have to agree. With the door closed, there is barely room to turn around; it would be nearly impossible for someone larger.

With our upcoming itinerary featuring exotic destinations such as Cape Town and Casablanca, today's pause at the coastal town of Eden feels a bit anticlimactic. Presumably only added to the agenda to make up for missing port stops when our schedule was changed, the shore excursions offered by Virgin Voyages were limited, expensive and easy to forgo. Instead, we have decided to catch the complimentary shuttle bus into the town centre, then make our way on foot back to our ship. It is clearly a popular idea; boarding the shuttle, we are lucky to get seats. With bodies hovering above us, as our bus jolts its way up a steep incline, I scroll through my phone.

'Eden is only 478 kilometres south of Sydney. It has the third-deepest natural harbour in the Southern Hemisphere. There is a long association with whaling here – there is even a whale museum. The main industries are fishing, forestry and tourism.'

'The museum might be worth a look,' Darryl replies as our shuttle approaches the main street. 'It's a much smaller place than I was expecting.'

Two hours later, confirming Darryl's first impression, we have seen all there is to see of the town of Eden. We have walked its main street, popped into its supermarket (something I enjoy doing in the places we visit), and skipped the whale museum. Its appearance, combined with the fifteen-dollar-per-person entry fee, just didn't entice us.

We did, however, find a great viewing area on our walk back to our ship: Eden Rotary Lookout, whose impressive views made us pause.

'Below is Twofold Bay,' I read from a convenient placard. 'The third-deepest natural harbour in the Southern Hemisphere.'

'It's also one of the best whale-watching spots on this coast,' a bystander adds. 'You should visit in spring. Humpback whales will stop here on their way back to Antarctica to rest or nurse their calves. It's a remarkable sight.'

'Every year we get more and more whales passing Brunswick Heads,' I reply. 'It's amazing to see their numbers grow. But they don't stop.'

Unlike other cruise lines, Virgin Voyages has forgone the traditional large dining room and buffets in favour of over twenty different

NEXT CHAPTER TRAVEL

eateries. From specialised restaurants like Gunbae (Korean barbecue), Extra Virgin (Italian) and The Test Kitchen (a laboratory-like dining experience), to pizza bars and ice-cream shops, all are included in your fare. Since becoming vegetarian, this variety really appeals to us, and tonight's cauliflower steaks at Razzle Dazzle (a mostly vegetarian venue), cement our positive opinion.

Dining in smaller venues also means we can keep to some kind of timetable for evening entertainment. Darryl has read that there is a magician performing tonight in the Red Room, *Resilient Lady*'s live performance space. But it only takes a few moments after the lights dim to realise he has made a mistake. Tonight's entertainment is not a magician, but a hypnotist, currently asking for volunteers.

Now, it is interesting how receiving a cancer diagnosis can shift your whole perspective; make you realise how precious life is, and how little time we might have to enjoy it. It's a real wake-up call to do what you can, while you can.

Before being diagnosed, I would never have volunteered to be hypnotised. But tonight, knowing I may never get this chance again, I am the first to raise my hand.

'I'll send you the video; it's hilarious. She's up on stage trying to *Riverdance*, and when she attempted ballet, her shoe flew off.'

It is later that evening and I am lying in bed, trying to drown out Darryl's laughter as he recounts the performance to our son, Pierce.

'And then she tried milking a cow – only her hands were up over her head...'

Grinning under the covers, I realise I honestly do not care how I looked on that stage. What matters is that I said yes to living.

It is going to take five days of sailing to reach Fremantle, near Perth, our next port of call. We will be travelling south of the Australian continent, through a stretch known for its strong westerly winds, the Roaring Forties. Once sought after during the age of sailing, today these winds are more useful powering wind stations in Tasmania and New Zealand. And while solo yachtsmen may still welcome them, I am not looking forward to their arrival.

This morning, in the very early hours, the clocks went back an hour – our subtle reminder that we are once again on the move. Adjusting our watches forward or back every day or so is something we have become very used to on our adventures, and I am eager to start doing so again.

Unlike past cruises, where a daily paper guide was slipped under our door, *Resilient Lady*'s agenda is digital. Using an app on our phones, we can peruse the day's schedule, book events, reserve restaurants and track our account. This morning, I used it to secure tickets for a show called *Another Rose* for tonight, noted a guest lecturer in the Red Room later today, and reserved a spot at the ship's book club.

'It's a completely different program than I am used to,' I say to Darryl a little later. 'I love that there's a book club, but there's no shuffleboard, no quoits, no port talks. If I wanted to exercise every morning – which I don't – there would be plenty of options. But looking at this agenda, I'm not sure there's enough to keep me occupied for six weeks.'

'You've got to remember, this isn't a regular half-world cruise,' Darryl reminds me. 'It's three small cruises strung together. You can't expect them to offer everything.'

He's right. The cruise we had originally booked from Sydney to Greece was actually a unique repositioning offer. Virgin, which usually runs seven- to ten-day cruises for adults-only, affluent, party-seeking guests, had put together three back-to-back itineraries totalling forty-three days to return *Resilient Lady* to Europe.

Since most of Virgin's typical clientele does not have forty-three days to spare, the deal was snapped up by a very different demographic: retirees. Catering to this older crowd was already going to be a challenge, but when the entire itinerary changed due to the situation in the Middle East, it became even harder. With fewer port stops, more consecutive sea days, and an older guest list, Virgin needed to completely overhaul its usual activities program. Scanning the app now, I find myself wondering whether they have done enough.

In the days that follow, as the Roaring Forties surprisingly, but happily, fail to materialise, the temperature drops with our lower latitude, and Tasmania, Victoria and South Australia slip past, I put that worry aside and focus on settling into our neighbourhood.

Being relatively experienced cruisers, we quickly re-establish routines. Before breakfast, I stretch, grateful for the ever-changing view through our balcony doors. After breakfast, we walk the deck or I use one of the gym's many treadmills. Mid-morning, I either attend something from the day's program or read, while Darryl settles under cover with his laptop to track the stock market (thanking the ship's free wi-fi). Lunch is usually a tofu salad from The Galley, Virgin's version of a modern food hall.

One afternoon, we come across a shuffleboard table, an indoor version of the usual deck game, which quickly becomes a favourite. I also learn that playing a car-racing machine on a moving ship makes me dizzy. Dinner is at a restaurant or The Galley before a show or an early night.

'Loads of people cancelled this cruise when the itinerary changed,' a linen-clad lady announces matter-of-factly.

I am sitting in a comfortable lounge chair alongside five others. It is our first session of book club and since we have barely started the assigned novel – *A Gentleman in Moscow* by Amor Towles – it has been a good chance to chat and compare experiences.

'I thought as much,' someone replies. 'We were told before boarding that we would need reservations for every restaurant, but we have just walked in each time.'

'Same here,' another adds. 'The ship is built for 2,700 passengers and around one thousand crew. Currently, and I think this will be the case for all three legs, there are only about 1,200 of us on board.'

'I know. It's great, isn't it? Same number of staff, half the passengers. I've never had such amazing service.'

'The activities program is a bit hit and miss, though,' I contribute.

'True. It's great if you're into morning fitness or trivia. I think they assumed Aussies just love gyms and games,' someone laughs.

'I guess we do,' I admit. 'But I have to say, the shows are amazing. We saw *Another Rose* the other night. It was unlike anything I have ever seen on a ship.'

It is true. Virgin does not just do performances differently; they do them on a whole new level. Not afraid to explore diverse sexual orientations and gender identities, the part-cabaret, part-musical, part-acrobatic spectacle we saw was both incredible and unforgettable.

'Wait until they put on *Persephone*,' Kayla, our book club facilitator, mentions. 'That's usually everyone's favourite.'

'I think the ship's performers, the Happenings Cast, is an interesting concept,' says a woman who looks to be in her late eighties. 'I like it.'

From what I have seen so far of Virgin's twelve-member entertainment troupe, each with their own unique theme or speciality, I tend to agree. They are a fresh take on the traditional cruise entertainment team: contemporary, engaging and full of personality. With titles like The Hostess, The Charmer, The Foodie and The Flare, they reimagine what onboard entertainment can be.

'And who would have thought I'd live to see drag queens working on cruise ships,' she adds, referring to The Diva, one of the more flamboyant Happenings Cast members.

Edging ever closer to Perth, Easter passes with surprisingly little fanfare, the clocks go back a few more times, and I finish my first book club book read. Finally, on 2 April , a day after crossing the invisible line where the Southern and Indian Oceans meet, we wake to see *Resilient Lady* gliding into Fremantle Harbour.

CHAPTER 3

Eight Days to Reach Mauritius

I have only ever been to Western Australia once before, and that was to catch a ship to Singapore with my family when I was eleven. Our final destination was England, where we would be living for the following year, and to get there, my father had found a ridiculously cheap cruise that covered the Australia–Singapore leg.

Arriving at Fremantle port to board this vessel, we immediately discovered why the upcoming cruise was so inexpensive: we would be sharing our voyage with thousands of live sheep. Standing, waiting to board, we could actually see the miserable, bedraggled animals in their cages. They took up more than half the ship, and already the smell was overpowering. It was certainly a memorable trip – one I have never forgotten.

Returning to Fremantle all these years later, Darryl and I had discussed what we might like to see or do. A look around Perth appealed to me, but was quickly dismissed by Darryl.

'It's just an Australian city like most other cities,' he had reasoned. 'You would probably spend most of your time looking at shops, and I would spend most of mine waiting for you. How about visiting Rottnest Island? Looking for a quokka?'

Accessible by ferry from Fremantle or Perth, Rottnest Island is a car-free destination situated about 19 kilometres from the Australian mainland. Although Aboriginal artefacts dating back some 30,000 years have been discovered here, it was first documented and named in 1696 by Dutch explorer Willem de Vlamingh. Finding it heavily populated with quokkas, small marsupials about the size of a family cat, de Vlamingh had mistaken them for large rats. Hence the name Rottnest, or 'Rats' Nest' Island.

While spying a quokka in its native habitat is our main motivation for visiting, stories of the island's natural beauty and pristine beaches have also added to its appeal.

'What do you think of this photo?' It is later that evening, and I have just posted a picture of myself crouching beside a furry quokka to my social media profile. 'Doesn't matter, I've posted it anyway.'

'Well, we got to get up close with a quokka,' Darryl replies. 'What did you think of Rottnest Island?'

'I liked it. Felt a bit like stepping back in time. And the beaches were beautiful. But I hadn't realised it was once used as prison and labour camp for Aboriginal men and boys. Or how harshly they were treated here.'

'And as an internment camp for enemies during World War II,' Darryl reminds me. 'I like how some of the old buildings are still used today as holiday accommodation.'

'Interesting, too, the damage caused by its salt industry.' I add. 'The deforestation. No wonder it looks so barren – limestone protruding everywhere.'

'I was surprised by the number of pushbikes,' Darryl continues. 'I probably shouldn't have been, given that it's mostly car free, but I felt sure our tour bus was going to hit one, especially the ones coming straight at us. The roads are supposed to be one-way.'

'And you're not allowed to beep your horn,' I laugh. 'Well, I was surprised there is no permanent water on the island in summer. Poor quokkas. Luckily, they can go three months without it.'

'I didn't know cats and dogs had wiped out all the quokkas on the mainland,' Darryl muses.

'And how about bumping into all those couples from home,' I exclaim.

I am not exaggerating. Our day, independently booked rather than organised by the ship, had started with a forty-minute smooth ferry ride over sapphire-blue waters. We disembarked at Thomson Bay, the main settlement for Rottnest Island. While waiting for a small tour bus to introduce us to much of the island's 19 square kilometres, we had struck up conversations with those waiting alongside us. Some were wearing Virgin Voyages-emblazoned bracelets, so we knew they must also be sailing on the *Resilient Lady*. Surprisingly, within minutes we discovered not only were many of them from our ship, but there were also some from our region back home. One couple was from Mullumbimby, another from Ballina, and a third from Lennox Head. All three of these towns are less than a thirty-minute drive from Brunswick Heads.

'It shouldn't be that surprising,' Darryl replies. 'This cruise started in Australia. But it *is* the first cruise we have done where nearly all the passengers are Australian. Normally, there are only a handful of us.'

'I've noticed that too,' I reply. 'I am wondering what it is going to be like after having sailed mostly with Brits.'

Thanks to the extra sea days added by our revised itinerary, our next leg, crossing the Indian Ocean between Fremantle and Mauritius, takes eight long days. I spend most of the first day updating our Darma Travels website with a new blog post, while Darryl tries out the hammock on our balcony. Dinner is eaten at The Test Kitchen, and by the time we have conquered all six of its creatively prepared, decoratively plated courses in the laboratory-inspired restaurant, we are ready for bed.

Day two is spent playing bingo before eating a decadent vegetarian ravioli at Extra Virgin, while day three has everyone talking about some passengers currently aboard a Norwegian cruise ship.

'Their cruise stopped in Africa,' a couple tells us at breakfast, 'and instead of booking the ship's shore excursion, about six of them booked their own tour.'

'But they were late returning,' the husband adds.

'So the ship left without them,' his wife says, eyes wide.

'They have spent the past forty-eight hours rushing around Africa, trying to catch up with their ship. They have only just made it. It's probably cost them a fortune.'

It is a particularly relevant story, given we are currently en route to Africa and many of us have booked private shore excursions. As is another story playing out right now on our televisions. All major news channels are reporting that a tourist has been killed while on an African safari. A bull elephant went rogue, attacked a jeep and killed a woman. With many of us hoping to partake in an African safari ourselves, the story does make us think.

Day four brings FaceTime calls from both Pierce and Paige. While neither has much news to report, the quality of the internet out here in our remote Southern Indian Ocean location is pretty impressive. Day four also sees me return to book club, where the discussion is more about Kayla, Happenings cast member and our book club facilitator, than it is about our book. Curious to know how she landed her position as The Flare, we listen, spellbound, as she recounts Virgin Voyages' rigorous recruitment process: how she had to host various skits, attend numerous call-backs, undergo intense safety training, and ultimately give up her life in New York City.

Day five, and we are halfway across the Indian Ocean, the Earth's third-largest ocean and its warmest. The clocks go back another hour, making it the seventh time they have done so over the past thirteen days. With no passenger laundry facilities on board, today we use some of our onboard credit to have our washing done for us. At fifty dollars for a large bag, it is expensive, but since we were given nearly one thousand dollars in incentive credits, it doesn't really matter.

Heading north-west and drawing closer to the equator, the days are heating up, and this morning's laps around the deck were interrupted by a sudden burst of equatorial rain. In the evening, following a few drinks out on the back deck, we head inside to see what Scarlet Night, Virgin Voyages' signature sailing event, is all about. With Darryl wearing a crimson T-shirt, and me in my red *Sesame Street* Elmo turtleneck, we stand out a bit among others' glamourous attire, but the high-energy party isn't really our scene.

Day six and I wake, feeling quite guilty about those two drinks I had on the back deck last night. Alcohol can increase estrogen levels, and since my hormone-positive breast cancer diagnosis, I have been extremely careful with what I put in my body. The guilt is compounded by the fact that Verzenio heavily compromises the liver, so adding alcohol isn't ideal. Still, I remind myself, I want to enjoy life.

'Stuff it,' I mumble, throwing off the bed covers. 'I am not going to let cancer stop me from having a margarita or two every now and then.'

It is interesting I felt this way this morning because, just a few hours later, after I finish my morning laps, a fellow passenger stops me.

'Is your name Emma?' she asks.

'Yes.'

'I have just finished reading your breast cancer book,' she says. 'I recognised you from the photo on the back.'

It turns out Robyn had the same type of breast cancer as I did – invasive lobular carcinoma – and also underwent a double mastectomy, followed by chemotherapy and radiation. With so many similarities, she tells me, she really enjoyed my book. It is the first time someone has recognised me in this way, and I walk away from the encounter, absolutely glowing.

Day seven, the day before our arrival in Mauritius, and I realise that if we leave the bathroom door open, its degree of swinging is a good indication of the sea state outside: rough seas and the door swings erratically; calm seas and it barely moves. This morning, it is somewhere in between.

Today, we begin a new book at book club, *Circe* by Madeline Miller, and I learn to make friendship bracelets at craft class. Dinner is at The Wake, which, due to its limited vegetarian options, will likely be our only visit. The night wraps up with a comedy show in the Red Room featuring a comedian named Patty... or so we think.

At some point on the cruise, we had heard whispers of invite-only events.

'You get slipped a card,' one of our lunch companions had murmured. 'Maybe under your door, at dinner – you never know when.'

'And if you do get a card,' someone else added, 'you are not allowed to tell anyone what happened. They even take your phone so you can't take photos. It's top secret.'

Making our way back to our room after Patty's show, one of the Happenings cast members, The Charmer, waylays us.

'Are you up for an adventure?' he murmurs, slipping Darryl one of those coveted cards. 'Be outside the Ground Club in thirty minutes.'

Needless to say, it is with some excitement and curiosity that we shortly present ourselves at the Ground Club. Our feelings are compounded when, with a group of around fifteen other passengers, we are led through staff-only areas, down twisting stairwells and into the bowels of the ship. I will stop here. It would spoil the occasion for anyone else if I said more. Suffice to say, it was memorable.

Day eight, and our long, uninterrupted days at sea are finally over. Outside, I spy land. We have arrived in Port Louis, the capital of the African island nation of Mauritius.

CHAPTER 4

Home of the Dodo

Mauritius was a country I had heard of, maybe even dreamed of visiting one day, but knew almost nothing about. We were ecstatic when we learned that our changed itinerary would include a stop here and, consequently, I had performed a Google search, trying to brush up my knowledge. All I really remember now is that Mauritius lies about two thousand kilometres off the east coast of Africa and has a population of around 1.2 million: a vibrant mix of Indian, Creole, Chinese and French heritage. Once reliant on agriculture and textiles, its economy now leans more on tourism and information technology.

What struck me the most from that search, though, was that Mauritius only gained independence from the United Kingdom in 1968 – just fifty-six years ago. English remains one of the country's main languages, alongside French and Mauritian Creole. It is always a relief to learn that English is widely spoken. It means we can communicate more freely with locals, making any visit easier, more enjoyable and more educational.

Mauritius also ranks highly on the Human Development Index, which may be why Virgin Voyages had no trouble securing a solid line-up of shore excursions. Today, we are taking full advantage of one.

It is not long after breakfast when we find ourselves sitting aboard a modern, air-conditioned coach, cruising along a wide, well-signed motorway. I have the window seat, and from it I take in the tropical scenery. Nearby, hibiscus, ginger and bougainvillea plants abound, while in the distance, coconut palms jostle for space with majestic mango trees. As is often the case in tropical countries, the thick, lush vegetation gives the landscape a slightly unkempt air; it is not easy taming well-watered foliage.

Leading our tour is Gregory. Brightly dressed, he has the largest smile and skinniest beanpole legs I have ever seen. Assisting him is the beautiful Enza. Both look quite young, and as we make our way to our first stop, the Hindu site of Grand Bassin, Gregory's commentary on the education system helps explain their youth.

'Mauritius has both public and private schooling,' he explains. 'After high school, we have three choices if we want to continue our education: university, IT school or hotel school. Enza and I went to hotel school.'

'IT school?' someone asks. 'Is Mauritius big on IT?'

'It employs over twenty-four thousand people,' Gregory replies, 'making it one of the biggest industries in Mauritius. We also rank first in Africa for cybersecurity and telecommunications. We often win tech competitions. So, yes, IT is very big here. And do you know what else is big?' He laughs. 'Beer. We drink a lot of beer. The best are Phoenix and Blue Marlin.'

'How about wine?' someone calls from the back of the bus.

'Yes, we make wine,' Enza chimes in. 'But not from grapes. We make it from lychees.'

'But this is interesting,' Gregory continues, reclaiming the conversation. 'Lychees used to take just two months to grow, from December until the end of January. But now, because of climate change, it takes four months. They start appearing as early as October, but they are not ready for picking until late January. It is a very obvious sign of climate change.'

Mulling over how often climate change gets mentioned during our travels, I let Gregory's conversation wash over me.

'We have just five towns in Mauritius and two hundred villages. Most of us know three languages: Creole, English and French. We have no predators here. No snakes. Mauritius was home to the dodo.'

'The dodo came from here?' I sit up, my interest piqued.

Extinct since the late seventeenth century, I have always been fascinated by the dodo. Flightless, with stubby legs, yellow feet, a stout body, large naked head, and a black, yellow and green beak, its comical appearance, along with its great name, has undoubtedly fuelled my fascination. I am thrilled to be visiting the place where it once roamed.

'Maybe I can find a dodo souvenir,' I whisper to Darryl.

It has taken a little over ninety minutes to reach Mauritius's most sacred Hindu site, Grand Bassin. The flat coastal plains are long gone; for the past half hour, we have been winding steadily upward through dense, green forest. Sitting 550 metres above sea level, Grand Bassin, a volcanic crater lake, is both breathtakingly beautiful and spiritually significant. It is symbolically linked to the Ganges River and holds deep meaning for the island's Hindu community. Ornate shrines line the water's edge, incense rises from small altars, and worshippers quietly come and go. Home to several temples and large statues, it also serves as an important pilgrimage destination.

As we alight from the bus and make our way towards a 33-metre-high statue of Lord Shiva, one of the tallest of its kind in the world,

Gregory shares that if we had arrived just a day earlier, we would not have been able to visit.

'Yesterday was the festival of Maha Shivaratri,' he tells us. 'During this festival, half a million Hindus make the pilgrimage here.'

Grateful not to be sharing the sacred grounds with five hundred thousand others, we take our time, appreciating how the area's natural beauty blends seamlessly with the man-made temples and imposing statues and simply enjoying being outside beside a mesmerising, glassy lake, its surface dotted with colourful Hindu deities.

Just before reboarding the bus for lunch, I experience one of the highlights of our entire adventure. A holy man, dressed in traditional Hindu garb, gently winds red and yellow thread around my wrist, intoning incantations as he does. Known by many names – *kalawa* being one of the most common – this sacred thread is a symbol of protection and wellbeing.

I still wear it today.

The journey from Grand Bassin to lunch is equally interesting. The higher we climb into the mountains, the narrower the road becomes, until it feels as though we are corkscrewing our way along a goat track. At each tight corner, I close my eyes and clutch my new *kalawa*, silently praying we do not meet oncoming traffic. Thankfully, it works and we arrive safely at our 'bird's nest' restaurant.

Interspersed with visits to one of Port Louis' most significant landmarks, St Louis Cathedral, and a model ship-building shop (Mauritius is renowned for manufacturing these), I find my dodo souvenir. It is a replica of this odd, flightless bird, carved from gleaming moonstone, and I discover it at a roadside stall somewhere within the stunning confines of Black River Gorges National Park. With much of the country's rainforest lost to deforestation and overgrazing, this park protects what little remains. And while I will always remember the incredible views of cascading waterfalls and the cheeky, fornicating monkeys, it is my little stone dodo I will treasure the most.

Returning to Port Louis, I'm lucky enough to have a window seat again, I soak in the passing scenery: the wide bitumen roads and the long, unkempt grass growing beside them. The abundance of beautiful foliage, sadly marred by an undergrowth of plastic drink bottles. It is clear that Mauritius is steadily developing, but equally clear that poverty still lingers.

Seeing this, and remembering past travels, makes me realise something: ensconced in our little pocket of Australia, it is easy to forget just how many more people in the world live with far less, and how those struggling to get by far outnumber those who are well off.

'We are travelling alongside Madagascar, down the Mozambique Current. That's why it's so rough.'

I have just returned from book club and am filling Darryl in on our main topic of conversation: the weather.

'It will probably stay like this for a few days.'

'Well, if it is going to be rocky, then I'm glad there are a whole lot of other ships around,' Darryl replies.

He has raised a good point. Up until Mauritius, we had barely seen another vessel. Now, we are spotting quite a few – mainly cargo ships, their containers stacked like turtle shells. They are providing an enjoyable distraction.

'I am guessing we have now joined the main shipping route to Cape Town.'

'And it's probably even busier now that most ships are avoiding the Suez Canal,' Darryl agrees.

'Have you noticed how every staff member on any ship we have sailed seems to have a bad-weather story?' I say. 'Get ready for a few new ones.'

Over the next two days, as the rough weather continues – and while Sheldon, our cabin steward, tells us how he once lost his phone overboard on a rough crossing, and Raj, a waiter, shares tales of seasick passengers – we make the best of life aboard a rocking ship. A guest speaker boarded in Mauritius, his speciality is all things African and we attend his talk on South Africa in the Red Room. Normally, speakers are expected to wrap up within an hour; this one is still going strong at ninety minutes, introducing us to the concept of 'African Time', a relaxed, forgiving approach to punctuality common among locals.

Although hesitant, we brave his second lecture on Durban, but I do not absorb much. I am far too distracted by a large drip falling steadily from the ceiling.

'It can't be a good thing, water dripping on us on a boat,' I mutter to Darryl as we exit. 'And also, the room was freezing.'

It is not the first time I have complained about the cold on this ship. Presumably to help stop the spread of germs, the indoor temperature is kept low. I have never had to live in such a chilly environment for so long, and I am slightly disgruntled about it – not just because it is uncomfortable being cold all the time, but also because I only bought one jumper with me.

Our final evening before arriving in Durban, we have dinner in The Galley. Sitting alone at the table beside us is a pale-looking gentlemen. Striking up a conversation, we learn he is a comedian who boarded at Mauritius.

'But I haven't been able to perform any of my shows,' he moans. 'I've been too seasick.'

CHAPTER 5

On Safari in Africa

We are currently standing on one of the upper decks of the *Resilient Lady*, watching a helicopter lower the female port pilot onto our ship. She is here to navigate us into Durban Harbour, and it is the first time we have ever seen a pilot arrive this way. It is an incredible feat to witness, and it only heightens my excitement. I am thrilled because we are about to set foot on African soil, something I never expected to do.

While the thought of visiting Africa, and maybe doing a safari, was a long-held dream, I had given up on it ever becoming reality. Our altered itinerary changed all that.

Africa has fifty-four sovereign states, and during this cruise, we will visit three ports across two African nations: Durban and Cape Town in South Africa, and Walvis Bay in Namibia. My only knowledge of today's stop, Durban, comes from snippets shared during that recent chilly port talk:

'Durban is the third-largest city in South Africa after Johannesburg and Cape Town... It has a population of 4.2 million, with over 51 per cent identifying as Black African... Around 25 per cent are Indian or Asian. Many Indians came here to work on the sugar plantations... Almost half the residents speak English as their first language... 38 per cent of Durban's population is under the age of nineteen.'

But perhaps the most thought-provoking detail:

'Durban Port is a dangerous area. Remove all your jewellery before disembarking and take care of your belongings.'

Hearing that final piece of advice makes me glad we have booked a guided tour.

It is a little after 10am when our pilot successfully docks us at Durban Harbour. Unlike our previous ports, here, all passengers and crew must present themselves at immigration. It is a long, slow, painful process, with the customs officials clearly operating on African Time, and we are feeling rather disgruntled and anxious by the time we exit the port's security gates and step into the crush of bodies surrounding them.

'Look for a sign with our name on it,' I yell to Darryl over the noise of the crowd. 'They're called African Sun Safaris.'

We are feeling slightly worried because this isn't a Virgin Voyages shore excursion, but a privately organised tour we booked through GetYourGuide. It was much cheaper and more comprehensive than anything the ship offered. Today we are supposed to visit a game reserve, then, later, a lion park. We just hope they have waited for us.

'Over there,' I finally say, pointing to a relic of a minibus parked in a street of tired, run-down buildings. 'The guest lecturer wasn't wrong,' I add. 'How dodgy does this place look?'

It turns out we need not have worried about missing our tour. With the area so crowded and the bus so innocuous, it takes some time before we can even depart.

'Couldn't find the bloody bus through the bloody crowds,' mutters a red-faced Australian man.

'We thought we had booked a private tour, not a minibus,' an unhappy American couple grumble. 'We will be complaining about this.'

'Welcome to Durban, I am Timbu,' says our guide, trying to calm tensions. 'Today we are going to have a great day.'

His words seem to work, and everyone begins to settle. That is, until his next line: 'We running late now. Doesn't matter, our driver go extra fast.'

We have learnt that a popular reason for doing a safari in Africa is to try and spot what is known as The Big Five – that is, an elephant, lion, leopard, rhino and buffalo. With only half a day here, we won't be able to see them all unfortunately, but we *will* be seeing some. Our first stop, Tala Game Reserve, should provide the rhinos, along with many other animals, while our second stop, a lion park, promises lions and elephants.

It is an hours-long journey to reach Tala and, as promised, our driver barrels along at breakneck speed down a Swiss-cheese highway. Normally, I would be worried about going this fast in these conditions, but today, the scenery outside keeps me distracted.

'It's so similar to home,' I marvel. 'Lantana bushes, macadamia nut trees, sugar cane plantations, cows grazing in fields, farms selling eggs… I'm surprised.'

'But we don't allow hitchhikers on *our* motorways, and we don't have signs like *that*,' Darryl replies, pointing to a large, weather-beaten placard.

'Cows for the next six kilometres,' I read aloud, laughing. 'No, our highways definitely don't allow cows.'

It is a couple of hours later, and with bodies aching in places they never have before, that we clamber down from our weathered olive jeep. We have just spent the better part of that time zigzagging our way around Tala Game Reserve. Traversing tracks that resembled dry riverbeds and grasslands ten feet tall, we have had the most incredible time.

We have seen curious antelope and swift wildebeests. Funny warthogs, bumbling hippos, and those important rhinos. We have had beautiful zebras run in front of our vehicle, and mesmerising giraffes flutter their long lashes at us. It has been an unforgettable experience, amplified by Timbu's colourful commentary.

'Baby hippos born underwater. They swim to surface to get first breath... Rhinos get horn cut off every two years. Stop poachers. Giraffe no have voice box.'

(I later learn that this last part isn't quite true. Giraffes *do* have voice boxes – they just don't use them very often.)

Of course, there is the obligatory gift shop, slightly more rustic than usual.

'What have you bought?' Darryl groans a short time later.

'Some hippos carved from stone,' I reply, opening my palm to reveal the small, brightly coloured figurines. 'To go with my dodo.'

'We'll end up with a menagerie to carry at this rate,' Darryl mutters, clambering back aboard our minibus.

'Timbu, why are there so many houses still under construction around here?' I call out as we make our way to our next destination.

'Lots of Zulus live here,' Timbu replies. 'Zulu king give people land. But building a house expensive. People live in city and work. They take many years to build on their land. They come every week and build a little more.'

'South Africa has an election coming up,' someone else mentions a short while later. 'How do you think it will go?'

'I think we get rid of ANC,' Timbu replies. 'They very corrupt.'

The African National Congress (ANC), a political party founded in 1912, is well known for its role in fighting apartheid. It has been the ruling party in South Africa since 1994, when its legendary leader, Nelson Mandela, was elected president. Like many long-serving governments, its time in power seems to have bred corruption and discontent. Today, Timbu is voicing what, a month later, turns out to be a popular belief: it is time for the ANC to go. Although not defeated outright, in May 2024, the ANC lost its parliamentary majority and was forced to form a coalition to remain in government.

Tala Game Reserve gave us one of the Big Five. A short time later, a lion park, whose name we never did learn, gives us two more. We do not even need to alight from our minibus; instead, it is ushered through some heavily guarded gates and onto another spine-jolting track.

While it is not quite the same as seeing lions and elephants in the raw African wild, the animals here do roam free, and it is a heart-stopping moment when our bus comes across a pride of lions digesting their lunch under some shady trees. Lazing and chewing not three metres from my window, they leave me frozen, mesmerised – until the urge to grab a photo kicks in.

A short time later, that same breathtaking feeling returns when we encounter African elephants.

'Africa has two types elephant,' Timbu tells us. 'Bush elephants – bigger. Tusks curve out. Forest elephants – smaller. Tusks straighter. This bush elephant. Biggest land animal on Earth.'

Many years ago, my mum gave me a small elephant pendant carved from ivory. I wore it on a chain around my neck, and from that moment on, I have adored elephants. I even have a tattoo of one. Stepping off the bus, and being allowed to get within metres of these incredible animals, has made my day.

We have a few more hours in Durban before our ship is due to depart and, rather than spend them onboard, we decide to stay on shore a little longer. It is apparently much too dangerous to walk around this area, so we make use of a complimentary shuttle bus that ferries passengers to a local shopping centre.

Travelling just a few kilometres, our brief journey gives us a riveting insight into this port-side section of Durban. Along the waterfront, cranes and machinery dominate, and the air is thick with the smell of diesel and salt. Away from the harbour, crowded streets are choked with traffic and sidewalks crammed with bodies. We do not see any white faces and many of the grand colonial-era buildings look tired and neglected.

'This must have once been a really nice area,' I comment. 'Times and conditions have certainly changed.'

'Probably all part of what Timbu was talking about when he mentioned the ANC,' Darryl replies. 'Any money meant for investment and maintenance has disappeared elsewhere.'

Walking around the shopping centre a short time later gives me another insight into Durban, and probably much of Africa. We have travelled to many parts of the world, and I tend to pigeonhole them into two broad categories: the Eastern one and the Western one. Every country we have ever visited seems to fall within one of these two divisions. But Africa, I discover today, does not. It is distinctly different – maybe a blend of the two, maybe something else entirely. It is an interesting revelation, and I wonder if more compartments will open to me as our travels continue.

It takes three days to sail from Durban to Cape Town, and each day brings something different. Day one, we are forced to change cabins. A grating creak in the ceiling has escalated into full-blown caterwauling, making it impossible to sleep. A conversation with fellow passengers at breakfast reveals we are not the only ones affected.

'So far, thirty cabins have had to be changed,' we are told. 'Not good for a brand-new ship.'

'At least we get to stay on the same deck. It's only a few doors along from our original room,' I reply.

'And it has exactly the same layout,' Darryl comments. 'It is easy to forget we're even in a different room.'

Day two brings thunder and lightning. It is the first time I have experienced a storm at sea and, tucked away in our cosy cabin, I find it more exhilarating than anything else. The storm continues to fester for most of the day, but with a gym and things to keep us occupied, it barely impacts us. I actually use the enforced time indoors to visit the ship's hairdresser for a much-needed haircut.

Day three, we cross the point where the Indian Ocean becomes the Atlantic. Travelling further south than we ever have before, we also run into some fog. It only lasts around ninety minutes, but it is a blanket of fog that swallows everything around us. Visibility is reduced to barely a metre. It forces the *Resilient Lady* to slow considerably, her foghorn sounding every two minutes. Hearing the answering blasts from other ships makes for a particularly memorable experience.

That afternoon, day three brings another standout event.

'*Persephone* is on in the Red Room later,' I read from the program on my phone. 'Kayla, my book club facilitator, said it's the most popular show on board. Why don't we go a bit early with our books so we can get a seat?'

Which is exactly what we do. Only, upon arriving at the Red Room, we find the seating has all been stowed away and the room is already full. Instead of sitting, we find ourselves packed shoulder to shoulder, books still in hand, straining to see the stage.

Some time later, the lights cut out, music crashes overhead, and a swarm of writhing, twirling performers engulfs the room, weaving among us.

It's raucous, raunchy, utterly fantastic. Our eyes dart in all directions, trying to keep up with the mayhem.

Loosely based on the Greek myth of Persephone, whose abduction to the underworld led to the creation of the seasons, the show is given a bold, futuristic twist. Gods and goddess entice us, acrobats swing overhead, and underworld ghouls gleefully thrust their groins at everyone.

Forty-five crazy minutes later, it is all over – and going to a stage show will never feel quite the same again.

'Amazing show,' I say to Darryl as we make our way back to our room. 'But I felt like an absolute dill standing there with my book in my hand.'

Tomorrow's arrival in Cape Town will mark the end of leg one of our three-sector cruise. While some passengers will disembark and new ones will board, there will still only be around 1,200 of us, meaning we will continue to enjoy an unusually generous staff-to-guest ratio.

At the end of each cruise sector, passengers must spend all of their onboard credit or forfeit it. With each of our three sectors offering generous allowances, we have actually struggled to use ours and I suspect we are not alone. That evening, the ship buzzes with welcome news: unspent credit will now carry over to the next leg.

Lying in bed later that night, I cannot sleep. My mind is spinning with ideas for how to spend this growing credit, my stomach is bubbling with excitement for Cape Town. But most of all, it is the foghorn – which is back and bellowing every two minutes – that is keeping me awake.

CHAPTER 6

On Top of the Table in Cape Town

'**We must have arrived because** we're not moving. But I can't see anything outside,' is how Darryl greets me the following morning. 'I can't even see over the side of the ship.'

Despite my trouble falling asleep last night, I must have drifted off eventually; I didn't hear Darryl get up or step out onto the balcony.

'What time is it?' I mumble sleepily. 'Our tour's at eight.'

'Just after six,' he replies. 'I wanted to wake early and watch us sail into Cape Town. That first view of Table Mountain getting closer is supposed to be spectacular – but the fog's so thick I can't see a thing.'

'I booked the early-morning cable car tour to the top of Table Mountain because I had heard the afternoon ones can get cancelled when fog rolls in,' I groan, starting to wake more fully. 'I never expected the *morning* to be affected. I'll be devastated if we can't get to the top – it's a once-in-a-lifetime Bucket List thing. Well, we do have our hop-on bus tickets. At least we can still use those.'

We count ourselves incredibly lucky to have been given this chance to visit Cape Town. Years ago, the idea was not so far-fetched, but as we grew older, and given its distance from the east coast of Australia, any real hope of getting here slowly faded. We never imagined an affordable cruise line would choose this bottom-of-the-world route, but with the shipping industry thrown into disarray by what is happening in the Middle East, two slightly rusty Australians have arrived. Shame we can't see anything.

Nestled between the rugged slopes of Table Mountain and the glistening waters of the Atlantic Ocean, Cape Town is one of the world's most iconic cities. Founded in the seventeenth century by the Dutch as a supply station for ships travelling between Europe and the East, it is now known for its laid-back atmosphere, diverse population, stunning beaches, world-renowned winelands and natural beauty. Despite its legacy of institutionalised racial segregation and discrimination under apartheid (1948-1994), Cape Town has emerged as one of the world's most popular travel destinations, drawing visitors from across the globe.

Cape Town's most famous landmark is Table Mountain, a flat-topped peak that dominates the skyline. Rising over one thousand metres, with views stretching across the vibrant city, sparkling ocean and dramatic coastline, it is a must-see for anyone visiting here. While it is possible to hike to the summit, there is also an aerial cable car for those who prefer an easier route.

Our plan was always: gaze at Table Mountain as we sail in, scale her mid-morning, then explore the rest of the city on the hop on bus. A plan that nature seems intent on ruining.

Despite having lived in London in our twenties, neither of us has ever experienced fog like this – both in quality and quantity. Hanging thick like a dense, white blanket, visibility is reduced to just a few metres and the air feels heavy with moisture. For hours, our ship sits marooned just outside Cape Town harbour, sounding her horn every two minutes (as maritime law dictates in such conditions), with the muffled replies of similarly stranded vessels echoing back.

Eight o'clock, our tour's departure time, comes and goes. Ten o'clock, then twelve. By one, everyone has given up. With only one scheduled day here, our dreams of setting foot on Cape Town soil are gone. We will be forever condemned to telling the story of how close we got to scaling Table Mountain.

Then, teasingly, at two o'clock, the fog lifts and quickly dissipates – but it doesn't matter. We all know it is too late. The tours have been cancelled. All we can do is stand on *Resilient Lady*'s top deck as she finally berths and watch Cape Town – every bit as spectacular as we had hoped – unfold before our eyes. Watch the cable car start back up again on picturesque Table Mountain. Watch new arrivals prepare to board, and watch those who are leaving disembark. It is incredible how disappointed I feel.

'Hello, ladies and gentlemen, this is your captain speaking.'

Unlike other cruise ships, our captain doesn't make announcements. In fact, he's virtually invisible. No-one knows what he looks like, what he sounds like – anything. So, when his voices comes over the loudspeakers, it immediately captures everyone's attention.

'It appears many of you are disappointed at not being able to visit Cape Town,' he sympathises. 'Well, we have had a change in schedule. Instead of departing this evening, the *Resilient Lady* will now remain berthed overnight and depart tomorrow afternoon instead. All tours cancelled today will be rebooked for tomorrow. This additional day in Cape Town will, however, change our onward plans. We will no longer be stopping at Praia in Cape Verde.'

At first, we all stand there, too stunned to speak, trying to process what we have just heard. The silence only lasts a moment before the ship erupts into cheers. Still standing on one of the ship's upper decks, I am jumping with excitement, laughing with happiness.

'We still get to scale Table Mountain! I'll have to see if we can use our hop-on bus tickets tomorrow instead. I'm sure they'll understand. Yes, we are going to see Cape Town!' I fist-pump the air.

'What will missing Cape Verde mean?' Darryl asks when we eventually calm down.

'Not much,' I reply. 'It's a tiny island nation off the west coast of Africa. It would have been nice to tick another country off the list, but I'm not too concerned. I wonder if this means more sea days, though. Cape Verde was the stop between Namibia, where we're heading next, and Tenerife in Spain. It was already going to take eight days to get from Namibia to Cape Verde, then another two to Tenerife. I suppose now it will be ten straight days at sea – the most we have ever done.'

'Let's worry about that later,' Darryl says. 'For now, let's just go ashore and have a look around.'

'We have to go ashore anyway,' I remind him. 'With our passports. We need to check in for this leg of the cruise and have our bracelets updated. Luckily, we get to keep the same cabin. I know some passengers who had to change rooms due to the ceiling creaks – now they have to move again.'

The Cape Town Cruise Terminal is situated at the bustling V&A Waterfront. Named after Queen Victoria and Prince Alfred, it offers a mix of modern shops and attractions housed in renovated warehouses, as well as cultural landmarks, high-end boutiques, waterfront restaurants and local craft markets.

It is a fun, lively place, which we wander and make great use of for the remainder of the afternoon. Shops are browsed, soulful street performers enjoyed, photographs taken. A designated viewing area allows us to watch fat Cape fur seals sunbathing, while a nearby café offers an early dinner. Walking back to our ship, we pop into one of the many diamond shops for which Africa is renowned. While the merchandise is stunning, the pieces I like are eye-wateringly expensive.

Some time that night, I wake to the sound of more foghorns. It is disheartening – I don't want fog to ruin another chance to explore this city, but knowing there is nothing I can do about it, I roll over and go back to sleep.

'Apparently, this fog is common in Cape Town,' I tell Darryl the next morning. I have woken early and spent a few minutes Googling. 'More common than I thought. And it is often called the "tablecloth" because of the way it drapes over Table Mountain like a thick, white cloth.'

'I can understand now what you were talking about,' Darryl says a little while later.

We have disembarked the *Resilient Lady* and are currently onboard a large coach, making our way through a soupy city. Overnights fog is starting to lift, but it still obscures much of everything. As Google had foretold, it has draped itself over the monolith and town like a giant piece of white linen.

'I still think everything looks incredible,' I reply.

Looking from my window, despite the misty conditions I have been impressed with what I have seen.

'Actually, it reminds me a bit of Sydney,' I continue. 'Only cleaner. I've seen three street cleaners in the past two hundred metres. Even the street names are in English, although the words aren't familiar – how do you pronounce *Bloem* Street?'

'Is that the cable car?' Darryl interrupts, pointing ahead. 'Look how fast it goes – and how steep it is. I'm not going up there.'

We have arrived at the base of Table Mountain, situated three hundred metres above sea level, the starting point for the mountain's aerial cableway. Now much closer, Darryl has just fully taken in the swaying cabins as they ascend rapidly to the now fog-free summit. He is clearly eyeing their speed and angle with suspicion.

'It's that or hike,' I laughingly reply.

Fortunately, Darryl's desire to reach the top of Table Mountain overrides his concerns, and after a short queue, we enter one of the 360-degree rotating capsules. Holding sixty-five passengers each, the system is designed to carry eight hundred people per hour on the 1,067-metre journey.

'Wow.' I gape, nose pressed to the cabin window. 'What a view. We're above the fog now – look how much thicker it looks out to sea. Once it clears, you can see Robben Island, apparently.'

Robben Island, located off the coast here, is where Nelson Mandela was imprisoned for eighteen of his twenty-seven years of incarceration. No longer a notorious prison for political prisoners and anti-apartheid leaders, it has become a symbol of the struggle for freedom and human rights. When planning our visit to Cape Town, it had been a tough choice between Table Mountain and Robben Island.

'I will never, ever forget this.'

It is sometime later, and Darryl and I are perched on weathered, lichen-covered rocks on the edge of a cliff. Below us, rocky peaks, scarred with splashes of greenery, rise from what looks like a calm sea – but is actually the dense fog stretching as far as the eye can see. We have spent much of our time following Table Mountain's wheelchair-accessible pathways but have now diverted off the main track to rest.

'I agree,' replies Darryl. 'There is always something I take away from our adventures. This view will be one of them.'

Eventually – reluctantly – we manage to tear ourselves away from our incredible sitting spot and make our way back to the cable car for our descent. Cleverly, the exit route passes through a gift shop, and as I purchase a keepsake T-shirt for Darryl, I strike up a conversation with a young family. With five children ranging in age from five to sixteen, their sheer exuberance, along with their filming paraphernalia, had caught my attention.

It turns out they are an American family who travel the world You-Tubing their adventures. They gift me a rubber wristband emblazed with their channel name, Our Backman Family, and later, I look them up online. After watching some of their vlogs, I can only wish I'd had the gumption to do something like that. To receive an education that way, life's lessons taught through experience – would be amazing. I can't help but wonder what kind of adults those children will grow into.

While we could return to our ship on the same coach we arrived on, we have decided to use the hop-on bus service that has served us so faithfully in so many cities around the world. I had already contacted them and successfully transferred yesterday's unused tickets to today.

Sitting atop our open-roof bus, I am freezing, the fog hasn't completely dissipated at ground level, but I am completely enthralled. Not just because I am finally seeing parts of Cape Town, but because it is fascinating… and it is reminding me so much of Australia.

'Apart from the cold, we could be in Bondi or Vaucluse,' I laugh at one point. 'Lavish mansions, golden beaches – well, maybe not the one thick with seaweed. But certainly Sea Point and Clifton Beach could be suburbs of Sydney.'

'Big blue sky, like ours… when you can see it,' agrees Darryl, pointing to a break in the fog.

Riding the bus has been a fun way of exploring Cape Town, but eventually, chilled and hungry, we hop off at the V&A Waterfront.

'African Time really is a thing,' Darryl comments a short time later.

We are sitting in a café, waiting for our falafel and salad lunch. The café isn't busy, maybe a quarter full, and there are seven staff members on duty. But five of them are laughing and chatting together, happily ignoring the customers, while a sixth is poking around on his phone. Only one person seems to be doing anything at all, which explains the 45-minute wait for our food.

Still, the slower pace has its upsides – it sets the tone for the rest of the afternoon and allows us to wander Cape Town's craft shops at leisure. On each of our adventures, I have managed to find some small, relevant gift to bring back for friends and family. Previous trips have taught me it is wise to buy them in countries where your dollar stretches a bit further – and not to leave it too late. Cape Town is full of shops selling native souvenirs that reflect the culture and artistry of Africa, making our last stop for the day the easiest gift buying I have ever had to do.

'Tell me, why do you need thirty-eight small, beaded animals?' Darry asks. 'They'd better not all be for your growing menagerie.'

'No,' I reply indignantly. 'Only the beaded elephant is mine. And maybe the giraffe… and zebra. The rest are for my Bowling Club Girls.'

CHAPTER 7

The Namibian Desert

Four weeks into our adventure, and as the *Resilient Lady* slowly makes her way northward, tracking Africa's west coast, we both wake up with runny noses and sore throats. Learning Covid is currently rampant onboard, we are relieved when our tests (brought with us) come back negative.

Outside, the temperature is hovering between a chilly 13 and 17 degrees Celsius, and a damp fog still lingers. All this makes hibernating in our cosy cabin the ideal option, so the day is spent lying in bed – me working on my latest blog, Darryl flipping between movies on TV.

Every now and then, one of us ventures upstairs to The Galley and returns with comforting supplies: an Impossible burger and chips, poke bowls, berries and yoghurt. It is good that we can rest today and treat our colds – because tomorrow, we will be arriving in Walvis Bay, Namibia.

The place where the desert meets the sea.

Situated in southern Africa and bordered by Angola, Zambia, Botswana, South Africa and the Atlantic Ocean, I had heard of Namibia but knew little about the country. Some quick Googling months earlier unveiled some interesting facts.

'Its economy is driven by mining,' I had summarised to Darryl. 'Especially diamonds and uranium. Then it is agriculture and tourism. It gained independence from South Africa in 1990, after a long struggle that included German colonisation. And it is home to the Namib Desert, which I hope to visit, one of the oldest deserts in the world.'

'How about the language?' Darryl had asked.

'English is the official language,' I had replied, smiling. 'But Afrikaans and various indigenous languages are also spoken. And how about this? Namibia is celebrated for its peaceful governance and for being a leader in sustainable tourism and conservation.'

'Well, I am definitely looking forward to visiting,' had been Darryl's final summation. 'It's where *Mad Max: Fury Road* was filmed.'

Now, months later, and with Namibia just over the horizon, I am incredibly excited to soon be arriving. On the Facebook page set up specifically for passengers on this one-off cruise, the administrators had mentioned a private tour company, Paulus Jamba Tours, that specialised in local excursions here. After contacting them and learning of an itinerary that included pink flamingos, pink salt lakes, desert dunes and cultural dances, it had been an easy and exhilarating decision to book with them.

Early the following morning, we find ourselves with eight other passengers, a guide and a driver rambling around Walvis Bay. As usual, I have my nose pressed to the window, drinking in the sights – which, so far, are startling. Sand everywhere, and not a single blade of grass to be seen. Big brick houses fronted by sandpit lawns. Large, wide, sand-covered streets. An enormous public library. Date palm-lined avenues.

'This area all owned by the Chinese,' Brendan, our guide, offers, seeing my confusion. 'They have many oil rigs just offshore, and they own many of the mines too. Later, we visit more normal area.'

It is cold – which we learn is unusual – and it is overcast, which, we are told, is common.

'We do not get the sun every day,' Brendan continues. 'It is often cloudy, and fog is normal along the coast in Namibia. It is desert's lifeblood. It provides the water for many animals to survive.'

'How about rain?' someone asks. 'Do you get much here?'

'The north of Namibia has rain, and the countryside is very green. But not here, not in this region. It has not rained here since 2015.'

Travelling further afield along more sand-covered roads, still not seeing grassy yards, green parks or any trees apart from the date palms, it is easy to believe that it truly doesn't rain here.

'It's incredible,' I murmur to Darryl. 'I don't think we've ever been to a place with so much sand. I think even the UAE had more greenery. I can't imagine growing up here – no lawn to kick a ball around on, no trees to climb or rest under.'

'No. The UAE was the same. But have you noticed the houses are built without gutters and downpipes?' Darryl, the former plumbing inspector, points out. 'No need for them if it doesn't rain.'

I have mentioned before that there are always places on our travels that I will never forget – locations or sights so remarkable, they become etched into memory like vivid snapshots of wonder. Petra's Treasury in Jordan was one such place. China's Terracotta Warriors, another. The Suez Canal, a third. Today, Namibia gifts me two more: witnessing colonies of vibrant pink flamingos in their natural habitat and later, experiencing the raw beauty of the eighty-million-year-old Namib Desert.

I have been so focused on listening to Brendan, absorbing his views on his country, that I had not realise we had stopped at some beautiful wetlands.

'Namibia is very corrupt country,' he had told us indignantly. 'You can go to university, but you'll only get a job if money changes hands under the table. If you can use your hands, you'll be okay. But if you use your head to get a degree, then you will not get the job you want. Namibians are also very selfish,' he had continued. 'Everyone is out for themselves. We do not try to group together to make a better country for our youth.'

Pondering his words, acknowledging that corruption seems rife in so many of the countries we have travelled, especially the poorer ones, it takes me a moment to realise what we have stopped for, what I am actually looking at.

'Are those flamingos?' I eventually cry. 'Look at them. Look how many there are – they're gorgeous.'

And indeed, they are. We have pulled up beside a vast, mangrove-lined lagoon. Overhead, the sky is blanketed in thick, creamy clouds, and the horizon is softened by an opaque mist. Stretching before me are miles of mudflats, currently exposed by the low tide but usually covered by a thin layer of seawater. It is an environment rich in algae, brine flies, and crustaceans – perfect feeding grounds for the beautiful flamingos I can't stop staring at.

It takes some doing but eventually we manage to tear ourselves away from this magical, captivating place. It really has been a special experience seeing so many of these elegant, vibrantly coloured birds with their long, spindly legs gathered in one area, but Namibia has other treasures to show us.

Which she does, as over the following few hours we travel further and further afield. First are her salt lakes – an arresting pink in colour, caused by salt-loving bacteria that thrive in the high-salinity water. It is interesting noting the number of small commercial salt works harvesting the commodity.

It is also quite surreal to step off our minibus and walk across the crispy salt surface, gazing out over miles of vividly pink water.

Next is Dune 7, located in the Namib Desert I had so wanted to see. One of the tallest sand dunes in the region, it is a popular spot for sand-boarders and adventurous climbers. We are content to just sit at its base and simply take it all in.

Later, it's lunch at Swakopmund. Founded in 1892 during the German colonial era, its architecture and street names still reflect those origins, as does much of its food.

'Strudel,' says Darryl, reading the menu. 'Yum. I'll have that.'

Early afternoon and we see the other side of Namibia – the side not financed by Chinese oil interests or German tourism. The overcrowded shantytowns with no power and no running water – only communal toilets, and water brought in manually.

'Namibia is facing a housing crisis,' Brendan tells us. 'But the government is trying to fix it. They are building housing, but you must buy them.'

'How much would a house here cost?' Darryl asks, curious.

'About fifty to eighty thousand dollars,' is the reply.

At one of these settlements, we do stop. Entertainment has been laid on for us in the form of cultural dancing and a small market. It is a chance to support the local community directly, so most of us either contribute to the hat that's passed around or purchase a small souvenir. Much to my delight – and Darryl's dismay – I pick up yet another figurine to add to my growing menagerie: a small, beaded pink flamingo.

'Brendan, there are a lot of crosses next to the road,' someone calls, as we venture deeper into the stunning Namib Desert.

'People don't bother to get their licence here,' he replies. 'They just buy them.'

A comment we all reflect on with alarm as sand-covered bitumen gives way to jarring, compacted-sand roads, and the landscape becomes even more alien and spectacular.

'This is how I imagine the moon would look,' I marvel to Darry when eventually we stop and alight. 'An ancient landscape of jagged gullies, stark gravel plains, and sand everywhere. Not a blade of grass to be seen. Barren, but beautiful.'

'Except you wouldn't find that on the moon,' Darryl laughs, pointing to a trestle table laden with beer, soft drinks and platters of finger foods.

'Oh,' I reply, startled. 'No. Actually, I'm surprised to even find it here.'

'Have you heard of the Skeleton Coast?' Brendan asks later, as we begin our return to the ship. He is referring to a famous, rugged stretch of Namibia's coastline.

'It is close to here. It got its name from all the shipwrecks and whale skeletons found along the shore. Very interesting. Maybe you all return and see it another day?'

'Namibia has been incredible to visit,' I whisper to Darryl. 'Spectacular and memorable. But I am not sure it is one of those places I would want to return to. At least... not in a hurry.'

As I predicted, we now have ten sea-days ahead of us before reaching Tenerife, an island off the coast of Spain. Unlike Darryl, who is quite content spending time on board, I hate it. I would much prefer to be stopping somewhere new every other day. As that's not an option, I resolve to make the most of it and, as the days progress, I start to find these slow days at sea not so bad after all. Even *Resilient Lady*'s inadequate entertainment program doesn't seem quite so terrible. Its lack of activities means there is no pressure to be anywhere or do anything.

The only commitment I make is to my exercise. The gym for arm work, the decks for leg work. It helps that our colds have gone.

'I think all the dust and sand of Namibia dried up my nose and cold,' I mention to Darryl. 'It is the only way I can explain how it disappeared so quicky.'

Being confined to a ship has also made it easy to continue a practice we started during my chemotherapy – a routine that not only got us out of the house each day but also made me feel so much better: buying a strong daily coffee.

Chemotherapy destroyed my energy levels and left me constantly nauseous – side effects my current medication, Verzenio, also causes. A large coffee each morning helps. It kickstarts my stamina and settles my stomach.

I have obviously been consistent with this ritual, as the café staff now greet me by name each day. This morning, I discovered they have even created a button on their till with my name and coffee order. It made me feel quite special.

Heading slowly and gradually northwards now, the sun has reappeared and the days are warming. Three tiny birds, which appear to have boarded back in Namibia, have captured passengers' attention with their flittering antics. The pools are once again well used, and the sun loungers are full.

I am still attending book club, though we now have a new facilitator, Meggi. She is an actor, and when she is not running book club, she performs the lead role in another incredible onboard show, *Lola in the Attic*. Watching her completely mesmerise the audience in a three-act performance one evening, I am doubtful I will see a better live show again.

Liberia, Ghana, Côte d'Ivoire. Sierra Leone, Guinea, Senegal. Exotic names of incredible countries. I can't believe we are passing within kilometres of them.

Cocooned within our floating bubble, the troubles of the outside world start to fade. The events in the Middle East feel distant. The only time this changes is when we hear about the Bondi stabbings.

News that six people have been fatally stabbed in a Sydney shopping centre and others, including a baby, injured, jolts everyone back to reality.

Anzac Day comes and goes, as does another crossing-of-the-equator ceremony – my fourth.

'It's obvious we are in the Northern Hemisphere now,' I mention to Darryl one morning. 'It is only when we are travelling in this hemisphere that the mornings are so dark. The sun didn't rise until eight this morning. It's never like this at home.'

Day eight, and somewhere outside is Cape Verde, the country gladly forsaken for our extra time in Cape Town. Today, dolphins surf our ship's wake, and cargo ships pass frequently. A large rain cloud, unwilling to release us from its grip, has kept most passengers indoors. This enforced enclosure, combined with so many days at sea, seems to be a breaking point for some.

'We got on in New Zealand,' says a lady I meet in the lifts. 'This is week six for us, and we are over it. The ship's not designed for this length of cruise.'

'I've been seasick since Sydney,' another woman tells me early one evening. 'When I heard we were going to be at sea for ten days straight, I tried to get a flight from Namibia to Tenerife. Couldn't do it. It was going to cost too much, and with no direct route, it would have taken thirty-six hours.'

The rain hasn't bothered us that much. I have spent the afternoon on our outside hammock, reading and enjoying the waterworks. Our cabin change gave us an extra-large balcony, and it has been quite fascinating to watch the rain and passing ships while cosily swaying with the ship's movement.

Darryl has been making full use of the free ship-provided wi-fi. Prior to this cruise, he flatly refused to use the internet for communication, always preferring a phone call. But so far out to sea, that's not possible – so he's been forced to try Messenger and WhatsApp.

He seems to like it because, when I finally leave the comfort of the hammock, he is full of news from home.

'Paige has resigned her job and is going travelling not long after we get back,' he tells me, one of several updates.

Monday, 29 April – the last of this long stretch at sea. While I have managed to keep myself reasonably occupied, spending such a prolonged period cooped up onboard a ship is something I hope never to have to do again. I woke with a nasty headache, a side effect of my medication, so most of the day has been spent recovering in bed.

Tonight, for dinner, we tried *Resilient Lady*'s vibrant Korean barbecue restaurant, Gunbae. Focusing on shared meals cooked over a flameless tabletop grill, its barbecuing element had meant we were reluctant to try it. Vegetarians and barbecues do not always mix well. Turns out we need not have worried – tonight's meal of grilled vegetables and sautéed mushrooms is our best yet.

'I wonder if the three tiny birds get off the ship tomorrow,' is the last thing I mumble to myself before falling asleep.

CHAPTER 8

Santa Cruz de Tenerife

Not surprisingly, after so many days at sea, the atmosphere at breakfast this morning on board the *Resilient Lady* is jubilant.

The constant movement of the ship has stopped, and from our harbour location we get the most welcome and stunning views of Tenerife's capital, Santa Cruz de Tenerife. The foreground is a mix of buildings that blend coastal and island architecture, while the background is dominated by sharp, rugged hills under a vibrant cobalt sky.

'It always surprises me how alike these island ports are,' I mention to Darryl over my bircher muesli. 'This could be Papeete in Tahiti, or Puerto Quetzal in Guatemala.'

'They do all start to look alike,' Darryl agrees. 'What do you know about this place?'

'Not much about Santa Cruz – we will hopefully learn more on our tour this morning. But I do know Tenerife is the largest of Spain's

Canary Islands. It was conquered by the Spanish in the late 15th century – and while its primary language is Spanish, it is not a colony of Spain. Rather, it's an autonomous region that follows Spanish law.'

'And its economy?' Darryl prompts.

'Now you're testing me,' I laugh. 'Luckily, I did some reading on Tenerife last night. Like most of these island getaways, agriculture use to be its main source of income, particularly wine and bananas, but today it is tourism. I remember when we lived and worked in London, everyone wanted to come here on a mini break. But you know the most interesting thing I discovered?'

'What?'

'The name "Canary Islands" originates not from the bird, but from a Latin term that translates to "Island of Dogs". *Canaria* means canine. And the canary bird actually took its name from these islands – not the other way around.'

As well as being happy to once again have solid ground beneath my feet, I am quite excited to be visiting here. As I mentioned to Darryl over breakfast, it was a popular holiday destination when we were living in London over thirty years ago. Many of my friends and work colleagues vacationed here, but we, unfortunately, never made it. It feels good to finally be remedying that.

Today, we have opted for one of the excursions organised by Virgin Voyages, rather than booking something independently. We will be exploring the north of the island, with a stop at the UNESCO-listed city La Laguna for cheese and wine. We will also pause at Mirador de Humboldt for photos, and later finish the day strolling the streets of Santa Cruz de Tenerife.

'Hurry up, hurry up. We are already running late.'

It is mid-morning and Fanny, our German guide, is once again chastising us all.

The tour had started well, with around fifty of us boarding a large, comfortable coach. Leaving Santa Cruz far behind, 120 kilometres-per-hour motorways had us shooting up lush, green, winding hills, climbing higher and higher. The views over deep, dark valleys, rugged mountains and a dramatic coastline became increasingly spectacular.

When she introduced herself, I had been pleased to note that Fanny was German.

'I always find German guides particularly efficient and professional,' I had whispered to Darryl.

But it had only taken our first stop for cracks in Fanny's demeanour to start showing.

'We are about to arrive at Mirador de Humboldt – named after the famous explorer Alexander Von Humboldt. It is the best place to take a photo of Mount Teide, the highest volcano in Spain and one of the tallest active volcanoes in the world. You—'

'Excuse me, Fanny, but is there a toilet?' someone interrupts her.

'Yes,' someone else calls out. 'We need to use one as well.'

'There is a café that has a toilet,' Fanny replies grudgingly. 'But there is only one, so please be quick.'

Unfortunately, many people had needed to use this one toilet, and what was meant to be a quick ten-minute photo opportunity stretched into a forty-minute wait.

'I don't mind waiting,' Darryl had whispered to me. 'The view's amazing. I wasn't expecting to see volcanos amidst banana trees and grapevines. But look at Fanny – she is not looking happy.'

'Quick, quick. We are running very late now.'

It is sometime later and, after a scenic drive along narrow, winding roads through plantations of mangoes, oranges, tomatoes, potatoes and chestnuts, we are exploring La Laguna. Once the capital of the Canary Islands and now recognised as its cultural heart, the place looks incredible. Built on a grid layout, like many of the Latin American cities, this fifteenth-century World Heritage site has retained much of its charm, along with some well-preserved architecture.

Or so we think it has. It has been difficult to tell, given the pace Fanny has set.

'That is the Cathedrale of La Laguna. It dates back to 1511. And that is the Casa de los Capitanes Generales. A seventeenth-century building, it showcases classic Canarian architecture. But we do not have time to look inside. Hurry, hurry, hurry.'

'This is ridiculous,' I eventually pant. 'It looks like such a wonderful place. Look at this square and these tree-lined streets. Look at those great shops. But we are going too fast to appreciate anything.'

'We are here, but we are still late. You will have to be quick with your wine and cheese.' Fanny has finally come to a standstill, but the berating has continued.

'I will see you later back on the bus.'

'That has got to be the worst guide we have ever had.'

It is a few hours later and Darryl and I are sitting in a café back in Santa Cruz. We have managed to successfully order two soymilk coffees using bad Spanish and are now laughing over the morning's ordeal.

'She wasn't *that* bad,' Darryl grins.

'She was. I'm exhausted.'

'We did learn some things,' Darryl continues. 'We now know the island of Tenerife is shaped like a duck, and all its beaches have black sand – except one, which has white sand imported from the Sahara Desert. We also know they have a big problem with Airbnb, and that there are 320 volcanos here. Finally, although *you* couldn't eat or drink it, the wine they make and the cheeses they produce are first class.'

'Okay,' I grudgingly admit. 'Fanny *did* teach us a few things. But I still maintain she was the worst guide we've ever had. She didn't tell us *anything* about Santa Cruz.'

Fortunately, there is such a thing as Google, and as we sip our coffees, I quickly read about the city we are currently visiting.

'It was first discovered in 1494 by Spanish conquistadores, but it wasn't until the sixteenth century that it truly developed – when its strategic location and growing port facilitated trade and commerce... It is known for its annual Carnival... The city displays a mix of modern and colonial influences, with wide boulevards and historic squares...'

'You didn't have to Google that last bit,' Darryl interrupts. 'We're sitting in one.'

'Santa Cruz also has great shops.'

'It doesn't say that,' Darryl interrupts again.

'No. *Google* doesn't say that.' I grin. 'But I bet it does.'

It's a bet I would have won – had Darryl taken it.

It is the following morning, Wednesday 1 May – a date special to me because it marks the anniversary of my father's death. A man who not only instilled in me my sense of adventure and the need to explore the world, but also gifted me the desire to write about my travels. Every now and again I still dip into his journal, detailing our overland journey from England to India, via, Iran, Afghanistan and Pakistan, undertaken when I was just a year old.

It is a cold, windy day. The pools are empty, and I haven't seen the three tiny birds that have been with us since Namibia. I presume they disembarked at Santa Cruz de Tenerife, probably wondering where on earth they were.

Tomorrow, we arrive at Casablanca, a city I am incredibly excited to be visiting. But today is for uploading my latest blog, attending book club (we are currently reading *The Immortalists* by Chloe Benjamin), and reviewing our onward travel plans. Our two weeks exploring Türkiye has finally come together. I have found a small agency based in the city of Kaş called Amber Travel, who have been helping me with arrangements. Early this morning, I made final payment for our upcoming train journeys, making our Türkiye visit real – there is no backing out now.

There are only eight days left of this cruise, our six weeks are nearly over, and it feels like everyone is ready to disembark. It has been too long a voyage for the entertainment provided and the limited number of ports offered. Fortunately, the remaining eight days include four stops; otherwise, I think people would really start to crack. As it is, many are turning to alcohol, the bars filling by ten each morning.

Now that we are nearing Europe, the seas are full of vessels. I have downloaded an app called MarineTraffic onto my phone, and each time another ship passes by, it is fun to look them up. My favourite liner so far has been one called *Aida*. It actually trailed us all the way from Cape Town to Tenerife, then docked alongside us. Just before boarding yesterday, we managed to speak with some of her staff and discovered she was empty of passengers. Built to accommodate 5,000, she is remaining at Santa Cruz de Tenerife for a refit. It is clearly a big job; the crew we spoke with were struggling to load over a thousand new televisions.

Over the past weeks, we have been consistently winding our watches backwards and are now nine hours behind Australia – the farthest we will travel back in time on this adventure. Tomorrow, as we reach Morocco, we will wind them forward by one hour.

Darryl mentioned a few weeks ago that, of all the trips we have taken, this one has messed with our body clocks the most – and I agree. Constantly adjusting the time, plunging southwards then steeply northwards, crossing equators, jumping between seasons – it's a wonder our circadian rhythms are keeping up.

CHAPTER 9

Disappointed by Casablanca

I am not sure why I am so excited to be visiting Casablanca, Morocco's largest city. Finding our ship was going to call here, I had done some research – and the overwhelming message from travellers was to leave as soon as you arrive. Or skip it entirely.

I had even discovered that the immortal movie *Casablanca*, produced over eighty-two years ago and still universally famous, wasn't even filmed here, but rather on a Hollywood lot. But still, excited I am.

'I just can't help thinking of exotic deserts, exciting souks or markets, luxurious carpets, arrogant turban-topped men riding scary camels – whenever I hear the words "Casablanca" or "Morocco".' I try to explain my enthusiasm to Darryl. 'I have always wanted to visit. I have actually always wanted to do a train journey through this country, like

Chris Tarrant did on one of his *Extreme Railway Journeys*, but this will do for now.'

'It will be interesting to see if the city lives up to your expectations,' Darryl replies. 'Given what other travellers have said. What have we got organised?'

'The Virgin Voyages shore excursions were expensive,' I reply. 'And limited in where they went. So, I booked a tour through Viator. They will pick us up at ten near the port gates and show us most of Casablanca's main sights – the Hassan II Mosque, Rick's Café, Pigeon Square, some souks for shopping. A few other places too, but I can't remember all their names.'

'Ten o'clock? But that's not for another three hours. Feels a bit of a waste of time.'

'It is. Virgin have again provided shuttle buses from the port into the city. We could catch one of those, have a quick look around the centre, then get back here in time for our excursion?'

'We'll need to make sure we get back in time,' Darryl replies enthusiastically.' But let's do it.'

While I have found our daily activities program lacking, and the *Resilient Lady*'s layout not as convenient as other ships we have sailed, I have been appreciating her little extras – like the free wi-fi and the complimentary shuttle buses provided at each port.

This morning's free transporter is actually waiting at the foot of the ship's gangway, eliminating the 500-metre trek to the harbour's congested exit. Sitting on our coach, we pass through secured gates and see frantic guides searching for passengers amid curious onlookers and pushy touts.

'It's looking pretty chaotic out there,' I say to Darryl. 'Hopefully we will have no trouble later finding our guide and tour.'

It is a twenty-minute journey from the cruise terminal to United Nations Square, our shuttle's destination, and as we travel, I start to get a sense that Casablanca is a little more modern than I was expecting. Less *Arabian Nights*, more concrete jungle with pollution-spewing cars. Less turban-topped men atop spitting camels – more western-attired youth astride discordant scooters.

'I really don't know why I was expecting it to look more Arab, more exotic,' I wryly acknowledge to Darryl. 'It's nothing like that at all. It's much dirtier, bigger and busier.'

'You're probably confusing it with Fes or Marrakesh. Pictures of those places gel a little more with what you have described.'

'I think you're right. I think I was hoping Casablanca would have some elements of those two cities. We haven't *seen* it yet. Maybe later. Although… I do like the design of some of the buildings. Look at that Art Deco one over there, with the rounded wrought-iron balcony. And that building with the tiles and arches – they are filthy but they are gorgeous. Underneath the dirt and the pollution, Casablanca's architecture appears to have good bones.'

'Good morning. Where are you from?'

We are currently standing in the middle of United Nations Square. A bustling public area lively with street vendors and cafés. It links the beautiful, iconic Boulevard Mohammed V with the Medina (old city) and we have just been waylaid by a cheerful, smiling man.

'You English?' he continues.

'No. Australian.'

'Ah. Australian. A long way from home. Perhaps you would like to buy a carpet?'

'No, thank you. We're fine.'

'Come. You do not have to buy. Just have a look. I have a friend who has a bazaar. Lots of things to see. Silk carpet. Leather handbag. Silver jewellery. Oil for your hair.'

It is the typical scenario in every city we have visited – a peddler pushing for business. The kind of person we would normally politely run from. Someone to avoid. But this time, realising we only have a very short time here, wanting to see everything we can and knowing we will never buy a carpet, we decide to follow what turns out to be a chef called Rashid.

Feeling slightly alarmed as he leads us further from the square, into chaotic traffic and down jammed alleys, it is with some relief when we eventually arrive at a large, colourful shopping emporium. Relief is compounded when Rashid turns to us, smiles, then begins to walk away.

'I am a chef, not a seller. I just bring you here to have a look. If you buy, my friend will be happy. If not, then it is fine.'

While we do not buy anything, we do have fun – first, when browsing all the incredible goods, then later, when trying to find our way back to our shuttle bus.

It is a few hours later, and we have found our tour and are on our way to another Casablanca landmark. As feared, it was every bit as difficult as expected finding our minibus amongst the jostling crowd and dozens of tourist coaches surrounding the harbour exit – but eventually we did, with a few minutes to spare.

On board, many of our fellow passengers had been thoroughly disgruntled.

'Been sitting here for an hour, just waiting to go somewhere,' was the general refrain.

Telling them that we had already been into the city, had a look around and had managed to return on time did not help matters. I had to laugh, though, when overhearing a couple in the seat behind me. They had just caught their first glimpse outside the terminal gates.

'Oh. It looks like a big city. I was expecting a country town.'

Turns out I wasn't the only one with thwarted expectations.

'Just up ahead, you will get your first look at Rick's Café.'

Having kept us entertained with stories – including how and why he had two wives – while pointing out some of Casablanca's notable sights, like the walls of the Medina and the scenic waterfront La Corniche neighbourhood, our guide, Ahmed, now gestures towards perhaps the city's most legendary attraction: the famous, fictional bar from the 1942 film, *Casablanca*.

'But you all do realise, of course,' Ahmet continues, 'that there never was a real Rick's Café. That the film was made in Hollywood. That what we are about to see was designed by a clever American woman, Kathy Kriger, and opened in 2004.'

While I had recently learnt this, others on our tour clearly had not.

'What?' exclaims someone from the back of the bus. 'You mean Humphrey Bogart was never here? But I've told everyone I'm going to see the *real* Rick's Café.'

'Well, it *is* Rick's Café,' someone else replies. 'And it *is* real – it's just not the café from the film.'

While some tours included the interior of Rick's Café, and perhaps even hearing someone play 'As Time Goes By' on the piano, ours did not. Instead, we made do with a quick photo stop before continuing to our next location.

'I want to give you a quick history of the Hassan II Mosque before we arrive,' Ahmet tells us. 'We will stop there for a while and go inside, but I think it is good to know a little about a place before seeing it. The Hassan II Mosque is one of the largest mosques in the world. It was built on reclaimed land and it can accommodate twenty-five thousand worshippers inside and eighty thousand outside. It took six thousand artisans just six years to build, and it was completed in 1993.'

Arriving at a promontory overlooking the Atlantic Ocean a short time later, I step off the bus and realise that Ahmet's words have not fully prepared me for the sheer scale of the place. With a vast square opening on to a calm ocean, sprawling plazas paved with intricate mosaic tiles, and the largest minaret in the world, the Hassan II Mosque complex is absolutely enormous.

EMMA SCATTERGOOD

'And all this took only six years to build,' I hear someone mutter.

'The prayer hall roof is retractable, allowing worshippers to pray under the open sky, and the minaret is topped with a laser that points toward Mecca,' Ahmet explains.

We have just finished our tour of the interior and are now struggling to put our shoes back on (shoes are not permitted inside mosques), before heading down to the basement to view the ablution area.

'A mosque's ablution area is a designated space for *wudu* – the ritual washing performed by Muslims before prayer to ensure physical and spiritual cleanliness,' Ahmet continues. 'Worshippers would normally sit at these fountains and wash their face, hands, arms and feet. But these ones down here aren't actually used – they are just for show.'

'It's interesting,' I whisper to Darryl. 'This area is for show, and I can't imagine the Mosque filling with 125,000 worshippers often. It kind of feels like all this was designed more as a tourist attraction than a fully functioning place of worship.'

'Especially when they are offering guided tours throughout the whole place,' Darryl agrees.

It takes some time to reach our next destination, Mohammed V – or Pigeon Square, as it is more commonly known. Not because it is far away, it is actually quite close, but because of the circuitous route we travel to get there.

A route that winds through affluent suburbs where mansions are tucked behind security-manned gates, while, paradoxically, the streets and footpaths in front of them are in a terrible condition. A journey through districts where to cross at a pedestrian crossing means taking your life into your own hands, and alongside Arab League Park, the biggest green space in the city.

At the Church of Notre Dame of Lourdes, a prominent Catholic church known for its modernist design and stunning stained-glass windows, we do stop – but for some reason it is closed. So we have to continue.

'Mohammed V Square,' Ahmet announces. 'Better known as Pigeon Square, for obvious reasons. It is a popular meeting place for both locals and tourists, so we will stop here for a little while.'

Standing amongst the large number of well-fed pigeons in this square, Darryl and I manage to steal a quick, private conversation with Ahmet. Our discussion bounces between religion, education, women's rights and colonialism.

'Public education is free here, even university… Morocco is an Islamic country, with ninety-nine per cent of the population identifying as Muslim and less than one per cent Christian… Even though we are Islamic, we are more moderate in our practices compared to, say, Saudi Arabia. Here, women have more rights – they do not have to wear the hijab… The French ruled Morocco from 1912 until 1956, when we gained independence.'

I am still reflecting on this conversation some time later – surprised that such a heavily populated Islamic country can be so liberal in its outlook, cheered by its attitude toward women and delighted that, if I wanted to, I could probably find a decent croissant.

'I thought we were visiting some *souks*,' someone on our bus has called out.

'Yes, we are meant to be stopping at the Habous Quarter markets,' someone else grumbles.

'Unfortunately, we have run out of time,' Ahmet apologises. 'The traffic has been worse than normal. I need to get you back to your ship but we do have time for a quick stop at a small bazaar. It has leather goods, handbags, shoes, spices, carpets, ceramics – everything.'

Bitterly disappointed to be missing the Habous Quarter, known as the New Medina, built by the French and famous for its relaxed *souks* and handcrafted goods, there is a fair amount of disgruntled mumbling amongst the tour's passengers. This only subsides when we arrive at a shopping emporium stuffed to overflowing with traditional Moroccan wares.

'What's that?' I ask Darryl a short while later.

'A little carved stone camel,' he replies. 'It's for your menagerie.'

We are currently heading northwards, tracing the eastern coast of Spain. Some time during the very early hours of this morning, we passed through the Strait of Gibraltar, the narrow waterway connecting the Atlantic Ocean to the Mediterranean Sea. While some passengers stayed up late, eager to glimpse the iconic Rock of Gibraltar, a massive headland guarding the northern horizon, we stayed cocooned under our doonas.

It is not the first time we have traversed this strait. Back in 2017, we journeyed through here, only, instead of entering the Mediterranean, we were exiting. It was also broad daylight at the time.

From the moment we woke this morning and gazed upon majestic snow-capped mountains, mountains I had been so excited to see back in 2017, it was obvious we were back in the Mediterranean. Unlike the vast, empty Atlantic Ocean, the Mediterranean Sea is full of life.

But it is not just outside that feels different. Inside, the change of atmosphere is even more pronounced. With only six days left until we arrive in Athens, and the European continent now within reach, passengers are excited. Onward travel plans are being discussed, the laundry is running hot, and goodbyes are starting to be said. Tomorrow's arrival in Barcelona marks the end of the cruise's second leg.

CHAPTER 10

Discovering Gaudí in Barcelona

While this isn't my first time visiting Barcelona, my grandparents used to live a few hours south of here, it has been decades between visits, and there is very little I remember of the city. I do vaguely recall staring up at some unfinished cathedral, but at the time I was far more interested in sampling another dish of delicious chicken paella than wandering through a dusty old incomplete church. Fast forward a few decades: the grandparents are long gone, I'm not so keen on paella anymore, and that cathedral – Antoni Gaudí's Sagrada Familia – is still unfinished. But my interest in it has completely reversed. In fact, it is the main sight I want to visit here, and, I discover a few hours later, a very popular choice.

It is just after breakfast when we find ourselves drifting past a fascinating historic fortress and into busy Barcelona Harbour. Although this is technically our second visit to a European Union country, Tenerife being the first, Barcelona is much bigger and the end of the second leg of our cruise. Therefore, we are expecting some delay with immigration. The general assumption among passengers is that while Tenerife was happy to ignore any custom formalities, Barcelona, being on the Spanish mainland, certainly would not.

Turns out we are all wrong. Not long after docking, we have disembarked, passed through an unmanned immigration hall, and are now waiting for the customary shuttle buses to transport us into the city centre.

The queue for the bus is long and as we inch closer to its head, it is interesting to note that a lot of the conversation mirrors our current thoughts.

'Strange our passports weren't checked or stamped for EU entry.'

'Hope that doesn't become a problem later on.'

'What are you doing in Barcelona today?'

'Catching the hop-on bus.'

With Virgin Voyages offering no shore excursions, and as we were already fans of hop-on buses, it had been an easy decision for us to tour Barcelona this way. We had already purchased tickets online, figured out where to board and, with over thirty sightseeing stops across the city, I had even highlighted a few key ones to jump off at.

'I want to see Gaudi's Sagrada Familia first,' I had told Darryl. 'I've also marked the Gothic Quarter, Las Ramblas, the Boqueria Market, and maybe the Olympic stadium – if we're not too worn out by then.'

While Barcelona's history spans some two thousand years, beginning as a Roman settlement, remnants of which are still visible today, when I think of the city, four things come to mind: Catalonia, Franco, the Olympics and Gaudi.

Catalonia refers to an independent region of north-eastern Spain with its own language, culture and deep-rooted history. Barcelona is its capital. Renowned for its unique identity, strong local governance and rich traditions, Catalonia has long pushed for greater autonomy, particularly since Franco's time.

Francisco Franco was a Spanish dictator who, with help from Nazi Germany, rose to power and ruled from 1939 until his death in 1975. His reign was marked by mass executions, censorship, political repression, restricted personal freedoms and the enforcement of conservative Catholic values.

Under Franco's dictatorship, Catalonia suffered greatly. The Catalan language was banned, Catalan leaders and intellectuals who opposed Spanish nationalism were persecuted, imprisoned or exiled, Catalan institutions were closed. While Franco's death did see Spain transition to a democracy, and conditions improve for the Catalans, tensions have reignited in recent years with Catalonia once again pushing heavily for independence.

In 1992, Barcelona hosted the summer Olympic games. With significant urban development, greatly improved infrastructure and a revitalised waterfront, the city was transformed. It became the European place to visit.

Personally, it was not the city's physical makeover I remember most, but Sarah Brightman singing the official Olympic anthem, 'Amigos Para Siempre'. That haunting song has stayed with me forever.'

And finally, Gaudi – the legendary architect whose 142-year-old masterpiece we are currently on our way to see. Antoni Gaudi, a visionary who helped shape and was shaped by the Art Nouveau movement, left a profound mark on Barcelona. He has many notable works here and his Sagrada Familia, a Roman Catholic basilica begun in 1882, has become the symbol of the city itself.

Knowing I hadn't given the building the attention it deserved all those decades ago, I am excited and eager to be rectifying the matter today.

'It's busy, isn't it? Can you see where to go?'

Our shuttle has just dropped us at one of Barcelona's largest and busiest squares – Plaça de Catalunya. It's the meeting point of the new and old parts of the city, and the starting location for both routes offered by the hop-on bus. Unfortunately, the sheer volume of milling tourists, jostling locals and weary commuters has made it difficult to locate any sort of bus stop.

'I can easier understand why locals have started telling tourists not to come here,' I answer Darryl. 'Why some of them have begun retaliating with force. These crowds are ridiculous.'

It takes some searching, but eventually, a massive snaking queue correctly guides us to our bus boarding point. Gratefully sinking into our seats, earphones in place, we begin to watch the passing landscape with interest.

'I hadn't realised Gaudi had such a wide influence here,' I mumble to Darryl, as the commentary in my headset explains that the museum, the residential building, the park, the shopping avenue, the gardens, and even a pavilion we have passed, were all affected by the architect in some form or another.

'I was expecting a few buildings with Gaudi's stamp, but not this many. Speaking of Gaudi – look, there's the Sagrada Familia.'

If you look at a map of Barcelona, you can't help but notice that a large part of the city is laid out in an obvious grid pattern. Long, wide streets intersect equal-sized octagonal blocks. Designed by urban planner Ildefons Cerdà in the 1850s and 60s, this 'Eixample' (meaning extension) was created to ease overcrowding and poor living conditions, while improving traffic flow, visibility and ventilation.

Alighting at Gaudi's masterpiece in the heart of the Eixample, it is thrilling to finally gaze upon its quirky spires, Modernist gargoyles, and unmistakably lumpy physique. I can even understand why George Orwell once called it 'one of the most hideous buildings in the world' – it is bizarre, overwhelming and oddly beautiful all at once. But what rapidly leaves the biggest impression on us isn't the building itself – it is the way the Eixample grid system here completely fails.

The Sagrada Familia does not sit neatly within one of Cerdà's octagonal blocks. Instead, it spills across several, broken up by small plazas and sliced through by narrow, traffic-choked streets. Add to this the fact that the basilica is still under construction, with scaffolding and temporary fencing eating into what little space remains, and the result is chaos. One of the world's most iconic landmarks surrounded by a crush of tourists, all jostling for position, cameras raised, in an area far too cramped to hold them.

'This is ridiculous. I'm glad we didn't bother purchasing tickets to go inside as well,' Darryl eventually complains. 'Imagine how crowded that is. Let's go.'

We have just spent the past forty minutes battling our way around the perimeter of the building, dodging traffic and failing to snap a decent photo. Darryl, with his walking stick, has found it especially tough going. Beginning to realise that the locals really do have something to worry about when it comes to overtourism, I am happy to comply with his suggestion.

While our glimpses of FC Barcelona and the former Olympic site (now a marina) are noteworthy, and our stops at the bohemian neighbourhood of Gràcia and the village-like district of Sarrià are memorable, it is how we spend our afternoon that elevates Barcelona to a city worth returning to.

Alighting one final time at Plaça de Catalunya, our plan is to make our way on foot back to Barcelona Harbour via the Gothic Quarter and La Boqueria Market. From what we have heard, both neighbourhoods should appeal to us more than the modern, structured areas of the city.

Characterised by a maze of narrow cobblestone streets, medieval buildings and leafy plazas, the Gothic Quarter is considered the historic and cultural heart of Barcelona. Dating back to Roman times, it offers a mix of ancient history, contemporary art galleries, boutique shops, a Gothic cathedral, and more. Little wonder it is a cherished destination for locals and tourists alike.

'Yes, this is definitely my favourite part of the city,' I sigh some time later.

Wandering aimlessly, we have managed to purchase a souvenir tote bag in one of the gorgeous boutique shops, browse an eclectic art gallery, and even discover remnants of an old Roman wall. We are now standing in an ancient cobblestone lane dripping with baskets full of colourful flowers. A guitarist is playing somewhere nearby, his music drifting between the buildings.

'But I still can't get over how disappointing the Sagrada Familia was – at least this makes up for it.'

'This area is full of shops,' Darryl states bluntly. 'No wonder you like it. But I agree. This is definitely more us. Anything Roman or built from sandstone usually is.'

With breakfast feeling like a distant memory, it is as a welcome sight when, a few minutes later, we find ourselves at La Boqueria Market, Barcelona's most famous food market. Dating back to the thirteenth century, with stalls bursting with fresh produce, the atmosphere here is incredible – lively, exciting, exotic.

Spoilt for choice, we eventually settle on a couple of vegetable empanadas and eat them perched on benches while being serenaded by local musicians.

'So, apart from the crowds – what's your verdict on Barcelona?' Darryl asks when, revitalised, we begin our journey back to the harbour.

'Interesting,' I reply. 'One day here is definitely not enough, though. I would return – just to more thoroughly explore the Gothic Quarter.'

Back on board the *Resilient Lady*, a sea of fresh faces and a new injection of onboard credit are the first signs that we have commenced the third and final sector of our cruise. At dinner that night, we also learn that, having now completed two cruises with Virgin Voyages, we have reached Blue Level on their loyalty program.

'It gives you one load of free laundry. One free coffee per day. And a party,' our dining companions tell us.

'I don't mind the free load of laundry, and I love getting a complimentary daily coffee now – but I don't care much about the party,' I mention to Darryl as we prepare for bed.

'It's probably going to be the last time we cruise with Virgin,' he replies. 'They are apparently not returning to Australia next season, and as we haven't liked the ship as much as, say, the *Arcadia*, we may as well make the most of it and enjoy the party.'

I am not really listening to his reply. My attention has drifted to the sun, still shining brightly outside.

Fighting cancer and managing the exhaustion caused by treatment means I have become meticulous about maintaining a routine – especially with sleep and medication. For the past two years, I have ensured I am in bed by nine, taken a melatonin, and hopefully fallen asleep by 9.30. It is the only way I can function well the following day.

Mostly I am fine with this. But tonight, preparing to get under the covers while the sun continues to blaze outside, knowing people are still splashing in pools and sipping drinks on deck, I can't help but feel slightly ridiculous.

CHAPTER 11

Our Return to Malta

It is an early start the following morning when a FaceTime call from Paige wakes us. She is phoning to say that she has just purchased a handful of plane tickets that will see her heading overseas just one week after we return to Australia. Her excitement is contagious, propelling us out of bed and ready to start the day.

This is our second-last day at sea. Tomorrow we visit Malta, the day after is our final sea day, followed by Santorini and then Athens. As usual on these sea days, I spend a large part of it updating our website with our latest blog. While time consuming, it is rewarding, especially now that I am often stopped by fellow passengers commenting on it.

With only four more days until our cruise ends, and our account plush with new onboard credit, the early evening is spent putting it to use – purchasing sunglasses and aftershave from the ship's shops.

Darryl and I have been to Malta before. Seven years ago, Valletta's limestone harbour stupefied us with its beauty. Knowing just how beautiful, how impressive the view of the city is as you approach from the sea, we are on *Resilient Lady*'s upper deck early the following morning, keen to witness fellow passengers' reactions. They don't disappoint – the most relatable comment comes from a young couple.

'I thought Barcelona was good, but this is next level.'

Having already explored Valletta, Malta's capital city, it had not been easy deciding what to do this visit. Should we revisit a city we loved, or try something new? Eventually, after much scrolling through Virgin's shore excursions and GetYourGuide, a tuk-tuk tour of Gozo won out.

The Maltese archipelago, lying directly south of Italy and north of Libya, consists of three small islands: Malta, Comino and Gozo. Their strategic location in the middle of the Mediterranean Sea has given them a chequered history – Greeks, Romans, Arabs, Normans, Argonese, the Knights of St John, French and British, all having fought or ruled these islands at some point. While Malta is the largest and most developed of the three, and Comino is famous for its Blue Lagoon swimming spot, Gozo is a mystery to us.

'It would have been great to revisit Valletta,' I say to Darryl. 'But this tour sounds fun. Not only do we get to see another side of Malta – a different island – but we will be doing it by tuk-tuk.'

It takes forty minutes by boat to reach Gozo. Having spotted several sleek ferries in the harbour, we are a little disappointed when our vessel turns out to be a small, somewhat dodgy one. Darryl struggles to board it, and many passengers get soaked by sea spray. It is worth it however, to eventually arrive and spy a cluster of tuk-tuks waiting for us.

'How come everyone else gets to ride with their partner but we can't? Can't you make someone change tuk-tuks? Well, I am going to *complain*.'

With an average of five passengers per tuk-tuk, one couple has been forced to separate, and for the duration of our exit from the harbour, their strident complaining is all we can hear. Fortunately, we have boarded the vehicle driven by the youngest guide of the group. Full of youthful exuberance, his spirited driving soon puts us at the head of the convoy, leaving the complaining couple far behind.

A tuk-tuk is a small, three-wheeled motorised vehicle. With open-air sides, the ability to navigate places that are inaccessible to larger vehicles, and close proximity to the driver, we quickly discover it is the perfect vehicle for touring.

'Tell us a little about Gozo. What's in those terraces, and why is everything so brown?' one of our companions asks our driver.

It is a good question. With a population of 39,000 that swells to over seventy thousand in summer, Gozo is not a heavily developed island. For the past fifteen minutes, our journey has taken us along small winding roads, bordered by brown, barren, rocky fields broken into neat terraces. Large, plump hay barrels are a frequent sight.

'It hasn't rained much this summer,' comes the reply. 'Each year, we seem to get less and less rain, and the summers are getting hotter and hotter. In winter it is cold and windy – the temperature can drop to ten degrees – but in the summer, it reaches 45. That's why it all looks so brown.'

'And the terraces? What's in them?'

'They are for the cabbages, onions, beans, tomatoes and potatoes.'

'If it doesn't rain much, how do they survive?' asks Darryl, ever the former plumbing inspector.

'Water is collected when it rains. But if it doesn't, then it gets piped over from Malta.'

'And the hay barrels? Where are the cows?'

'It's too hot for the cows in summer. They are kept indoors.'

Ours is the first tuk-tuk to arrive at our first destination: the Church of St John the Baptist. By the time the final vehicle arrives, we have already admired its massive dome, peered inside its impressive interior, and are on our way to our second stop: the Sanap Cliffs.

'This reminds me of the Slieve League Cliffs in Ireland,' I call to Darryl from my stunning viewpoint, one hundred and thirty metres above the Mediterranean Sea. 'These limestone cliffs will make a great cover picture for my blog on Malta – try and get a good photo.'

It takes some time to get the perfect shot, meaning our tuk-tuk is a little behind the others on departure. It doesn't matter. With a determined look on his face, our driver quickly starts overtaking those ahead until, once again, we lead the pack.

'If you look left, you will shortly see the Gozo salt pans. These salt pans have been used and operated for centuries, often by the same families. We will stop shortly, and you can buy some salt if you wish.'

While we don't purchase any salt, it is fascinating to learn a little about the harvesting process – how seawater is collected in the shallow limestone reservoirs that cover the coastline here; how the water evaporates under the sun's heat, leaving behind white salt crystals; and how the salt is then collected, dried and stored in caves carved into the coastal rock.

'That was fun,' I say to Darryl as we once again board our tuk-tuk. 'A smaller production than what we saw in Namibia, but probably more interesting to look at.'

Our tour includes lunch, which consists of a selection of traditional *pastizzi* – small Maltese pastries made from flaky filo dough and filled with ricotta cheese, mushy peas or spiced meat. We eat while sitting on one of Gozo's secluded beaches, engaged in lots of spirited conversation.

'We speak Arabic, French, Spanish and English,' one of the drivers replies in response to a question.

'Gozo has thirteen villages and sixty-six churches,' comes the answer to another.

'Have you seen much change lately?' opens a whole floodgate of responses.

'Our population has grown by forty per cent in the past seven years. It is too much.'

'We have migrants arriving – some legal, others illegal. From many other countries.'

'Who wouldn't want to live here? Education is free. We have everything.'

'But everything is stuck now.'

'What do you mean by stuck?' Darryl asks.

'Our roads are full now. So are our hospitals and schools.'

'You mean the infrastructure can't keep up with the increase in population?' someone else asks.

'Yes. And each year it gets worse.'

It is mid-afternoon when we arrive at our final stop for the day – Gozo's Citadella. Located in the capital city of Victoria, this historic fortress has been the island's defensive stronghold for centuries. While we enjoy the panoramic views from its buttresses and appreciate its winding streets, our most memorable experience comes from a conversation with another tuk-tuk driver. We bump into him while sneaking into a small pub for a fortifying coffee, and he is keen to share his knowledge of the place.

'This Citadel has served as a fortress and a refuge for centuries, but its most famous story happened in 1551,' he tells us. 'During the Ottoman-Habsburg wars, the Ottomans led a raid on Gozo. This Citadella was the island's last line of defence, and everyone rushed here seeking protection. They held out as long as they could, but the Ottomans were relentless. When it became obvious that surrender was unavoidable, some chose to jump to their death from the Citadella's highest point rather than be captured. Eventually, the Citadella fell, and the entire population – between five and six thousand people – was taken into slavery and sent to North Africa. The island was ruined and left almost deserted. It took decades to be resettled.'

It is a sobering story, and it occupies my mind for much of the ferry ride back to Malta. Not even our brief detour to the famous Blue Lagoon manages to dislodge it entirely from my thoughts.

CHAPTER 12

What Santorini is Really Like

It has taken six weeks, but departing Malta and entering the Ionian Sea overnight means we have now entered Greek waters – and have nearly reached our destination. We wake early on this final full sea day and head to The Galley for breakfast. From the crowds surrounding us, we surmise that many others had the same idea, and we are forced to share a table with another couple.

'We have noticed you around the ship,' the gentleman says to Darryl as he takes his seat. 'We were wondering what led you to need a walking stick.'

'Our son had an accident on his mountain bike nine days before this cruise,' his wife explains. 'We thought he might end up a paraplegic and wanted to cancel, but he insisted we go.'

'It's been difficult to enjoy ourselves knowing what he and his family are going through, but he seems to be doing okay. He's even managed to take a few steps using a walker,' her husband adds.

Familiar with what they are currently experiencing – in 2011, Darryl spent five months recovering in hospital following a life-altering motorbike accident – our conversation continues, and we learn that their cruise hasn't been entirely smooth sailing.

'I got Covid in Cape Town,' the wife tells us. 'But Virgin were great. I had to isolate for four days, but they gave me a separate cabin just down the hallway, and delivered all my meals. I could just phone for room service, and it would arrive at my door. I wasn't the only one, apparently – a number of passengers caught Covid.'

Thankful that we managed to avoid it, we make our farewells, but they remind us of something before leaving.

'This is our third cruise with Virgin Voyages, so we are Blue Level passengers now. They are throwing a party for us all this afternoon. Will you be going?'

While we do end up attending the party, we don't find it overly enjoyable. It is held at the Athletic Club bar on the *Resilient Lady*'s upper deck, which, like the rest of the ship, struggles with large crowds. It is open air, hot and packed. We do finally see who is captaining our vessel, a young man who looks as though like he hasn't long left high school, and we enjoy saying goodbye to acquaintances, but we don't linger.

The following morning, it is apparent by the number of sore heads that not everyone followed our example. An older couple with their daughter and son-in-law make us smile. They are from the Gold Coast, and we have spoken with them on many occasions. This morning, as our ship comes to a halt near the island of Santorini and prepares to send passengers ashore, we notice the four of them looking very pale and sorry.

'We all overdid it,' the eldest of the group mutters. 'It was all those free cocktails.'

Feeling incredibly grateful that we are not about to tackle one of our most eagerly anticipated stops with hangovers, we just laugh and head to our tender.

Santorini, population 15,480 and officially known as Thira, is a 76-square-kilometre island about six hours by ferry from Piraeus, the shipping gateway to Athens. Its iconic caldera, a submerged crater surrounded by steep cliffs, was formed around 1,600 BCE by one of the largest volcanic eruptions in recorded history. Famous for its unique landscape, which includes multicoloured cliffs and black, red, and white sand beaches, it is even more renowned for its whitewashed buildings, blue-domed churches, breathtaking views and spectacular sunsets.

Initially, it had been a hard decision on deciding what we would do here. With choices including wine tours, monastery visits, hot springs and catamaran cruises, we were spoilt for choice. Eventually, however, realising that the island was only accessible by tender, and shuddering at the idea of 1,200 passengers trying to board at the same time, we elected to take a ship-organised excursion. It promised some history, with a stop at the ancient site of Akrotiri (Greece's equivalent of Pompeii), dining in the picturesque town of Oia (pronounced Eee-ya), shopping in Fira, the island's capital, and a cable car ride. But most importantly, it guaranteed us a hassle-free, early tender ashore.

'I'm not sure about this road.' I am sitting in the front seat of a large bus. Out the forward window I see another bus heading straight for us; out the window to my right, the land drops away, hundreds of metres down to sea level.

'The view's amazing,' I add, 'but it's a bit unnerving coming head-to-head with another huge vehicle on such a narrow road – with such a sheer drop to the sea below.'

Formed by a dramatic volcanic eruption, much of Santorini is perched on towering cliffs. To reach the villages, visitors have a few options: climb 587 steps, ride atop a weary-looking donkey, take the cable car or do what we are currently doing – zigzag up a steep, narrow road in a bus.

It is a relief when we finally reach the top and I can sit back and enjoy the scenery. The landscape is rockier and starker than I expected. The greenery I do spot, and initially mistake for weeds, turns out to be grapevines, grown in a circular basket shape to protect them from the wind. Eventually, we arrive at what looks like a grass-covered knoll with a roof tucked into it. A nearby ticket office confirms we have reached Akrotiri.

'That was disappointing. I have always wanted to visit Pompeii and hoped this would satisfy my curiosity. It definitely hasn't,' I complain to Darryl an hour or so later.

'I mean, it's impressive that they even found the place at all, buried under sixty metres of ash for nearly four thousand years. And discovering pottery, tools – even a toilet – is fascinating. But really, I expected so much more. Maybe even ash-preserved human remains.'

'The guide said that, unlike Pompeii, the people here probably evacuated after early warnings about the eruption,' Darryl reminds me. 'And I didn't think it was that bad. The scale of the place is interesting. What we saw now is likely just a third of what's still buried. And considering it's nearly four thousand years old, I'm impressed they had such a sophisticated sewerage and drainage system.'

'You're probably right,' I grudgingly admit. 'It just didn't live up to my expectations.'

It takes around thirty minutes to travel from Akrotiri to Oia, and while we pass more of those low-lying clumps of grapevines, our route also hugs the edge of the caldera – offering stunning views of the Aegean Sea and terraced cliffs adorned with whitewashed buildings. When not clinging to cliffs, we pass through small traditional villages or cross open, rugged volcanic terrain. As we edge closer to Oia, the landscape becomes even more striking, with iconic windmills and blue-domed churches coming into view.

'This is as far as the coach can travel,' our guide advises, as the driver expertly reverses his rig into a tight cluster of other large vehicles. 'You have two hours here. I recommend trying the frozen Greek yoghurt, and for the those wanting the best photo opportunity, I will give you directions once we enter the village.'

Keen on both suggestions, we keep our guide in sight as she leads us upwards along a rough, overgrown trail. Surprised at how rustic the entry from the coach terminal into Oia is, it is a relief when the rocky path gives way to pavements, which soon become narrow streets lined with tempting shops and inviting eateries. But it is a short-lived relief, because, along with the shops, come the crowds.

Given that Oia's streets, squares and courtyards are narrow and compact, and that three or more cruise ships call at Santorini daily, with Oia as the main attraction, we expected congestion, just not to this frustrating degree.

'Look. There's a great-looking place that sells Greek yoghurt. Remember where it is,' I pant, struggling to keep our guide in view.

'Sorry, sorry – excuse me,' I mutter, pushing my way through a sea of people choking the cramped lane she has just ducked down.

'You go ahead,' Darryl mutters, his way completely blocked.

'I am not leaving you,' I quickly reply.

'This is just like being deceived by Instagram,' I groan a minute later. 'The photo shows a stunning scene – classic white buildings with blue domes and the Aegean Sea in the background. But the reality is you can't see anything for the crowds.'

'Exactly,' Darryl laughs. 'Let's give up on following the guide and explore on our own. Maybe you will find a better photo opportunity elsewhere – or back here later.'

'Sounds good. But first, let's go get one of those frozen yoghurts. That's if we can find them again.'

Successfully armed with cups of the delicious frozen dessert, we spend the next hour elbowing our way through the packed streets of Oia. We browse busy boutique shops, stand shoulder to shoulder at craft stalls, and duck into crowded art galleries. Twisting, congested lanes lead us to the crumbling remains of a Venetian fortress and, in an overflowing souvenir store, I purchase a cheap pair of earrings.

'To protect you against the evil eye,' the shopkeeper tells me winningly.

At every turn, crowds permitting, we pause to photograph the stunning scenery: the sapphire sea, the volcanic caldera, luxurious cave hotels with their tiny plunge pools, and of course, the iconic blue-domed churches. Finally, with the yoghurt long gone and the crowds becoming just too much, we stop for lunch.

'Now this is more like it – what I dreamt of when I imagined Santorini,' I say, my eyes drinking in our tableside view, the earlier mayhem completely forgiven. 'Sitting in a tiny Greek restaurant, eating mezze, surrounded by white buildings, and overlooking an endless sea – this is perfect.'

'No wonder Oia is one of the most photographed places in the world – with views like this,' Darryl replies. 'But would you want to come back?'

'No. Never,' I reply without hesitation. 'It's been fun, it's impressive, and I am glad to have seen it – but the tourists… they're killing the place. Remember Venice? That was bad – way too crowded. But this? This is worse. I hope they do something about it one day. At the very least, reduce the number of cruise ships that come here.'

Travelling a distance of eleven kilometres, it doesn't take long to reach our next and final stop for the day: Fira, Santorini's capital. It is another small, vibrant town perched on the caldera's edge, offering stunning views over the Aegean Sea and neighbouring islands. This time, when we alight from the coach at the town's boundary, our guide simply points to a tower in the distance and advises us to head toward it.

'That is where the cable car departs from,' she tells us. 'You won't get lost if you just keep walking uphill.'

Fira, with a maze of pedestrian-only cobblestone alleys and narrow, winding streets, is fortunately a little easier to navigate than Oia. It is also a shopper's paradise, with most walkways lined with enticing souvenir, clothing, leather and jewellery stores. Browsing these stalls, purchasing a sage-green linen top, and admiring the handmade leather handbags makes the uphill journey more enjoyable – until our path is abruptly blocked by a long, snaking queue.

'What's the queue for?' Darryl questions a familiar face from our ship.

'The cable car,' they crushingly reply.

Before 1982, the only way to reach the Old Port, where our tender back to the ship now waits, was by foot or donkey, down a steep path of steps. The cable car, generously donated by a wealthy shipowner, transformed the experience, providing a quick, safe and efficient way to scale the caldera cliff. While the descent itself takes just three minutes, it is another ninety before we are finally back aboard the *Resilient Lady*. Fifty of those minutes have been spent shuffling through that queue beneath a pounding hot sun – another clear example of how overtourism is affecting Santorini.

It's our final evening on board the ship. As is usual with cruises, our cabin will be needed by new passengers, meaning an early departure in the morning. With two nights of complimentary accommodation, plus transfers, included with our cruise, all we really need to focus on now is packing.

'I'm going to have to leave some things behind,' I sigh wearily. 'That's the problem with cruising first, then travelling independently. You need big bottles of shampoo and toiletries to get through six weeks on a ship – but they're too bulky for trains and buses.'

'Just make sure we have emptied the safe, and that we have got our passports and anything else we need,' Darryl replies. 'Are you sad this part of the trip is ending?'

'Not at all,' I say. 'I've loved how this cruise gave us Cape Town, Namibia and Morocco. But I'm tired of being cossetted. I'm ready to make our own way, make our own decisions. I'm looking forward to Greece, Bulgaria, Türkiye and India now.'

CHAPTER 13

We Made it to Athens

While it is easy enough to physically disembark the *Resilient Lady* the following morning, from the moment we step ashore and pass through the unmanned customs counters, bedlam prevails. Of the 1,200 passengers on board, nearly seven hundred of us have opted for the same post-cruise package: two nights' central accommodation and hotel transfers.

We have been advised of our hotel name – the President Hotel – and our transfer departure time: 10am. It should be a simple case of heading to where the coaches depart, looking for the one marked with our hotel's name and boarding. Instead, as we exit the departure hall, still curious that no one has checked or stamped our passports, we are swept up in a sea of bewildered passengers, all anxiously searching for their bus.

'Not enough buses have been booked,' a disgruntled couple tells us. Their transfer time was meant to be at 9.15am.

'Not only that,' someone else chimes in, 'no one's taken into account how much luggage everyone has. The buses are leaving half-empty because their holds are full and can't take any more bags.'

'And good luck even finding the coach with your hotel's name on it,' adds another. 'We've been looking for ours for over an hour. Our transfer time was 9am.'

'I'm a bit worried they didn't register our arrival into Greece,' someone frets. 'I hope we don't have any trouble leaving the country.'

It is chaotic and frustrating, but eventually, we manage to slip onto a departing vehicle. Accustomed to travelling light, we have far less luggage than most – so when a small space becomes available in one of the bus holds, ours are the only bags that fit.

'That was lucky,' Darryl mutters, settling into his seat. 'What a welcome to Greece.'

'I know from the Facebook page for this cruise that a lot of us are staying at the President Hotel,' I reply. 'It's not as central as we were hoping, but it is large and modern, with a rooftop pool and rooms with views over Athens. Hopefully ours will be ready.'

'If it's not, we should at least be able to leave our bags,' Darryl says.

'True. I've been thinking – we are at the President for two nights before moving closer to the centre of Athens, closer to the main tourist areas. Since we are a bit further out, we should figure out how to use the Metro system. Let's do that this afternoon – catch the Metro into the centre.'

Athens, home to over three million people, is one of the world's oldest cities, with a recorded history stretching back more than 3,400 years. Often called the cradle of Western civilisation and the birthplace of democracy, it has long been a centre for art, philosophy, politics and culture. These days, it is a vibrant mix of old and new, where ancient ruins sit beside modern shops and busy cafés. Like much of Greece, the city was hit hard by the 2008 global financial crisis. Debt soared, unemployment spiked and protests filled the streets. But with a renewed focus on tourism and innovation, Athens is gradually bouncing back.

This isn't our first visit to Athens. In 2017, we spent a day here as part of a cruise from Singapore to England. Back then, we joined ship-organised tours that focused mainly on the Parthenon and Olympic Stadium. Now, with five nights planned for this visit, we are looking forward to exploring the city a little more thoroughly. While we intend to revisit the Parthenon, this time we want to wander the streets and explore the famous neighbourhoods of Plaka, Monastiraki and Kolonaki. Mastering the Metro system will help for the first few days, after which, having booked into accommodation closer to these districts, we will simply walk.

It is a little after noon when our bus deposits us at the President Hotel. Fortunately, our room – heavily curtained, with an elevated bed – is ready. It doesn't have the view we had hope for, but its generous size makes up for that. Keen to get moving, we dump our bags and head out again. Before leaving the hotel, I do find where the closest Metro station is, along with the location of a supermarket and the phone number of a nail parlour.

'It's been over seven weeks since I had them done,' I explain to Darryl. 'I didn't want to bother bringing nail polish or remover this time, so I'm just going to visit salons. Hopefully I can get an appointment for this afternoon.'

Like most metro systems, the Athens network proves quick and easy. We buy two-day travel passes at a handy kiosk and board a surprisingly clean and modern train. Before long, we are walking across the polished marble and stone slabs of Syntagma Square, Athens' central plaza and home to the Greek Parliament.

Once the gardens of a royal palace, the square now features a grand mid-19th century fountain, broad marble steps, shady trees and plenty of benches, making it a perfect spot to pause and get our bearings. One thing we have learned while travelling is the value of always having internet access. Our Airalo eSIM, purchased back in Australia, has worked almost everywhere (Namibia being the only exception), and once again proves its worth as we fire up Google Maps to orient ourselves.

'Plaka's in that direction, the Parthenon is down there, Ermou, the main shopping street, is that way. But the place we are staying at next, Neo Luxury Suite, is just a block away. Why don't we go check it out?'

'I'd prefer that to visiting the shopping street,' Darryl readily agrees. 'And since the accommodation you book is usually impossible to find, it would be good to locate it now while we are bag free.'

An apt comment, as we discover shortly. Booked through Booking.com, our self-contained apartment, located on a popular side street, proves very difficult to find. It is only when we seriously study the address that we unearth it.

'There,' Darryl says, pointing to a brass plaque hidden among many others on a solid door.

'It's locked but wait – someone's opening it.'

Standing on the footpath, we watch with interest as an elderly couple exits the building.

'We are looking for the Neo Luxury Suite,' I say. 'Is it through there?'

'It is,' the gentleman replies. 'We are staying there too, but we check out early tomorrow. Your host will leave a key in the container here, and you will be given a code.'

'Just be aware the locks and keys are really old,' his wife adds. 'We found them very fiddly. It took us ages to unlock this door – and the one to our apartment.'

Having managed to phone and secure a booking that afternoon at Marbelle Nail House, a salon not far from the President Hotel, we reboard the Metro a short time later. A convenient supermarket near the station allows us to stock up on water and snacks, and I leave Darryl enjoying them in our room while I attend my nail appointment.

It does not take long, once I have settled into my chair, to remember that – just like in Australia – a nail salon or hairdresser offers one of the best ways to connect with locals. It is a perfect window into everyday life. For the ninety minutes it takes Nara, the salon's owner, to do my nails, I am treated to a fascinating mix of stories and insights.

'I have owned this salon for four years,' she begins. 'Before that, I trained first as a computer technician, then as an English teacher. But it is no use being a computer technician in Greece unless you are a man. And teaching doesn't pay well. I only earned eight euro an hour. It is better owning my own business, but getting staff is a problem – especially since Covid.'

'Staffing is a problem in Australia too,' I manage to offer.

'Retiring isn't going to help me,' Nara continues. 'You only get 480 euro a month when you retire.'

'Do you have unemployment benefits here?' I ask.

'The unemployed get five hundred euros a month, but only for a year. After that, it is cut off.'

While we are talking, an elderly lady enters the salon. Nara gestures toward her.

'She is one of my regulars. She comes in every month for a pedicure. She is from Mariupol, in Ukraine. For years, she lived half her year in Greece and the other half in Ukraine. She holds citizenship in both countries, but recently Russia told her she must chose Russian citizenship – or risk not being allowed back into Mariupol. She doesn't know what she is going to do.'

While it is great to be back on land and travelling independently again, it does mean our easy access to free restaurants has disappeared. That evening, we feel the loss as we head out in search of dinner. Being vegetarian, it is not always easy finding a suitable place to eat, especially in meat-loving nations like Greece, but eventually we settle on a small, basic kebab shop nearby. It looks a little untidy, with plastic tablecloths, and we hesitate at first, but the cheerful greeting from the owner wins us over. It turns out to be a perfect example of why you shouldn't judge a place by appearances – the fluffy falafels and homemade hummus we are served are cheap and delicious.

'We have a tour of the Parthenon booked for tomorrow. We then move to the Neo Luxury Suites the day after.' It is later that night and I am studying Itinerary Four, the Excel spreadsheet containing our entire program, as we lie in bed. 'Unfortunately, the tour won't pick us up from this hotel. We will have to catch a taxi or the metro closer into the city.'

'I'm really looking forward to actually walking up the Acropolis and around the Parthenon,' Darryl replies sleepily. 'I physically wasn't able to in 2017. I had to view it from a bus window.'

Marvelling at what an odd pair we make, Darryl with his injuries, me with my cancer diagnosis and medication issues, I fall asleep, feeling incredibly grateful. Grateful that, despite the hardships, we have made it back to the other side of the world. Grateful to once again be doing something we love. This really is our *next chapter travel* – and somehow, it feels even more meaningful than before.

CHAPTER 14

Revisiting the Parthenon

We could very easily still be aboard the *Resilient Lady*, we think the following morning as we jostle for space in front of a groaning breakfast buffet. Not only is it as busy as The Galley often was, but it is full of the same people, with many familiar faces surrounding us.

With only an hour before our guided tour of the Parthenon departs from a central city location, we don't linger. After a quick coffee, some fruit and toast, we jump into a taxi, alighting at the tour organiser's main office. After forty minutes of waiting, it is a relief to finally see the minibus arrive – and a complete surprise to spot who is already on board.

'Where did you catch this bus?' I cry to Debra and Nardean, two *Resilient Lady* acquaintances we had left still eating breakfast at the President Hotel.

'It picked us up from the front of the hotel,' Debra replies.

'They wouldn't pick us up,' I exclaim indignantly. 'They made us come all the way here to their main office.'

'Are we all on the same tour?' Darryl asks. 'That might be the reason.'

'We are doing the Parthenon this morning, then the southern beaches this afternoon,' Nardean replies.

'We are just doing the Parthenon tour this morning,' I say.

'That's probably why they wouldn't pick you up,' Nardean laughs. 'We are more important.'

Located on Acropolis Hill in Athens, the Parthenon is not only an iconic symbol of ancient Greece, but also one of the most famous landmarks in the world. Constructed between 447 and 432 BCE, the huge rectangular building, made primarily of marble, and with forty-six outer columns and twenty-three inner ones, was built to honour Athena, the patron goddess of Athens. Originally a temple housing a massive gold and ivory statue of Athena, it has had many lives over the centuries: treasury, a Christian church, a mosque and, in 1687, an ammunition store. It was during that time, when a war with the Venetians led to stored gunpowder being ignited, that it became the ruin we mostly see and love today.

I say mostly, because in the 1970s a long-term restoration project began. Focused on reassembling fragmented columns, restoring sculptural elements and stabilising the structure, it is a massive, ambitious and ongoing project, befitting such a symbol of ancient democracy, culture and power.

Boarding the minibus, still feeing slightly nonplussed at our needlessly rushed morning, it doesn't take long to traverse the narrow, congested Athens streets and arrive at the foot of the Acropolis. Excited by the sight of the ruins standing ceremoniously above us, we quickly disembark and cluster around our guide.

'Here are your Whispers,' she tells us, handing each of us an ear-set. 'With an average of 23,000 people visiting here each day, you wouldn't be able to hear me otherwise. It will take us about twenty-five to thirty minutes to reach the top and the first part is steep. There are also some steps that are higher than normal. But we will take it slowly. Just make sure you stay with me.'

Unlike yesterday, today is wet and cold with periodic showers of rain. The crowded path is quite slippery and we are grateful our guide has set a slow pace. The large limestone steps that mark the gateway onto the Acropolis are especially hazardous, and it is a relief to reach the summit.

'Apart from the Parthenon,' the voice of our guide rings through our ear-sets, 'you will notice there are some other buildings here. That is the Erechtheion, a temple dedicated to Athena and Poseidon, and known for its caryatids – the sculptured female figures that serve as columns. Over there is the Temple of Athena. I'll leave you to wander on your own shortly, but does anyone know how Athens got its name?'

'Through a contest,' someone offers.

'Correct,' replies our guide. 'According to myth, both Athena and Poseidon wanted to become the patron saint of the city. Each offered a gift to its people: Poseidon, being the god of the sea, gave the gift of a saltwater spring. Athena, the goddess of wisdom and warfare, planted an olive tree representing peace and prosperity. The citizens chose Athena's gift, seeing it as more beneficial – and so the city was named Athens.'

It is a great story that highlights many things, especially the blurring of myth and reality. It also reminds me, once again, how little we know about our own country's history. Australia's First Nations people may very well have myths, gods and legends like this – but sadly, we were never taught them in school. I ponder this for a while, only pushing the thought aside when the incredible sweeping views in front of me take over my full attention: the sprawling cityscape at my feet, the rich Aegean Sea, and lumpy lone Mount Lycabettus in the distance.

And right in front of me, the elegant and perfectly proportioned rectangular temple ruin – golden, worn and timeless.

'What did you think? Was it worth the climb?' I ask Darryl some time later, as we slowly follow our guide back down the slippery path.

'Despite the weather and the crowds, I enjoyed the visit,' he replies. 'And strangely, even though it's a ruin, you can still sense how grand it must have once been. It's hard not to be impressed. I am especially happy that I got to walk through it this visit – not just view it from a bus window.'

'I enjoyed it in 2017, but found it even better today,' I say. 'Maybe because I was also seeing if through your eyes, or maybe because our guide today was better. I'm not sure. I'm looking forward to the Acropolis Museum now, though. It wasn't part of our tour in 2017.'

Opened in 2009, the Acropolis Museum is a modern architectural masterpiece of glass and floating concrete. Housing artefacts taken from the Acropolis, such as the famous Parthenon frieze and the original caryatids from the Erechtheion (the ones on-site are copies), its reputation meant we made sure it was included in today's tour. Conveniently located at the base of Acropolis Hill, it is not long before our minibus drops us at the tail of a snaking queue leading to its entrance.

Fortunately, our guide has contacts, and we are very quickly ushered into the building, where we reinsert our earpieces.

'The museum has three main floors,' she begins. 'The ground floor displays artefacts uncovered during excavation – pottery and sculptures. There's also a glass floor where you can look down at the ancient ruins that lie beneath the museum. The first floor features items found at the Acropolis like small sculptures, and the top floor has been built to mimic the exact layout of the Parthenon. Here, you will see the frieze, sculptures and other relics, displayed in the same positions they originally occupied.'

'But not all of the them,' someone cheekily interjects. 'What about the Elgin Marbles?'

'Yes, not all of them,' our guide agrees. 'Do you all know what the Elgin Marbles are?'

'I don't,' someone from the back of our group calls out. 'What are they?'

'Between 1801 and 1812, Lord Elgin, a British diplomat, removed a number of sculptures, friezes and other artefacts from the Parthenon. Claiming he had permission from the Ottoman officials, he sold the collection, which later became known as the Elgin Marbles, to the British government, which placed them in the British Museum.'

'The legality of his actions has been questioned,' the person who raised the topic adds. 'And Greece has been asking for their return for years.'

'It is true,' our guide continues. 'And one day, it is hoped the collection will be reunited and displayed here, all together.'

It takes some time to explore all three floors, and while the museum does an incredible job expanding our understanding of the Acropolis site, by the end of the tour, we are ready for something less cerebral. Learning that Plaka, one of the oldest and most popular districts in Athens, is within walking distance, we say goodbye to our guide – and Debra and Nardean. As they are flying back to Australia tomorrow and we are moving to new accommodation, it is unlikely we will ever see them again.

As usual when preparing for an adventure such as this, I had tried to thoroughly research the cities we would be visiting, looking to find those areas most suitable for us to stay or visit. Many hours had been spent on Athens, many books borrowed from my local library, much time scouring the internet. Eventually, I came to the conclusion that Athens could be broken into eight main districts, but we would focus on just three.

Plaka – one of the city's oldest and most picturesque neighbourhoods. It is not only conveniently located near the archaeological sites but also filled with cafés, tavernas, souvenir shops and boutique hotels.

Monastiraki – just west of Plaka. A livelier area known for its flea market, rooftop bars, shopping and exploring. A place where ancient and modern Athens apparently coexist.

And Syntagma – where we got off the Metro yesterday. The political, social and commercial hub of the city, and the area I chose for us to stay after leaving the President Hotel. With great shopping, the changing of guard at the Greek Parliament, lovely gardens, beautiful buildings and slightly fewer crowds, Syntagma seemed like a good fit.

Today, strolling along Dionysiou Areopagitou Street, the pedestrian walkway that connects the Acropolis Museum to Plaka, it is fascinating to watch what I had studied on paper and online come to life in front of me.

'I didn't expect that easy walkway from the museum, but Plaka was just as I imagined,' I say later that evening, sitting in bed eating a quinoa salad from the supermarket we had spotted earlier, using our travel cutlery brought from home. 'Cobbled paths, lots of tavernas, ancient structures suddenly looming in front of you. I liked it. And the souvenir shops were great.'

'You always like the souvenir shops,' Darryl replies dismissively. 'I found it too crowded. Like most old parts of a city usually are.'

After a busy few days, it is nice waking the following morning knowing all we need to do today is move to our new accommodation. Breakfast is followed by a stroll around the neighbourhood, which, being a Saturday, has many blocked-off streets. Filled with market stalls, we browse, fascinated, among the juicy oranges, succulent olives and plump tomatoes. The smell of baked goods fills the air and vendors call out, trying to tempt us with cheeses, souvenirs and handmade crafts. It is a wonderful glimpse into the local culture and flavours of Athens.

Mid-morning finds us in a taxi on our way to the Neo Luxury Suite. The taxi is a Tesla, the first either of us has ever ridden in, and we spend more time commenting on the vehicle than on the sights passing by, like the National Gallery, Lycabettus Hill and the Greek Parliament. A welcome phone call along the way advises that our room is ready and, after locating our key, we are grateful for the advice given by the elderly couple two days before. The locks are indeed fiddly, and without their warning we may have given up on them. Instead, after some perseverance, we gain entry to our room and find the one-bedroom apartment superb. With a tiny balcony overlooking the busy street below, a separate dining area and a fully equipped kitchen, it is perfect for us. Along with information on local supermarkets and eateries, our host has even left us some coffee, jam, bread and biscuits.

'This feels like we are back travelling again,' I say to Darryl, dropping my bag and collapsing onto the sofa. 'Hotels are great, but an apartment in the heart of a place is much better.'

'I know what you mean. I much prefer being able to organise our own food rather than having to go looking for it all the time – and being able to do our own laundry,' Darryl replies. 'And these little flats are great. How was the tiny ancient lift?'

'It straight away reminded me that we were back in Europe,' I laugh, referring to the minuscule lift with the sliding grille door that has brought us to this fifth-floor apartment. 'Where elevators are a modern afterthought to old buildings.'

Now staying right in the heart of Athens, that afternoon it is easy to simply stroll the streets. Monastiraki gives us a fascinating flea market to explore, along with Hadrian's Library, an Ottoman mosque and a Byzantine (Eastern Roman Empire) church. Plaka provides a restaurant where we dine on mezze dishes and are offered mousse made from carrots for dessert. Every corner we turn holds a surprise, and more often than not, if we glance skyward, our senses are jolted by the sight of the great Parthenon looming over us.

Before arriving here, I had wondered whether Athens would be similar to central Rome. Our walk shows me it is not. While both cities are full of old buildings, Rome feels more concentrated, its ancient ruins sitting grandly at the heart of things. Athens is different. The old and the new seem more spread out, more casually blended – ancient temples, modern shops, everyday life all sitting comfortably side by side.

After a long day, it is a relief to return to our apartment. The little supermarket recommended by our host – tucked into a narrow, four-storey historic building, unlike the single-storey suburban ones we are used to – provides us with some basics: almond milk, muesli, fruit, chips and toothpaste.

'Delphi tomorrow,' I say later, as we prepare for bed. 'Centre of the world and home to the famous oracle of Delphi.'

CHAPTER 15

The Oracle of Delphi

Waking, I find messages from both Pierce and Paige on my phone, wishing me a happy Mother's Day. I laugh – I had no idea today was Mother's Day in Australia. And given that we are about to visit a place where a female voice once held such weight, it feels quite auspicious.

Before making our way to where today's tour will be departing from, however, there's something I need to do: book a couple of train tickets. It is rare when we travel that I haven't already organised most of our onward journey, but traversing Greece, I quickly learned, would be different. For starters, there are far fewer trains here, and the ones we could catch were virtually impossible to book from Australia. Secondly, with no trains, much of the travel is done by bus – again, not easy to arrange from overseas. Finally, one of the excursions we want to do, traversing the Corinth Canal, is tidal dependant. And if we can't do it, there's no point travelling to, and staying in, the area from where it departs.

What all this means is that, for the first time in a long while, we will be winging it. We have an itinerary, and accommodation has been earmarked at various places, but if transportation can't be sorted, or the Corinth tide is unfavourable, plans can be changed or cancelled.

This morning, knowing that the Greek train-booking website works far better when actually accessed from within Greece, I manage to secure some tickets for next week that will take us to Thessaloniki, in the north of the country. Tomorrow, I will look into bus tickets for the journey from Athens to Nafplio, our next stop.

Tickets sorted, breakfast consumed, coffee purchased along the way, we eventually find ourselves back at the office where our Parthenon tour departed from two days ago. A total coincidence, but given how professional that tour was, it feels fortuitous.

Boarding a much larger, more comfortable coach, we are again handed some Whispers by today's guide, Dozia.

'Good morning,' she welcomes us in excellent English. 'I hope you are all looking forward to your visit to Delphi. It will take us three hours to travel there, but we will stop for a break in about two. I hope you enjoy the journey. While I will be pointing out some interesting things along the way, please feel free to ask me any questions.'

Settling back in my cushioned seat, eager to see what Greece actually looks like, I empty my mind and let the passing scenery capture my full attention. Having commenced our visit deep in the city's centre, my initial view of busy streets, remnants of ancient ruins and modern apartment buildings gradually shifts to areas dotted with olive trees, small shops and local businesses as we reach the outer suburbs. A bit later, the rolling plains of the Attica countryside come into view – open grasslands and fields of olive groves, vineyards and citrus orchards. Small villages with red-tiled roofs and traditional

Greek houses occasionally dot the landscape. Spotting a larger town in the distance, Dozia points it out.

'The city of Marathon,' she tells us. 'Where the marathon race gets its name. Does anyone know the story?'

With no one forthcoming with an answer, Dozia continues. 'In 490 BCE, the Persians invaded Marathon but were defeated by the much smaller Athenian forces. It was a great victory, and a messenger named Pheidippides was sent to Athens to deliver the news. He had to run a distance of approximately forty kilometres or 25 miles. When he reached Athens, it is said that he yelled, "We have won!" before collapsing and dying from exhaustion. This story inspired the creation of the marathon during the first modern Olympics, which were held in Athens in 1896. The distance of the race was to be the same as what Pheidippides ran.'

'But the marathon isn't forty kilometres,' someone points out.

'It isn't now,' Dozia replies. 'During the 1908 London Olympics, it was changed to 42.195 kilometres, so the race could finish right in front of the British royal box.'

Continuing onwards, our winding road passes through the fertile Boeotian plains, where fields of olives, fruit trees and solar panels stretch into the horizon. Thebes – one of the oldest continuously inhabited cities in the world and the birthplace of the mythical Greek king Oedipus – passes us by, and eventually, we begin to climb.

'Mount Parnassus,' Dozia calls out, as the lush greenery lining our winding road gives way to rugged, characterful cliffs and dramatic, spine-tingling gorges.

'Arachova – where the inventor of the Pap smear, Georgios Papanicolaou, came from,' she adds, as we pass stone houses clinging to steep hillsides, surrounded by forests of fir, olive and walnut trees.

Finally, just as I begin to wonder whether we will ever arrive, tiring of the never-ending winding switchbacks, the road levels, and the ancient ruins of Delphi emerge, rising naturally from the rocky landscape.

'Time for your Whispers,' Dozia advises us we alight the coach into air that's much cooler than the plains below.

'Delphi, one of ancient Greece's most sacred sites,' she continues, sweeping her hand over the view before us. 'Considered the navel of the world, it was home to the Sanctuary of Apollo from the eighth century BCE until late fourth century CE. People came here to worship the god of prophecy, music and light.'

'And the Oracle?' someone calls out.

'She was a priestess called the Pythia, and she served as the voice of Apollo,' Dozia replies. 'She delivered cryptic prophecies while in a trance-like state. People came from all over the world to seek her counsel. Modern researchers believe her trance-like state may have been caused by inhaling toxic gases emitted from a crack in the earth. I'll leave you now to explore on your own. There is a museum just along the road. We will meet there in two hours.'

Although a challenging site, with crumbling paths and ancient ruins spread across multiple steep terraces, the breathtaking views of the surrounding landscape, and the knowledge of who has walked here before, make its hardships easy to overlook. At the Temple of Apollo, where the Oracle of Delphi once delivered her prophecies, we sit for a while, perched upon broken ancient limestone columns.

'I don't think I will ever forget this Mother's Day,' I say to Darryl. 'Sitting here on Mount Parnassus, amongst the ruins of Delphi. I have always heard of the Oracle of Delphi but never knew anything about her. Now, I not only know where she lived – I have walked the same paths she did. It feels a bit surreal.'

'I agree,' Darryl replies. 'It's hard to comprehend what these ruins represent sometimes. That two thousand years ago, this was a thriving place – people came from all over the world to be here.'

We are still sitting there, drinking in the view, lost in the past, when my phone rings. It is Paige. And as she tells us about life back in Australia and shares her future travel plans, we are soon brought back to the present.

'Can anyone tell me what type of column this is?'

We have moved on from the ruins of Delphi and are now following Dozia through its nearby museum. Full of unearthed artefacts, it is interesting – but nowhere near the calibre of the Acropolis Museum. Hearing her question, little do we realise at the time, but by the end of this adventure, we will have seen hundreds more relics from dozens more ancient sites, and answering it, identifying column styles, will come easily.

'Doric?' someone correctly offers, albeit a little uncertainly. 'It doesn't have the spiral scrolls like an Ionic column, and it's not as ornate as a Corinthian one.'

It is another three-hour journey back to Athens, and it is close to seven o'clock by the time we re-enter our apartment. Too tired to go in search of dinner, we turn to an old travel staple, big bowls of muesli, and eat them sitting on our little balcony, reflecting on the day as we watch the hustle and bustle of the Athens streets below, with a sea of stars above.

True to yesterday's promise, I scroll my phone over breakfast, yet another bowl of muesli, searching for onward bus tickets from Athens to Nafplio in the Peloponnese region of Greece. It doesn't take long to realise the easiest way to get them is in person, at the coach station. Since we will be departing tomorrow morning, I book an early Uber instead. This will ensure we arrive at the correct place with ample time to secure tickets.

With our final day in Athens stretching free ahead of us, we mull over how best to spend it.

'We could just stroll Ermou Street again,' I suggest facetiously.

'Definitely not,' Darryl replies. 'I've been wanting to see the change of guard at the parliament building. Let's do that.'

'I was kidding about the shopping street,' I laugh. 'But what I would like to do is catch the hop-on bus. One of the routes heads out of Athens along the coast. We have seen the landscape north of the city on our way to Delphi, and tomorrow we will head southwest to Nafplio by bus. Today's hop-on route traces the Argo-Saronic Gulf to the east – it might be nice to see that too.'

'It would give us a good sense of the area,' Darryl agrees.

Delaying only long enough to fill our apartment with drying laundry, we soon find ourselves back at nearby Syntagma Square. Conveniently, it is where both the hop-on bus and the changing of the guard take place.

Taking place hourly in front of the Hellenic Parliament and the Tomb of the Unknown Soldier, the ceremony honours Greece's fallen soldiers and is a proud display of national tradition. We have always enjoyed these rituals, the most memorable so far was in Moscow, but this one gives the Russian version stiff competition. With their uniquely Greek uniforms – pleated skirts, red-tasselled caps, shoes with pom-poms – and slow, deliberate movements, the guards' performance is almost theatrical. The leg swings and synchronised steps are so comical that we are still talking about them as we board the bus.

It takes 120 minutes for us to complete the Beach-Riviera route offered by the Athens hop-on bus company. It would have taken longer if any of the stops had enticed us to disembark, but we find the beachside areas somewhat underwhelming – untidy parklands, dishevelled streets, stony beaches, littered roadsides and endless apartment blocks. Instead, we stay aboard, letting the commentary entertain us.

Rich with stories of Greek legends like Socrates and Plato, and gods like Athena and Apollo, the narration brings history and Athens to life. But my favourite line comes from a more recent Greek icon – shipping magnate Aristotle Onassis: 'If women didn't exist, all the money in the world would have no meaning.'

Returning to the city, we spend the afternoon exploring some of Athens' central sites: the Temple of Zeus, the Temple of Hephaestus, the Roman Agora (Roman forum). And just when it starts to rain, a surprise highlight of our stay in Athens occurs.

Dashing into a nearby building – the Hondos Centre – to escape the downpour, we note it has a rooftop restaurant. Hungry, we head up and discover a reasonably priced cafeteria with sweeping views straight out toward the Parthenon. Having wanted the full rooftop dining experience with a Parthenon backdrop, but baulking at the cost, it feels like we have stumbled upon a hidden gem. Especially when we find the bain-maries full with Greek specialities: stuffed peppers, rice with pine nuts and sultanas, moussaka. Darryl is especially pleased when he spots a cake he's been told he must try.

'It's called portokalopita,' he says. 'It's a traditional Greek cake made with oranges and yoghurt, then soaked in orange syrup. You don't mind me getting a slice?' he adds, knowing I have been avoiding sugar and desserts since my cancer diagnosis.

'Go for it,' I laugh. 'These days I tend to live my dessert experiences through others.'

Later, back in our apartment, with *Clarkson's Farm*, a Netflix series we both love, streaming on my laptop, an email arrives.

'The tide is favourable next week,' I read excitedly. 'We have tickets to traverse the Corinth Canal.'

CHAPTER 16

Nafplio and the Peloponnese Region of Greece

It is not often we need to take a coach for onward travel. Years ago, while exploring countries like Thailand and Malaysia, it was commonplace, but these days we usually enjoy the comfort and spaciousness of a train. Unfortunately, as I have mentioned, train services in Greece are severely lacking. Whether due to lines that were never built, or austerity measures introduced after the 2008 global financial crisis forced their closure, the reality is that if we wish to use public transport in this country, buses will mostly have to suffice.

Knowing today's bus doesn't depart until 10am, and with an Uber already booked to deliver us to the terminal, it is a relaxed start to the morning. While Darryl dozes, I head out in search of coffee and pastries. We have noticed since arriving in Athens just how abundant bakeries are here. Filled to the brim with an incredible array of goods, they are perhaps the most well stocked we have encountered anywhere – I think they even surpass the famous French patisseries.

'Although,' I say ironically to Darryl a little later, speaking around a mouthful of flaky croissant, 'the sheer number of bakeries might explain why the average Greek physique is a little larger than the norm.'

Not used to coach terminals, there is a flicker of unease as, after a short journey, we watch our Uber drive away. It turns out there was no need to worry. Although everything is written in Greek, destinations are also noted in English. All we need do is find the small office advertising Nafplio – our journey's end – ask Google to translate 'two tickets please' into Greek, and board our bus.

'Why Nafplio?' Darryl asks as we settle into our front-row seats.

'It's the former capital of Greece,' I reply. 'I watched a couple of YouTube videos on it. It looked lovely and I thought it would be a nice place to base ourselves for a few days. It's in the Peloponnese region, and I thought, if we get time, we could do some excursions from there – or we could just do nothing.'

A large mountainous peninsula in southern Greece, the Peloponnese is known for its rich history, stunning landscapes and picturesque villages. Home to famous sites like Mycenae, Epidaurus and Olympia, the birthplace of the Olympic Games, it was a region I had not wanted to miss. In researching where to stay, well-resourced Nafplio, located on the coast and crowned with an ancient castle, quickly became the obvious choice.

'Former capital?' Darryl asks.

'Yes. The Ottomans, a Turkish dynasty, controlled Greece from the mid-fifteenth century until the Greek War of Independence in 1821. Nafplio became the first capital of this newly born Greek state. Due to its central location and cultural significance, the capital was later moved to Athens in 1834.'

'How did you remember all that?' Darryl probes.

'I wrote it down in case I wanted to use it in a blog,' I laugh.

Our journey takes a little over two hours, and with our front-row seats it is easy to admire the changing scenery. Leaving Athens, the large, well-maintained highway, with little traffic and long tunnels, passes through industrial zones and suburban sprawl, which gradually gives way to rolling, rock-covered hills, olive groves and vineyards. We follow the rich blue waters of the Saronic Gulf for much of the way, and a highlight is crossing the narrow waterway of the Corinth Canal. This crossing marks our official entry into the Peloponnese.

From here, the road narrows, the stony hills replaced by flat lands with olive and fruit trees.

'Have you noticed how courteous the drivers are here?' Darryl observes at one stage. 'Especially on the highway – they move over to let you pass, or give a little warning beep if it's not safe. You would never get that back in Australia.'

'I hadn't,' I reply. 'I've been too busy reading the road signs. Olympia, Kalamata, Tripoli, Sparta… they read like a food and history lesson.'

Just when we are starting to feel a little perplexed, maybe even disheartened, by the continually narrowing roads and shrinking villages, the olive groves thin, and a slightly larger town starts to appear.

'I was a bit worried when the bus dropped us off,' I laugh to Darryl five minutes later, rolling my bag along a smooth marble street. 'The town looked so dodgy and dusty, I was thinking, "What have I done booking three nights in this place?" But this is great.'

Indeed, Nafplio is getting better the further we delve into it. With Google Maps indicating our accommodation is somewhere near the waterfront, our stroll is taking us right through the heart of its stunning old town. Beautiful, low-set buildings with intricate marble facades house an abundance of enticing shops, while tempting cafés and inviting restaurants spill into charming bougainvillea-strewn alleys. Eventually, we find ourselves at Nafplio's waterfront and stop, drinking in the view of the sparkling Argolic Gulf, the enigmatic little castle located a few hundred metres offshore, and the marble promenade lined with cafés and tavernas.

'Wow. This looks incredible,' Darryl mutters. 'Are we staying near here?'

'Google Maps says this is where the apartment is,' I reply. 'But I can't see anything that looks like it. All I see are restaurants.'

As we have encountered so many times before, our accommodation proves virtually impossible to find – and it is only with the help of a friendly waiter from one of the restaurants that we get anywhere. He phones the provided number and, after a rapid conversation, leaves his post to guide us to the entrance of a nearby building. Shortly after, our host arrives and, following a warm welcome, directs us into another of those quirky European lifts.

Exiting the lift and entering our apartment, we can only both exclaim with delight. Spacious and airy, with a generous balcony looking directly out towards the water and castle – not only does it exceed all expectations but it is going to be the perfect place to relax for the next few days.

'The castle in front of us is Bourtzi Castle,' I read from an information pamphlet left in the room. 'It was built by the Venetians in 1473, and we can visit by boat if we want. The huge fortress on the hill above the town is Palamidi – built in the eighteenth century. It is nearly 999 steps to the top.'

'We are here until Friday,' Darryl says. 'I am not really interested in visiting either castle, I would rather take it easy for a few days – we have been busy.'

'I agree. The town looks great, and I am keen to explore it. The shops we passed on the way here, especially the linen and jewellery, looked amazing. And from what I could see, the walkway around the harbour looked fantastic as well. Why don't we find a supermarket, get some food in. Then just eat, walk and explore until we leave. I had thought of doing a tour to Olympia or somewhere, but we have seen quite a few ruins already – and there are more to come. I'm happy to leave them for now.'

Which is basically what we do. With the weather hovering in the mid-teens and the days cool and crisp, the conditions prove ideal for strolling the Arvanitia Promenade – the paved coastal path that winds along Nafplio's foreshore. Enticed by its easy walking, the turquoise waters, rugged cliffs and sightings of numerous well-fed wild cats, it is a walk we do more than once.

One morning, while I sit on our amazing balcony finishing a blog, Darryl goes off to get a haircut. We catch up on laundry using the washing machine in our apartment, once again taking pot luck with its foreign-worded settings, and we learn to appreciate Greek coffee: a thick, bitter beverage served in tiny, difficult-to-hold cups.

Always keen to explore a local supermarket, we find Nafplio's offerings a little lacking in fresh fruit and vegetables, but they do provide pasta, muesli, bread and soup. While we do eat out one evening, Greece, being such a meat-loving nation, does not cater especially well to vegetarians, so we actually prefer these simple meals on our balcony under the stars. Besides, eating at home means we can eat at a reasonable hour. Like much of Europe, the Greeks tend to dine very late. It is not unusual for them to sit down to dinner around 10pm.

'That can't be good for their digestion,' I mention to Darryl. 'Besides, I am usually asleep by then.'

Over lunch one day, we write postcards home, and I am in hysterics hearing Darryl ask for stamps at the local post office.

'Five stamps to Auuuustraleeea, please.'

'Why did you pronounce Australia that way?' I ask, still laughing.

'I didn't want them going to Austria,' he earnestly replies.

Nafplio's shops are thoroughly explored. While I do not buy anything, I marvel at the quality and variety of leather goods, linen clothing, jewellery, shoes and souvenirs.

'Like the bakeries, I think the Greek souvenir shops surpass the French ones,' I admit to Darryl, returning from one afternoon's foray.

Each evening, after watching more of *Clarkson's Farm*, we leave our curtains open, and fall asleep with the lights of Bourtzi Castle visible from our bed. And every day, we are reminded, thanks to signs in the bathroom, that much of Greece has old plumbing, and toilet paper should not be flushed. As in parts of Asia, it goes into the conveniently provided bin.

With our Corinth Canal crossing secured, it means I can finalise our onward itinerary, so one morning, I return to the bus stop and purchase tickets to our next destination: Loutraki.

Eventually, it is time to repack our suitcases with freshy laundered clothes and return to the coach terminal. Our bus is already waiting, and with tickets pre-purchased, it is just a matter of handing over our luggage, finding our seats and settling in.

CHAPTER 17

Loutraki and the Corinth Canal

True to what we are starting to realise – that Greeks are incredibly kind at heart – our driver stops not long after beginning the journey. A woman has missed the bus but manages to catch up and wave it down. As she boards, her thanks are waved off with a cheery grin and a big belly laugh.

It takes just over an hour to travel from Nafplio to the isthmus of Corinth, where a narrow bridge spans the Corinth Canal and separates the Peloponnese from mainland Greece. Here, we disembark, find a taxi and ten minutes later enter the seaside town of Loutraki. Much less touristy than Nafplio, more a place where Greeks from Athens spend a weekend than one frequented by overseas tourists, it had been booked for its proximity to the Canal.

'A hotel this time,' Darryl remarks as our taxi pulls up in front of the Excelsior Hotel.

'It was cheap, well located and on the seafront,' I reply.

After securing our key, learning that a five-euro per person buffet breakfast is available each morning, and stepping into our water-view room with a balcony, Darryl turns to me.

'My personal travel agent has done it again. This is great.'

Located in an area renowned since antiquity for its therapeutic hot springs; destroyed by an earthquake in 1928; known today for its pebbly but lovely beaches with crystal-clear water; and home to one of the largest casinos in Europe – we have arrived in Loutraki not really knowing what to expect. That afternoon, while searching for a supermarket, we find it is a mix of charm and urban sprawl, with many mid-rise apartment buildings, hotels and commercial establishments. The wide beachfront promenade our room overlooks, which is lined with cafés and restaurants, is lively and practical, if a little worn.

'What time is our Corinth Canal crossing tomorrow?' Darryl asks, after we have struggled to master yet another hotel safe and eaten another supermarket-bought dinner before retiring to bed.

'Someone's collecting us at 9.30am,' I reply sleepily. 'They will drop us somewhere, where we will catch a boat. It was all so hit and miss whether we could actually do the crossing that I didn't concentrate too much on the final details. I was just grateful to take what we could.'

Having traversed both the Suez and Panama Canals, it had been a bit of an ambition of ours to also cross the Corinth. When we were coming to Greece and I realised this could become a reality, I had started researching ways we could make it happen. It had taken months of searching to find a company that actually traversed the canal's length. Most tour operators considered walking or driving over the principal road bridge that spans the canal sufficient – do that, and you had 'crossed' it. Eventually, I stumbled across the local Loutraki tourism office website, which was able to help.

Completed in 1893 after centuries of attempts, the Corinth Canal is an intriguing man-made waterway that connects the Aegean Sea to the Ionian Sea. It essentially turns the Peloponnese peninsula into an island. With a depth of around eight metres, a width of 21 metres, and a length of 6.4 kilometres, the narrow chasm carved through solid rock cuts nearly seven hundred kilometres off the journey for those sailing the region. Though it is considered a marvel of engineering, its slender width makes it too narrow for modern ships. Thinking about tomorrow's adventure, excited that it's all come together and still not quite sure what kind of tour I have booked, I eventually drift off to sleep.

At five euros each, our morning's breakfast proves to be incredible value. Fresh Greek yoghurt and fruit, multiple pastries, strong coffee and juice – all consumed overlooking the sparkling blue sea. It bodes well for the day ahead.

'I am Panos. Today you crossing the Corinth?' True to what we had been told, a taxi arrives right on time at 9.30am. Long-time local Panos doesn't stop talking for the entire twenty minutes it takes to reach the mouth of the canal.

'My father used to drive boats along the canal, I grew up just here. My school was right there. I have travelled the canal thousands of times. You see these roads? Those hills? That embankment? All made from the rock and soil dug from the canal. Here is my phone number. You phone me when you are done.'

Appreciating the wealth of information Panos has just shared, we bid him farewell and join a large group of mainly Asian and American tourists currently boarding a sturdy-looking motorboat. Managing to secure a position at the back of the vessel gives us a rear-facing view – initially thought to be a less desirable spot, but we soon grow thankful for it.

With no one between us and the ship's edge, it is easy to view the vertical limestone walls that rise 79 metres above us. To note the visible layers of beige, brown and grey rock. To see where sections have crumbled. Gliding further into the canyon, our position allows us to readily admire the blue-green water and the sparse vegetation clinging to the cliffs.

It is a surprise to come across two submersible bridges and, less surprisingly, a railway bridge. Occasionally, when we remember to, we look up, startled to see how small the stripe of blue sky is in relation to the towering cliffs. Thinking we are on a one-way journey, the adventure becomes even better when, reaching the canal's end, we turn around and experience it all again.

'You like?' Panos asks as we clamber back into his taxi.

'We love!' I reply. 'It is something I will never forget. Another Bucket List moment.'

'You wish to bungee jump from it now?' Panos grins. 'Lots of tourists like to do the bungee jump.'

'Definity not,' we laugh. 'We are not really the bungee-jumping type.'

'Ah well, probably best not. Too much dust coming. You see the sky? Dust from the desert.'

Now that Panos has mentioned it, we realise the sky has changed during our short time on the water. It is no longer a bright sky-blue, but a dirty, faded orange that is steadily deepening in tone.

'Sorry, Panos – what do you mean? Why has the sky changed colour? Dust?'

'Yes. It happen each year now. Dust from the Sahara Desert in Africa. Will stay few days now. It becoming big problem.'

Back in our room, we realise it is not just the sky that has changed. Until now, Greece has been consistently pleasant in temperature, but today has turned hot – and tomorrow is expected to be even warmer. It is early evening by the time we think it suitable to venture out again – strolling first Loutrakis' main street, where we appreciate the quality and quantity of the bakeries, then the seaside promenade. Being a

Saturday, tables and chairs have been set up on the pebbly beach, and it is interesting to see couples and families making full use of them. We are more used to dining on sand rather than rocks.

'I had forgotten just how much people still smoke in Europe,' I remark at one point, noticing every café and restaurant has customers puffing away.

Dinner is memorable – not so much for the vegan pizzas we are served, but for the layer of dust covering every surface. It is impossible to wipe if off our table and chairs, and my white shirt needs a wash by the time we have finished.

'Our train tour to Meteora from Thessaloniki has been cancelled,' I read from my emails in bed that evening. 'They are offering a tour by coach instead – but it means a four-hour journey each way. Eight hours on a bus.'

Meteora is a region in central Greece known for its towering rock formations and the monasteries perched atop them. Constructed by monks between the fourteenth and sixteenth centuries, of the original twenty-four monasteries built, only six remain. It is one of those iconic sites you really should see when visiting the country, and I had organised a tour by train long ago. But eight hours on a bus? That just doesn't sound appealing.

'Maybe I'll have a look at what else we can do instead,' I sigh.

It is a slow start the following morning. Being a Sunday, most of the shops and businesses in Greece are closed – unlike in Australia, where many continue to operate seven days a week. Sitting on our balcony under another dirty orange sky, I can see only two people on the promenade below.

'If this was home, the beachfront would be full of people walking and exercising by this time of morning,' I mention to Darryl.

'It's different here, though,' he replies. 'I could still see people eating dinner at eleven last night. They were still sitting in the restaurants well past one.'

'Greeks stay up a lot later than us – and we get up much earlier,' I agree.

We had given some thought to what we want to do today. The Loutraki tourism office had offered a few suggestions: hire a boat, experience the hot springs, visit a nearby monastery. They all sounded good, but what we really wanted to do was to get some exercise – stretch our legs.

Our hotel receptionist had mentioned that it was possible to walk from Loutraki to Corinth, a town further along the coast and visible from our balcony. She had also said she had never done it herself, didn't know anyone who had, and had never wanted to. But we weren't going to let that dissuade us. Google Maps showed a narrow path and some roads connecting the two towns – that was enough to get us started.

Covering just over six kilometres, our slow, careful pace sees the hike taking a few hours. While there is nothing particularly spectacular about it, we arrive in Corinth with a satisfying sense of achievement. Undertaken under an increasingly steamy sun, our journey includes reaching the very end of Loutrakis' promenade, getting a close-up look at the massive concrete casino the town is known for, walking (often nervously) along the verges of narrow roads, carefully crossing a slippery, muddy submersible footbridge over the Corinth Canal, discovering the Hellenic Army military engineering school, finding a second promenade, and following it until we reach the centre of Corinth.

'It's funny how the simple things can turn out to be some of our most memorable experiences,' Darryl reflects over our muesli and fruit dinner that evening. 'I think I will remember that walk today just as much as yesterday's canal crossing.'

'I agree. But I am also going to remember that out of all the nice taxis at the rank for our journey back – the Mercedes, the Honda, the BMW – we had to get the Hyundai bomb. The only taxi whose oil light stayed on, whose ceiling was missing, whose rear-view mirror was literally held together with duct tape. And a driver who thought he was racing in the Formula One!'

'Don't forget the petrol light,' Darryl laughs. 'It was on too.'

'I have really liked Loutraki,' I continue. 'It's a town more popular with Greeks than with international tourists, and I think that has given us a better insight into everyday life here. I love how all the shops were closed today – except for the cafés. I love how everyone was just spending their Sunday afternoon relaxing and socialising. Sitting outside, having something to eat and a drink – and not just alcohol. Lots of people were having coffee.'

'Or ice-cream,' Darryl adds with a grin. 'The ice-cream shops were doing a roaring trade. I have enjoyed Loutraki too – but I don't mind moving on tomorrow.'

CHAPTER 18

Thessaloniki, Pella, Edessa and Naoussa

I am up very early the following morning. Today's train travel will see us traversing the length of Greece, arriving at the country's second-largest city, Thessaloniki. After four nights there, it will be on to Bulgaria, then Türkiye. With so much travel immediately ahead, I know that if I am to get the India leg of our adventure sorted, it has to be now.

I have been corresponding with a Delhi-based travel company, My Flight Trip, and its owner, Sunil, has been very helpful. With his guidance, we have mapped out a rough itinerary of places we wish to visit. This morning, while Darryl snoozes, I check through it thoroughly. While I feel a little apprehensive about some of the Indian train travel we will have to endure, overall, the program looks great, so I give Sunil permission to start booking hotels and train tickets on our behalf.

Speaking of feeling apprehensive, our journey today falls slightly into that category too. Just fifteen months ago, in February 2023, fifty-seven people were killed in a train accident on the same stretch of line we are about to travel. It was the deadliest train accident in Greek history, and to date, no one has been held accountable.

'Although, if we got jittery about every place an accident has happened,' I console myself, 'we would never leave home. We would never go anywhere.'

After another of those excellent-value buffet breakfasts – where we pocket some fruit for later – it is into a taxi, which delivers us to the Corinth train station. This taxi ride once again takes us across the Corinth Isthmus.

'The seventh time we have crossed the Corinth Canal,' Darryl tells me. 'And when our train crosses it later, that will make it the eighth.'

Today's travel consists of two train journeys: the first from Corinth to Athens, and the second from Athens to Thessaloniki. Sitting alongside an English lady who moved to Greece thirty years ago after marrying a Greek national, the first leg passes incredibly quickly as she regales us with stories of her life here. She is also very knowledgeable about the local flora, and it is fascinating to learn about – and see – the abundance of fruit grown in this region: apricots, apples, grapes, nectarines, tomatoes and more.

There is a thirty-minute wait in Athens for our onward train and it is memorable for our first-ever brush with a pickpocket. Although he knows he shouldn't when travelling, Darryl has put his wallet in his back pocket. Standing on a moving escalator, a thief tries to take advantage of Darryl's error. Fortunately, Darryl realises in time and prevents what could have been a major problem.

'I know,' he says remorsefully. 'I shouldn't have had it in my back pocket. I won't from now on.'

The second leg of our journey takes five hours and we spend it ensconced in a moving compartment along with four other passengers. By good luck, we both have window seats, with a little table between us. We use it to rest surprisingly good Greek coffees purchased from the train's buffet and we spend most of our time gazing out of the window.

Initially, the view is of rolling hills, olive groves and small villages. Midway into the journey, we reach the fertile plains of Thessaly, Greece's agriculture heartland, with open fields, rivers and distant mountain ranges.

'Rice paddies,' I say in surprise at one point.

'Yes,' replies one of our compartment companions. 'This area of Greece, with its rice fields, is sometimes referred to as the Vietnam of Greece.'

The Tempi Valley, a lush, narrow gorge with views of Mount Olympus and Mount Ossa, passes by, and eventually our scenery transitions to coastal views of the Thermaic Gulf. Before long, our journey ends, and we find ourselves arriving in the port city of Thessaloniki.

Founded in 315 BCE and named after the half-sister of Alexander the Great, Thessaloniki was, for centuries, a melting pot of Greeks, Jews, Turks and others. In 1917, a devastating fire virtually wiped out the city. While it was obviously unfortunate it lost so much of its historic centre, the disaster led to a complete redesign, and today Thessaloniki is a modern, lively place, with bustling markets, trendy cafés, wide boulevards and a vibrant nightlife fuelled by its large student population.

While we are happy to be spending time here, Thessaloniki is also a springboard: a place from which we hope to explore the surrounding region, and the departure point for Bulgaria – the next leg of our journey.

It is too far to walk from the train station to our apartment, so we hail a passing taxi.

'I love how we can use our credit card to pay for a taxi these days,' I sigh contentedly, settling into my seat. 'Remember what it used to be like? You had to make sure you had cash and the correct currency. Travelling is so much easier now that you can just swipe a card anywhere.'

It is a short journey, and we exit the taxi to find our accommodation's host, Vassali, waiting for us on the pavement. Guiding us through some impressively large wooden doors and into another of those exciting European lifts, we emerge onto the eighth floor.

'The apartment has just been renovated,' Vassali tells us, unlocking a nearby door. 'Everything is new, and you have two balconies. The front one overlooks the sea, and the rear one looks out over Thessaloniki.'

Somewhere behind me, I can hear Darryl muttering to himself. It sounds like, 'The travel agent has done it again', but I am too busy listening to Vassali as he points out more of the apartment's features to pay much attention.

'The television has Netflix, the apartment is fully air-conditioned, and here is the washing machine if you need to do any laundry.'

'It is a bit cooler this far north and not as dusty,' I reply. 'So I don't think we will need the air-conditioning, but we will definitely be using the washing machine.'

'Is there anything else I can help you with?' Vassali asks, handing over a large set of keys.

'We are vegetarian. Could you suggest a place where we could get something to eat?'

'I don't know of any vegetarian restaurants, but I will do a search and get back to you. I'll text you the details.'

'That would be great. Thanks.'

'It feels like this could be the urban equivalent of a treehouse in the Amazon jungle,' I say to Darryl a short time later.

Experienced at settling quickly into new accommodation, we have made ourselves a cup of coffee and are sitting out on the large back deck. With eight stories appearing to be the maximum building height here, we are looking down upon, or directly at, numerous other large residential balconies. They obscure the view of the streets below; instead, all we can see are washing lines, mops, flowerpots and the paraphernalia of apartment living. Pigeons flitter by, and their contented cooing fills the air.

'It's great,' Darryl replies. 'It's different to what you would normally expect to see right in the heart of a city. Obviously, a lot of Greeks live in flats.'

True to his word, in the late afternoon a text arrives from Vassali, recommending a vegetarian restaurant suggested by a friend. It is within walking distance, and after enjoying a satisfyingly healthy poke bowl, we stop by a conveniently located supermarket to stock our fridge and pantry.

'I need a haircut,' I announce to Darryl over our coffee and toast the following morning. 'And I've finally had an email from the person purchasing our Bulgaria to Istanbul train tickets. He has secured them, and they will be waiting at our hotel in Sofia.'

As I mentioned some time ago, purchasing sleeper train tickets from Bulgaria to Türkiye has been more complicated than usual. They are not available online and can only be bought in person, in Bulgaria, and only within twenty-one days of travel.

Totally baffled as to how we were going to manage this from Australia, The Man in Seat 61, had come to our rescue. Scrutinising this website, I found a link to someone who regularly helped travellers by purchasing tickets on their behalf.

Contacting this someone, he had introduced himself as Paul and asked us to deposit payment into his bank account – he would take care of the rest.

Not really having any other options, we had done so, and for months we have been half-convinced it was all a scam – that no tickets would materialise, and we would still be left with the problem of how to get from Bulgaria to Türkiye.

While we haven't got the tickets yet, this morning's email suggests it is all legitimate.

I am still left, however, with the problem of my hair.

'I am going to try and get a haircut today,' I continue. 'Hopefully I can find somewhere and get them to understand exactly what I want.'

'Show them some pictures,' Darryl replies flippantly. 'It will be easier than trying to Google Translate it.'

Secretly thinking this a great idea, I spend the remainder of the morning taking screenshots of hairstyles I think will be suitable, along with Googling nearby hair salons.

'Any English?'

A shake of the head eliminates the first of the two hairdressers I had thought might work, but a positive reply at the second – along with immediate availability – means that by lunchtime, I have been successful in my quest.

'Your picture idea was great,' I confess to Darryl later. 'I'll probably do it every time I get a haircut from now on.'

With our apartment located just metres from the Thessaloniki waterfront, we spend the remainder of the afternoon strolling the Nea Paralia – a lively, five-kilometre promenade complete with bubbling fountains, funky sculptures, pleasant parks and convenient benches. The city's most iconic landmark, the White Tower, a fifteenth-century fort whitewashed to symbolise cleansing and freedom, provides a great photo opportunity, while Aristotelous Square surprises us with its grand symmetrical layout and beautiful, elegant old buildings.

'I have been searching GetYourGuide,' I mention to Darryl as we prepare that night's dinner of fresh pasta and salad. 'I know I am going to regret not getting to Meteora, but I have found another tour we can do from here. It visits three places: Pella, the birthplace of Alexander the Great; Edessa, the city of waterfalls; and Naoussa, one of Greece's principal wine-producing regions.'

'It sounds great,' Darryl replies. 'When were you thinking of going?'

'How about tomorrow? They still have availability.'

With a tour departure time of 8am and the meeting point a twenty-minute walk away, it makes for a lovely start to the day – strolling the Thessaloniki streets and watching the city awaken. Throughout our time in Greece, we have noticed many large, shaggy dogs. Referred to as strays, yet clearly well fed and cared for by locals, they roam freely, lounging in parks and public squares, and across footpaths. This morning is no exception – on our way to Aristotelous Square, we are often forced to step around one, peacefully sprawled across the pavement.

'Good morning everyone, I am Marco, your guide for today. I come from Italy, and I speak Greek, Italian and English. Today's first stop will be Pella, birthplace of Alexander the Great. I presume you all know who he was, but for those who don't, I will give you a quick recap.'

'That's good,' I hear Darryl mumble beside me. Agreeing, I laugh quietly.

'Alexander the Great was one of history's greatest military leaders. Born in 356 BCE, he ascended the throne at age twenty and ended up creating one of the largest empires in history – stretching from Greece to India. Through his conquests, Greek culture spread across the known world. While that's a very brief summary, some another interesting points about Alexander: he was tutored by the great philosopher

Aristotle, and contrary to popular belief, never meet Cleopatra. She lived about 250 years after his death in 323 BCE.'

'And Pella?' someone calls out.

'Pella was his birthplace,' Marco replies. 'In Alexander's time, it was a thriving city, famous for its grand palaces, mosaics and advanced urban planning. While today it is little more than ruins, the accompanying museum houses complete mosaics found at the site. You will be able to see them as the museum is also included in today's tour.'

It takes around fifty minutes to reach Pella. While I sit and admire the view from my window, the fertile plains with wheat, corn and sunflowers; the dust-covered hills in the far distance; the traditional Greek villages with red-tiled roofs, Marco continues to impart information.

'Did you know that more than half of all the Greeks live in just two cities – Athens and Thessaloniki? Greece is the only Balkan country that hasn't experienced communism… In 1923, after the Greco-Turkish War, about 1.2 million Christians were relocated from Türkiye to Greece, and around five hundred thousand Muslims were relocated from Greece to Türkiye. The exchange was compulsory and based on religion, not ethnicity.'

Fascinated by the last piece of history, I have to shelve my curiosity for the time being as, outside, the ruins of Pella come into view.

'I didn't think much of the actual ruins,' I say to Darryl back on the bus some time later. 'But the museum was fantastic.'

'I agree. It was a great building,' he replies. 'All suspended concrete, designed to blend into the landscape.'

'I meant its contents – all those complete mosaics! It must have taken months to move them into the museum.'

'Oh, years, probably.'

Unlike much of the landscape we have seen so far in Greece, the scenery as we edge closer to Edessa, our next stop, is lush and green, dotted with apple orchards, vineyards and olive groves. Situated on a verdant hill, as our bus climbs slowly upwards, it is possible to see water cascading down in a series of waterfalls, with droplets of moisture floating through the air.

'No need for me to explain why Edessa is called the "City of Waterfalls",' Marco comments as a particularly large fall of water comes into view.

With lunch at a restaurant included in our tour, we spend a few hours in Edessa, strolling leafy parks, walking behind waterfalls, enjoying delicious food and marvelling at the sheer volume of liquid that gushes through the town.

'I wouldn't want to walk too close to that,' says one tour member, gesturing toward a nearby rushing channel of water that cascades powerfully over the cliff's edge.

'No, there are some terrible stories of people who have,' Marco tells us. 'Just last year, a lady was having lunch at a restaurant nearby. She finished eating, got up and jumped straight into this rushing stream. There's no hope for people who do this.'

It is a rather sobering story to end our visit to Edessa, and our group reboards the bus a little quieter than usual. We remain that way for some time, each quietly absorbing the changing view – the lush foliage and forests disappearing, replaced by rolling green hills draped with bushy grapevines.

Finally, just when it feels as if I could drop off to sleep, we pass through some gates and stop in front of a long, low building. A large sign indicates that we have arrived at the Ktima Kir-Yianni Winery.

'Good,' I hear someone behind me say. 'I was nearly asleep. I need a wine.'

'This vineyard is part of the Boutaris family, who have been involved with winemaking for over one hundred and forty years,' Marco tells us as we disembark the bus, glad to stretch our legs. 'Yiannis Boutaris was pivotal in putting Greek wines on the international map.'

Since my breast cancer diagnosis, I no longer drink wine, but that doesn't stop me from enjoying this part of our tour. Being outside amongst the elegant grapevines, visiting the production areas and poking through the cellars – all while learning a little about the winery's history. And when Yiannis pulls out a *bouzouki* (a traditional Greek instrument similar to a guitar), the copious glasses of tasting wine appear, and the group really awakens, I am more than content to sip my Greek coffee.

'I really enjoyed today,' Darryl tells me later that evening, as we cook up another dish of freshly bought pasta in our apartment. 'It gave us a whole different look at Greece – showed us that there are areas that are green with trees, not just rocky hills covered in small bushes everywhere.'

'And how about all the rice fields we passed on the way back?' I reply. 'Even more than we saw from the train. The south of Greece was so dry and dusty, yet here, there is enough water to grow rice.'

CHAPTER 19

The Bus to Bulgaria

Our final day in Greece. Tomorrow, we board a coach that will take us over the border and onward to Sofia, the capital of Bulgaria. With trains on this stretch of track halted in 2020 due to the pandemic – and still not reinstated – we have been forced to purchase bus tickets. Not being the greatest fans of travelling long distances on crowded buses, tomorrow's journey is one we have not been looking forward to. Pushing our concerns aside, we concentrate instead on how to fill these last hours.

'I was thinking we could just wander around the city,' I suggest. 'Maybe revisit Aristotelous Square? The port area sounds good, and also the ancient Agora.'

'I would like to catch up on some washing,' Darryl replies. 'Use the washing machine while we have the chance.'

'Good idea. My sneakers need a wash. If I wash them this morning, they should be dry by tonight. We also need snacks and water for the bus trip. We could grab those from the supermarket we found.'

'And dinner?' Darryl asks.

'Let's eat out somewhere.'

Thessaloniki has yet to fully awaken, so while my shoes wash, we eat our breakfast on our spacious balcony, enjoying the peace and tranquillity afforded by our upper-level apartment. The air is cool, and the noise of the streets below is muted. All we can hear are cooing pigeons and the occasional window being opened. It is a lovely way to start our day, and I am feeling relaxed and quite content when I return inside to pull my shoes from the washing machine.

'Oh no,' I gulp.

'What?' replies Darryl.

'I've cooked my shoes. Look at them,' I groan, holding up a shoe whose sole has come completely unstuck. 'The glue has totally melted on both of them.'

'What setting did you use?' Darryl asks pointedly.

'I have no idea. The machine is all in Greek. I chose one that looked fine. I had no idea the water temperature could get so high it would melt the glue.'

'Well, it has,' Darryl replies, slightly exasperated. It is not the first time I have suffered a washing machine mishap. 'You'll obviously need to get a new pair.'

'Yes,' I reply remorsefully. 'But the soles were starting to wear away anyway. They were getting a bit slippery.' I try to excuse myself.

'Mmm,' Darryl grunts. 'Hopefully you can find some new ones today.'

Surprisingly, we discover a few hours later that Thessaloniki is full of good shoe shops. It is easy to find a replacement pair, and their bag swings from my hand as we complete our explorations of the city. While the ancient Agora and its accompanying fourth-century Rotunda impress, and the narrow cobblestone streets of Ano Poli (meaning Old

Town) are worth the effort to reach, it is the port area we appreciate the most. Here, we walk among the renovated warehouses, stroll the pier and browse the market, where we can't resist purchasing a large bag of fresh, sweet apricots. Dinner is a falafel kebab eaten amongst the historic ruins and clusters of animated students at Navarinou Square. Returning to our apartment after a long day, we remember to grab some water and nuts from the supermarket for tomorrow's journey.

The following morning, at some ungodly hour, I awaken with a concerning thought: what happens if the cancer drug I am on, Verzenio, acts up as it often does? What happens if I really need to use a toilet during the six-hour bus journey and there's no toilet on the bus? Frozen with anxiety, I mull over the problem for some time, and it is only when I decide not to take my morning medication, nor eat or drink anything, that I can eventually fall back asleep.

It is a fitful sleep, and a relief when the Uber we have ordered arrives promptly at 7am. While Uber has a great reputation, it is slightly disconcerting having to put your trust into an online booking app – especially when vital onward travel depends on it.

There is a slight hiccup when, arriving at our bus terminal, we notice it is not the one stated on our ticket. Apparently, there are several main bus stations in Thessaloniki, and I have given our Uber driver the wrong one. Fortunately, he is a lovely elderly gentleman who simply shrugs his shoulders before delivering us where we need to be.

Familiar now with Greek bus terminals, it doesn't take long to locate our coach and board, noting as we do that, once again, we have been allocated front-row seats. With only a handful of passengers, it is a relatively silent exit from Thessaloniki, with most content to either close their eyes or, like me, gaze at the passing scenery.

Initially, the view is very similar to what I saw from the train a few days earlier: small towns, industrial zones, then fields of olive groves and vineyards.

The further north we head, however, the more the landscape starts to change. Farmlands dotted with herds of sheep and goats appear, only to be replaced by climbing hills, winding roads and lush forests.

It is about here that Darryl turns to me.

'Have you been paying any attention to our driver?' he asks.

'Not really,' I reply.

'Well, watch him. I have never seen one like him. That is the fifth phone call he has taken – and he doesn't have hands-free answering. He hit a barrier earlier, and I think he looks pretty old to still be driving long-distance buses.'

Arriving shortly after this at the Greek-Bulgarian border, I get a better understanding of what Darryl was talking about. Parking near what looks like a customs building, our driver simply exits the bus and saunters away. No explanation is given – there is no indication of whether we should stay on board or disembark.

Eventually, a bold young student goes in search of answers. Returning, he communicates to everyone that we need to get off the bus and present ourselves first at the nearby Greek customs counter, then at the more distant Bulgarian one.

With still no sign of our bus driver, we do as instructed. And, although we get asked some probing questions about our missing European Union entry stamps, we are more intrigued by the current situation to be worried about that.

Twenty minutes later, with our bus still sitting in Greece and us waiting in Bulgaria, our driver nonchalantly emerges from a café, hops in, drives it across the border, and parks alongside us.

'We go now,' is all he says.

Returning to my seat, I am about to heartily agree with Darryl about our driver's odd behaviour, when Darryl turns to me.

'We've lost a passenger. There was a lady sitting in that seat. Her bag is still there, but she isn't.'

Darryl is not the only one to have noticed, but despite being informed multiple times, the driver, unconcerned, continues with the journey.

Captivated by the contrast in scenery now that we have crossed into Bulgaria, the different style of houses, the more rugged mountainous terrain, the deeper, lusher forests, I miss the phone call that has the other passengers talking loudly and our driver looking slightly panicked.

'Someone's phoned him about the missing passenger, I think.' Darryl tells me. 'I couldn't understand the conversation – it was all in Greek.'

Intrigued now by how animated our fellow passengers have become, and how belligerent the driver looks, I pull out my phone and bring up the Google Translate app. With it, we learn that the missing passenger is currently chasing us in a taxi, and we need to stop and wait for her. Needless to say, there is an admiring cheer when she eventually retakes her seat – it is amplified when she loudly berates the bus driver.

Some time later, as the forested countryside fades and the landscape transitions to urban sprawl, we enter Sofia, the capital of Bulgaria and one of Europe's oldest cities, dating back seven thousand years. Not knowing what to expect, I am surprised to find it reminiscent of parts of Russia we have visited – a mix of Soviet-era apartment blocks, modern developments, and the domes of Orthodox churches visible in the distance.

'That wasn't so bad after all,' I reflect to Darryl as we exit our coach. 'I won't be so hesitant about booking bus journeys in the future.'

'It was actually quite entertaining,' he replies. 'Now what? Can we walk to our hotel?'

'Probably,' I reply, reaching for my phone. 'It looks to be about a twenty-minute stroll.'

When arriving at a new destination, walking to our accommodation is actually one of the things we enjoy most about travelling. Not only does it give us time to unwind and stretch our legs, but it is also the ideal way to orient ourselves and get a feel for our new surroundings. Usually following directions from Google Maps, we are never sure exactly what the route will entail. Sometimes, like once in Rome when the directed trail led to steep cobblestone hills covered in dog faeces, it can be awful. Generally, though, it's great. With cobblestone lanes making it hard to walk with our bags, leafy green parks and noisy passing trams, today's stroll into the heart of Sofia falls somewhere between the two.

CHAPTER 20

Wandering Sofia and Plovdiv

It is a little after 3pm when our walk terminates at the aging but comfortable Central Hotel. Checking in, it is an indescribable relief to find Paul has come through for us and our onward train tickets to Türkiye are waiting. What isn't so good is that the room with the kitchenette we have booked is now unavailable. With no real explanation offered, our complaints result in some vouchers for the breakfast buffet and vague directions to nearby restaurants.

'It was nice to be able to watch television last night.'

It is the following morning, and we are contentedly filling our plates with various vegetarian dishes available at the buffet. Having struggled to find many vegetable dishes in Greece, we are surprised and delighted to discover that Bulgaria does have a tradition of plant-based food.

'Especially having four channels to choose from,' I reply, spooning a large amount of grilled vegetables onto my plate. 'It is the first time since we left home we have been able to watch anything apart from the BBC news.'

'We found a supermarket last night and had a little look around. What did you want to do today?' Darryl changes the subject while taking a seat at a table.

'Well, I've booked a tour to Plovdiv for tomorrow. Today, I thought we could just have a bit of a look around. Get more of a feel for the place. From what I could gather yesterday, it looks to be an easily walkable city.'

Full bellies, a brilliant blue sky and a pleasant twenty-degree temperature make for ideal walking conditions, and the hours slip by as we comfortably explore Sofia. With many of its main sights easily connected by grand boulevards, lively streets and ancient cobblestones, the city proves readily traversable.

Strolling one large avenue, noticing the enormous Stalinist-style buildings that surround us, and observing how well swept it is, I am immediately reminded of our visit to Moscow. It's a memory amplified when, outside the Presidential Palace, we come across another change of guard ceremony. Not long later, we stumble upon the Serdica Archaeological Complex, a site that provides evidence of Sofia's varied rulers. Located less than a minute's walk from grand communist-era buildings, alongside a modern metro station, the Serdica Complex brilliantly showcases Roman streets, walls and remnants of houses dating from the second to fourth centuries.

'It's a very spacious city,' I remark at some stage. 'And it feels almost empty compared to others. I wonder what the population is.'

Googling this question brings up some fascinating results.

'Bulgaria has one of the fastest-shrinking populations in the world,' I read. 'It is currently just over 6.7 million, but since 1989, it has lost over two million due to low birth rates and emigration.'

'And the population of Sofia?' Darryl asks.

'It is estimated at 1.67 million,' I read. 'In comparison to the amount of infrastructure here, that's not much, really. No wonder it feels so eerily empty.'

Continuing on, this feeling of desertion increases rather than lessens. We reach St Alexander Nevsky Cathedral, a beautiful old building whose golden domes shimmer in the sunlight, and there are only a handful of people in the wide-open cobblestone square where it sits. It is the same when we reach Saint Sofia Church, an ancient sixth-century building that gave Sofia its name and which rests upon a Roman necropolis (ancient cemetery). There is no one else here. The only time we do find the crowds expected of such a city is when, searching for lunch, we happen upon Vitosha Boulevard. It is a lively, pedestrian-friendly street, paved with smooth stone tiles and lined with cafés, boutiques and restaurants. Sitting among the crowds at one of its outdoor cafés, gazing at the passing shoppers and the tourists, feels far more normal and much closer to our expectations.

It is a half an hour walk to reach the starting point of our tour the following morning and, while we could have braved a tram or caught an Uber, we are content to stroll. As it is a Sunday and just after 7am, Sofia is still asleep and with another perfect day unfolding, it feels like a privilege to be here, in this city, watching it come to life.

Our minivan is waiting and, before long, we find ourselves travelling along a slightly aged, somewhat second-rate highway on our way to Plovdiv, Bulgaria's second-largest city. It is a scenic drive through mountains, valleys and fertile plains, and as we journey, our guide provides some background information about the place we are about to visit.

'Plovdiv is one of the oldest cities in Europe,' he begins. 'It dates back over six thousand years and is often referred to as the City of Seven Hills because it straddles seven hills. Like Sofia, it has been inhabited by many different people, each leaving their mark. The most obvious marks are the Roman Theatre and Roman Stadium. While what remains of the stadium is only partially visible, the Roman Theatre is still used today to host concerts and culturally significant events.'

'Wasn't Plovdiv voted the European Capital of Culture recently?' someone from behind me asks.

'In 2019, yes, that is correct,' our guide responds. 'It also gained this award back in 1999. Now, we have arrived. We will be stopping shortly, and you can either take the guided tour of Plovdiv Old Town, which is included with your ticket, or explore on your own. Either way, we will all meet at the entrance to the stadium, located on the main pedestrian shopping street, at 3pm.'

'That gives us four hours here,' I say to Darryl, glancing at my watch. 'Why don't we take the tour and then look for somewhere to have lunch?'

Despite there being well over a dozen passengers on the bus, only four others join us on the guided tour of Plovdiv Old Town, and after a while, we begin to understand why. It is a place that can easily be explored on your own, with many of its sites either well signposted or self-explanatory. Persevering with our choice to use a guide, we walk on enormous, irregularly shaped cobblestones, whose uneven and worn surfaces make it particularly challenging, and learn that many of these pavers were laid in Roman times.

We stand in front of colourfully painted houses and are told that they were built in the eighteenth and nineteenth centuries during the Bulgarian National Revival – a time of cultural, economic and national awakening in the wake of Bulgaria's independence from the Ottomans.

We climb Nebet Tepe, one of Plovdiv's seven hills, and, after admiring the panoramic views of modern Plovdiv, learn that this was where the city was first settled. Finally, after glancing at the ancient Roman Theatre and purchasing a souvenir fridge magnet from a quaint gift shop, we thank our guide and search for a suitable place to lunch.

'I saw a restaurant while we were walking earlier,' Darryl tells me. 'It looked like it had great views over the city. And it sold beer.'

Retracing our steps, Darryl's restaurant turns out to be the highlight of our day in Plovdiv. With incredible views over the surrounding countryside, icy-cold beer for him and crisp, fresh lemon juice for me, we sit for ages. Eventually, we order a meal of vegetable stew and cannot believe our luck when the most delicious array of vegetables arrives, marinated in traditional spices and cooked in a special clay pot. It is our best meal to date, and we are still talking about it as we enter Plovdiv's new town to seek out what is left of the ancient Roman Stadium, find our group and reboard our bus.

Though we are somewhat tired from our long day, it doesn't stop us from strolling the streets of Sofia that evening. It is a public holiday weekend, and the city is alive with people enjoying themselves. Restaurants are full, and the parks and monuments host an extraordinary number of wedding parties posing for photographs. For dinner, we find a small restaurant located next to a six-hundred-year-old mulberry tree, and as we dine, we talk about our impressions of Bulgaria, knowing this will be our final night in the country.

'It's been memorable,' I sum up. 'So many stately buildings, so reminiscent of Moscow. So quiet.'

'Such good television,' Darryl laughs. 'Yes, it has been memorable. I'm not sure about Plovdiv, though. Its Old Town was advertised as being ancient when much of it was built just two hundred years ago. I'm glad to be able to say I have been to Bulgaria, but I'm really looking forward to Türkiye next. This time tomorrow night, we will be on the train to Istanbul.'

CHAPTER 21

The Overnight Train to Türkiye

The sound of a passing tram wakes me early the following morning and, lying in bed, I realise that we are not yet fully prepared for our overnight journey on a sleeper train. We still need to purchase some essential items, face wipes, bottled water and a small portable toiletry bag, that have proven vital on previous overnight trips. Mid-morning, while Darryl rests, I return to Vitosha Boulevard to pick up these supplies, along with another souvenir tote bag and a couple of tofu poke bowls.

The poke bowls are enjoyed in our room, and at noon we hand back our room key. Having completed all the sightseeing of Sofia that we wish to do, I spend the next few hours writing a blog post in the hotel foyer while Darryl reads. At 3pm, we make our way on foot to Sofia train station. Located alongside the bus station where we arrived, it is the same journey down cobbled lanes, over broken footpaths and through grassy parks – only in reverse.

Arriving at Sofia train station, it is disconcerting to find all of the signage in Bulgarian. Realising how lucky and spoilt we have been with English signage so far, it takes both The Man in Seat 61 and Google Translate to figure out how to read the large noticeboards. With many platforms having two trains departing simultaneously, The Man in Seat 61 advises that it is important to determine whether your train is leaving from the east or west end. Grateful to have given ourselves plenty of time, we eventually work out where we need to be and head to the correct end of our platform.

While waiting, we have an interesting interaction. A husband and wife, accompanied by their three young children, approach us to ask how we purchased our train tickets. They wish to take tomorrow's train to Istanbul but, as we already knew, tickets cannot be purchased online.

'We were told to buy them here at the station or at the local tourist office,' the husband explains. 'But the system is down, so the tourist office can't sell us tickets, and no one here at the station speaks English, so we haven't been able to purchase any.'

'We were told that the guard on today's train might be able to help,' his wife adds. 'But it doesn't seem likely. Guards don't normally sell long-distance tickets.'

Knowing that our method of purchase – using the mysterious Paul – won't help them, all we can do is wish them luck and move on. As always when travelling, it's one of those stories where we will never know the ending.

Our train, when it arrives, proves to be aged and shabby. On the outside, it is covered in colourful graffiti; on the inside, everything feels grimy and grotty to the touch. At one end of the carriage, we discover a pungent Western-style upright toilet; at the other end, an even more pungent squatting Asian one.

Nonetheless, our compartment has a set of bunks which we make up using the provided linen, and a small fridge containing complimentary juice and chocolate.

Surprisingly, after hours spent reading and window-gazing, we fall asleep as the sole occupants of our carriage – but, when woken at 12.30am by Bulgarian guards checking passports, we find the other compartments are now full. Somehow, we have slept through everyone else's arrival. At 2am, arriving at the Turkish border town of Kapikule and instructed to disembark with our luggage, we discover that, of the thirty or so passengers on board (not many, really), everyone is a Westerner. Slightly groggy, we all stand silently in the frigid night air before presenting first at customs, then at security. By a little after 3am, we are back in our bunks, rocked to sleep by the gentle movement of the train.

It is not a long sleep, unfortunately. Woken a little before 5am by some external commotion and realising that we are now in Türkiye, I am too excited to close my eyes again. I have long wanted to visit Türkiye, and the Basilica Cistern in Istanbul has been on my Bucket List for years. When I was one, I did actually travel through this country by motorhome, and hearing my parents talk about their adventures and interactions with the locals fuelled my desire to revisit it as an adult.

Today, that dream is coming true. And as I sit, watching the scenery flash by, the Sea of Marmara, rolling plains, and growing signs of industry as we approach Istanbul, I can only think how lucky we are to have made this visit happen.

'Our train terminates at an outer suburb of Istanbul called Halkali,' I mention to Darryl when he eventually wakes up. 'We can catch the Marmaray, the commuter train, into the city – or we could catch a cab.'

'What's the distance between Halkali and central Istanbul?' he asks.

'I'm not sure about the distance, but the Marmaray takes about forty minutes. Then we would need to walk to our hotel. I don't think I am up to searching for a hotel on foot. Let's just catch a cab.'

It is a little before 8am when our train terminates – right in the middle of peak hour – which, combined with road works, is why we find ourselves sitting in traffic for over ninety minutes. Despite the frustration of knowing how much quicker the commuter train would have been, our protracted entry into Istanbul does have its benefits. It allows us a long, slow look at the suburbs we pass through, especially the narrow, cobblestone lanes of central Istanbul, and it showcases the impressive skill of Turkish taxi drivers.

Istanbul, home to an estimated sixteen million people, is a massive city with a rich and diverse history stretching back to ancient times. While the earliest of its known settlements date to around 6,700 BCE, the city itself was founded by Greek settlers around 660 BCE under the name Byzantium. In 330 AD, Emperor Constantine the Great made it the capital of the Roman Empire, renaming it Constantinople. Growing into the largest municipality in the Western world, it remained Constantinople until it fell to the Ottoman Turks in 1453. Although it lost its status as Türkiye's capital to Ankara in 1923, with the founding of the Republic of Türkiye, Istanbul still retains its position as the country's largest and most influential city.

Despite all this, Istanbul's true heart lies in the Bosphorus, the strait that connects the Black Sea to the Mediterranean and uniquely divides the city into European and Asian sides.

When planning our journey to this vast metropolis, deciding which side to stay on, the European or the Asian – was not easy. Each offers a range of suburbs with their own special character and appeal. Eventually, I found help from a local agency, Amber Travel, who not only assisted us in choosing to stay in Sultanahmet, part of the Fatih district on the European side, but also helped us purchase upcoming train tickets and organise various guided excursions.

'The Fatih district is Istanbul's historic heart,' they had told me.

Our taxi finally deposits us at the Hotel Saba, the hotel suggested and booked by Amber Travel. Although it is nearing 10am, this highly visited area of the city still looks asleep – shops are closed, cafés are only partially full. Approaching reception, all we want to do is shower, rest, then find a good coffee.

'Apologies, sir and madam, I cannot find a reservation for you in the system. When did you make the booking?'

Appalled, we start wondering that if this reservation has not been made, what about the others? The onward train tickets, the excursions? It is a profound relief when, after a series of worried conversations, a manager approaches, advises that *he* is expecting us, and suggests we go and help ourselves to a complimentary breakfast at the hotel's buffet while our room is readied.

'Apologies, sir and madam, for the confusion. Please. Leave your bags here and go and eat.'

Sitting on the terrace of the hotel's rooftop breakfast area a short time later, discussing what could have happened if our booking hadn't been found, much of our conversation also centres on how friendly the staff appear, how courteous. We do not realise it yet but we have just had our first brush with Turkish hospitality. By the time we leave Türkiye – never having felt cheated and always welcomed – we will have learnt that this courteous, approachable attitude is simply a way of life here.

'What an incredible view. Isn't that the Blue Mosque?'

Full from my breakfast of salad, bread and cheese and coffee in hand, I am finally relaxed. I have recovered from our long train journey, the nightmare of the Istanbul traffic, and the fright of potential lost reservations. This easing of anxieties means I can now truly enjoy exactly where we are and appreciate what a remarkable location our hotel occupies.

Currently sitting on the roof of a five-storey building, I gaze to my right, where the Sea of Marmara sparkles like a well-cut sapphire, dotted with ferries and ships. To the left, partially obscured by leafy foliage, is the Hagia Sophia, while, slightly off-centre, the iconic domes and minarets of the Blue Mosque rise proudly against the crisp skyline.

'This is one of those moments I am never going to forget,' I sigh in contentment. 'To actually be in Istanbul, sitting on my hotel roof, with both the Hagia Sophia and the Blue Mosque visible… my expectations have been exceeded.'

'It is pretty incredible,' Darryl agrees. 'I didn't really have any expectations, but this is pretty good. What have we got planned for today?'

'Nothing, really. Hopefully our room will be ready so we can shower and change. Then maybe just have a look around, orient ourselves as usual. Amber Travel have booked us a guide for the next two days. She will show us some of the main sights. We chose well, really, deciding to stay in the Fatih district. It is the historic and cultural heart of Istanbul – referred to as the Old City. Most of what we want to see is located near here.'

A couple of hours later, having showered and rested, we venture outside and almost immediately realise just how fortunate we are. Stepping onto a narrow cobblestone street lined with quirky shops and now-bustling cafés, we find ourselves within seconds at Sultanahmet Square – once the ancient Hippodrome of Constantinople, and still the heart of the Old City.

With the Blue Mosque towering over us and the Obelisk of Theodosius, an ancient Egyptian monument brought to Constantinople in the fourth century, standing proudly nearby, it is a bit of a pinch-me moment.

'We seem to be pretty close to everything,' Darryl nonchalantly understates.

Walking a little further, past splashing fountains and manicured gardens where people rest on benches, the massive dome and reddish-hued, centuries-old walls of the Hagia Sophia emerge. The chatter from its long queues of visitors only adds to the buzz created by the milling tourists, gesturing guides and street vendors selling *simit* (Turkish bagels).

'Yes, I think we're in a good location,' Darryl again understates.

'Are you kidding?' I splutter. 'It's an incredible location. We've only been walking a few minutes and already we have seen some of the most amazing sights Istanbul has to offer. And look across the road – there's the Basilica Cistern! Nearly everything I wanted to see in Istanbul, a stone's throw from our room.'

Knowing that we will be revisiting this area more closely with our guide over the next few days, we don't linger in Sultanahmet Square. Instead, the remainder of the afternoon is spent wandering aimlessly. A nearby supermarket is earmarked for a return visit, as is a small, bustling bazaar. Located right behind the Blue Mosque, the Arasta Bazaar, originally created to finance the building of the Mosque, looks to offer a calmer shopping experience than its famous counterpart, Istanbul's Grand Bazaar. From what I could see as we quickly passed through, its goods also appeared to be of high quality. With copious free samples of delicious nougat being thrust at him, I know Darryl won't mind returning.

CHAPTER 22

Exploring Incredible Istanbul

Fresh from a night in a bed that does not move and excited for our 9am rendezvous with our guide, the following morning we are first at the hotel's breakfast buffet. Looking at the variety of dishes in front of me, the sliced tomatoes, diced cucumber, pickled vegetables, crumbly cheeses, sprightly lettuce, and an assortment of other savoury selections, I laugh to myself as I heartily fill my plate.

A few years ago, pre-cancer, a selection such as this would have filled me with horror – where were the hash browns, sausages, yoghurt and muesli I would have normally chosen? Now, with my diet completely changed and my body thanking me for it, I appreciate this smorgasbord of fresh, healthy offerings.

'Do you think we could get some washing done before meeting with our guide?' Darryl asks, as we once again claim an outside table on the hotel's rooftop dining area – our only company a pair of curious baby pigeons. The view, just as stunning as yesterday, stretches out before us.

'Good idea,' I reply. 'I read somewhere that if we leave it with reception before eight, it will be returned to us later that same day. I am fine for underwear, socks and T-shirts – I've been hand-washing those. But my long pants and jeans desperately need a proper machine wash. If I get them back today, I can wear them tonight.'

'What's happening tonight?' Darryl asks, looking puzzled.

'I haven't told you, but something I have always wanted to do in Türkiye was see the Whirling Dervishes. I've booked tickets for us to go tonight.'

'The what?'

'The Whirling Dervishes,' I repeat. 'It's a sacred ritual where men, dressed in white robes and tall felt hats, spin in a state of deep meditation.'

'You are kidding.'

'No. I know it sounds weird, but I'm hoping we'll enjoy it. It's something we will probably never get the opportunity to see again.'

'I'm pretty sure I am not going to enjoy it,' Darryl grumbles. 'No wonder you didn't tell me you had booked tickets. I don't think I would have gone otherwise.

Darryl is still looking disgruntled some time later but brightens when, at 9am, our guide meets us in reception. Friendly, bubbly, and with excellent English, Felize couldn't help but cheer anyone up.

'Welcome to Istanbul.' She smiles warmly. 'You have me as your guide for today and tomorrow. Today, I was thinking we could visit Topkapi Palace and the Blue Mosque. Tomorrow, I thought you might like to see the Hagia Sophia and take a cruise on the Bosphorus. Is there anything else you specifically wanted to see while you are here?'

'The Basilica Cistern and the Grand Bazaar,' I reply immediately.

'Perfect. We can fit the Basilica in this afternoon, and I can leave you at the Grand Bazaar afterwards. How does that sound?'

'Good,' Darryl says. 'But we need to fit in some lunch as well.'

'And another Turkish coffee,' I add.

'Okay – lunch and coffee too,' Felize laughs. 'Let's get going while it is still relatively early. In another hour or so, it will really start to get busy. Right now, the queues might not be too long.'

Located on the far side of Sultanahmet Square, our slow amble to Topkapi Palace gives Felize ample time to tell us a little about herself, as well as providing titbits of information on the sights we pass.

'The German Fountain,' she says, stopping beside an ornate, octagonal, domed structure. 'A gift from Germany to the Ottoman Empire in 1901. It had to be shipped in pieces then reassembled... I grew up in this district. My father had a book publishing house near the Hagia Sophia, so I know Istanbul well.'

'Is that why you became a tour guide?' I ask.

'No. I actually studied to become a teacher at university but found I didn't like teaching. I have eight-year-old twins, so working as a tour guide suits me better. The hours are easier.'

'Most guides we have met haven't ended up using their degrees,' Darryl muses.

'We have a saying,' Felize continues a few steps later, stopping beside one of the modern drinking fountains that dot Sultanahmet Square. 'Whoever drinks the water of Istanbul will surely return one day.'

'I read another one,' I reply. 'If the world were a single state, its capital would be Istanbul.'

'Yes,' Felize laughs. 'We have many sayings. Maybe because of its location – its connection between Europe and Asia.'

'The Blue Mosque,' she says almost seconds later, gesturing ahead. 'So named because of the blue tiles that adorn its interior walls. I had planned for us to visit later, but look – there are no queues. Let's take advantage while we can.'

Constructed between 1609 and 1616, the Blue Mosque is one of Istanbul's most iconic landmarks. An active place of worship, it also contains a *madrasa* (educational centre), a hospital, a primary school, a market, and the tomb of its founder, Sultan Ahmed I. Visited by such notables as Pope Francis and Barack Obama, the Blue Mosque is renowned for its twenty thousand stunning handmade ceramic tiles featuring tulips, its two hundred and sixty stained glass windows, its nine domes and its six minarets.

'Although,' Felize adds as, having gazed appreciatively at the mosque's magnificent interior, we now stand admiring its courtyard, 'there is a story behind the six minarets.'

'According to legend, Sultan Ahmed I wanted the mosque to have minarets made of gold. But the Turkish word for gold is very similar to the Turkish word for six. The architect misunderstood, and instead of building golden minarets, built six of them. Whether it is true or not, who knows – but it makes a good story.'

With the crowds around Sultanahmet Square now building, it takes a laboured fifteen minutes to wind our way through them and reach the entrance to Topkapi Palace. Here, while Felize arranges our entry tickets, we purchase a freshly baked *simit* from one of the many red-painted *simit* carts that occupy the Istanbul streets. Similar to a bagel, but crunchier and less dense, *simit* can be eaten plain or with cheese, jam or Nutella. Returning and noticing Darryl crunching his way through a sesame-crusted one, Felize offers a little more information about *simit* stalls.

'*Simit* carts in Istanbul are not just about selling food,' she tells us. 'They also demonstrate the city's culture of charity and generosity. Most *simit* vendors will follow the tradition of paying it forward – a customer can buy an extra *simit* and ask the vendor to hold it for someone in need.'

'I love that idea,' I reply. 'You said the city's culture of charity and generosity – what do you mean?'

'We don't allow people to go hungry or homeless in Istanbul, or anywhere in Türkiye,' Felize explains. 'Whether through state programs or cultural traditions of charity, food and shelter can always be found. Many cities offer free daily meals at public kitchens. *Simit* carts aren't the only ones to offer free food – bakeries and supermarkets often participate too.'

'And housing?' Darryl probes.

'Many cities provide free shelter and warm meals to those in need, especially during the winter months. Many mosques and religious charities also offer meals, clothes and a place to stay.'

Listening to Felize, and discovering that Turkish hospitality extends far beyond being friendly to tourists – that there is a deeply entrenched culture of helping others – my mind turns contemplative as we pass through the heavy stone gates of Topkapi Palace. Where did these values of hospitality and generosity originate? Does it have something to do with Islam or something older?

These are questions I shelve for the time being, but decide to ponder later.

Home to the Ottoman sultans for four hundred years, Topkapi Palace is a vast, sprawling complex of courtyards, gardens, domed halls and hidden chambers. Built in the 1460s, and now a museum and UNESCO-listed site, enter and you have infiltrated a world where sultans once trod, intrigue prevailed and opulence was commonplace.

In saying this, while it was lovely to wander its manicured gardens, scented faintly with roses, admire its cool, paved courtyards, marvel at the Imperial Kitchens designed to feed up to five thousand people daily, and ponder upon a small, innocent-looking fountain where execution orders were carried out, Topkapi Palace does pale in comparison to France's Palace of Versailles or Rome's Vatican. Unlike these places, where images of gluttonous wealth will stay with me forever, Topkapi Palace leaves only a few memories.

The first is the long, meandering halls of its Harem. Walking past the meticulous tilework that clung to its walls, the stained-glass windows that threw patches of colour onto the floors, and through the eunuchs' quarters, we learn this Harem wasn't all about pleasure.

'It was actually a highly structured political institution,' Felize explains, 'where women could rise to enormous power. Like Roxelana, a former concubine, who became the legal wife of Sultan Suleiman the Magnificent. And Kösem Sultan, a powerful queen mother who ruled the empire from behind the scenes for decades.'

The second lingering memory comes from its fourth courtyard – a peaceful, garden-filled retreat with incredible views out over the ship-laden Bosphorus. Standing here in Europe, it feels surreal that the mosques, towers and buildings I can see just a short, watery distance away, while part of the same city, are actually on a different continent.

We exit Topkapi Palace, and although it is not yet noon, it feels like an appropriate time to stop for lunch. Directing us to a little restaurant nestled in the centre of Sultanahmet Square, Felize looks slightly startled when we mention we are vegetarians but recovers quickly.

'I would normally suggest a beef kebab or kofte,' she laughs. 'But have you tried *pide*? It is a popular Turkish flatbread, a bit like pizza, that comes with a variety of toppings or fillings. I would suggest, seeing that you do not eat meat, you order a spinach *pide*.'

Eating what eventuates to be the first of many *pide* and enjoying yet another of those thick, heart-palpitating Turkish coffees, our topics of conversation range widely. From why I have a pink-ribbon tattoo on my arm – 'It is to commemorate my recent battle with breast cancer' – to why Felize considers herself a feminist. 'I am married with twins, but I would much prefer to live alone and not have to cook and clean for someone.'

Eventually, when the conversation dwindles, it is time to head to one of the most eagerly anticipated sights of our trip: the Basilica Cistern.

First revealed to me in the movie *Inferno*, starring Tom Hanks, the Basilica Cistern is an ancient underground water reservoir famous for its 336 marble columns, the two Medusa heads used as column bases, and its eerie, otherworldly atmosphere.

Having been a fan of caves and underground caverns since childhood, watching Tom chase a villain through this vast 'sunken palace', with its dull amber lighting, dripping ceilings, reflective watery floor, and hordes of slimy wet pillars, my attention had been captured immediately. One day, I vowed, I would see this dark, cool and damp place located in the heart of Istanbul.

Today, I am ecstatic. I am about to honour that vow, about to check another item on my seemingly never-ending Bucket List. Securing tickets and carefully making our way down a flight of slippery metal stairs, not even Felize's warning can curtail my enthusiasm.

'I will not be going any further,' she tells us, pausing at the bottom of the stairwell. 'It is not good to breathe too much of the air down here.'

Although mindful of her words, the surrounds are just too enticing, too mysterious, too long sought after, and so we leave her in search of the first of the Medusa Heads, then the perfect photo opportunity. It is only when both missions have been triumphantly completed, and the enormous, dimly lit chamber thoroughly explored, that we return to her side and ascend back into the open air.

'I can tell from your expression that you enjoyed your visit,' Felize laughs as we emerge once again into the sunlight and the milling crowds at street level.

'I loved it,' I reply. 'It was everything I had hoped for and more. And it was something I had wanted to do for years. Just like visiting the Grand Bazaar.'

'The Bazaar isn't too far from here,' Felize smiles. 'I won't come in with you, but I can leave you at one of its entrances. You should be able to find your way back to your hotel, I think?'

'Yes. That won't be a problem,' Darryl answers confidently.

'And we will see you at the same time tomorrow morning. Nine o'clock,' I add.

One of the largest and oldest covered markets in the world, Istanbul's' Grand Bazaar is a must-visit destination for any serious shopper. Reminiscent of a museum, with its domed ceilings, archways and intricately decorated storefronts, the bazaar spans sixty streets and hosts more than four thousand shops. Goods on offer include gold, jewellery, spices, tea, antiques, ceramics, textiles, leather products, rugs and much more.

Farewelling Felize at one of its entrances, mindful of her warning to note exactly which entrance, we find ourselves immediately swept up into a maelstrom of haggling vendors, shopkeepers spruiking carpets and hypervigilant customers. So intense is the atmosphere that, initially, we are too wary to attempt anything other than avoid getting lost in its maze of narrow, winding streets.

Eventually, feeling slightly bolder, we do accept an invitation from a stallholder to sit and have a cup of apple tea.

'We will sit, but we will not be purchasing a carpet,' we make clear.

'Yes. We understand. We just want to extend to you some Turkish hospitality.'

Despite frequently having to parry subtle suggestions that we should change our minds and take a rug home to Australia, the interaction is informative and friendly. We leave more knowledgeable about Turkish hospitality, carpets and apple tea – and they more educated on Vegemite, Australia and Steve Irwin.

In 2017, while visiting Lucca, a lovely walled city in Italy, I purchased a buttery-soft leather handbag. Able to be worn across the shoulder and close to my body, it made a perfect travel bag and accompanied me on our 2019 global adventure. Unfortunately, despite searching extensively, I have never found another like it. Today, Istanbul's Grand Bazaar changes that. Searching hard for the entrance we originally came through, we pass a really tiny stall selling the same style of handbag in many beautiful colours. Seeing it as not only fortuitous but a perfect Turkish memento, I stop and, despite Darryl's groans of 'Why do you need another handbag?', I successfully haggle for one in a muted mauve. It is so inexpensive and so gorgeous that the grin never leaves my face the entire walk back to our hotel.

'It was deep.'

We have just spent the past two hours sitting in a darkened room inside a 550-year-old Ottoman Turkish bathhouse, watching a dance that dates back some eight hundred years. Sitting silently, watching men in long white robes and tall felt hats, eyes closed, whirling in endless circles, the sound of chanting and drums echoing from the worn stone walls, I had snuck a glance at Darryl numerous times. With no acknowledgment from him, no hint at what he might be thinking or feeling, by the time the twirling is over and the final prayers of salvation complete, I am bursting with curiosity.

'Yes, it was deep,' he repeats. 'Good to have seen it, but it is not something I really want to watch again.'

We are still laughing and talking about the performance as we begin our slow trek back to our room. But as we become less fixated on what we have just seen, more aware of our surrounds, our voices quieten. Unlike our previous explorations of this area, which were undertaken during the day, dusk has fallen, and Sultanahmet Square has been transformed into something else entirely – a magical, incredibly beautiful place where the golden lights of the Hagia Sophia twinkle and blush against the darkening sky. Where streetlamps cast a soft glow on ancient cobblestone pathways, shimmering fountains gently trickle, and a gentle breeze carries the scent of Turkish tea.

'Oh, this is stunning,' I whisper, looking around me. 'I think Istanbul has just elevated itself to one of my favourite cities. I will never forget this. The lights of the mosques. The *simit* carts. The fountains.'

'It's strange. It is so alive, yet so peaceful,' Darryl murmurs in reply.

CHAPTER 23

Catching a Train to Ankara

Well nourished by another great breakfast of salads, bread and coffee from our hotel buffet, we are ready for Felize when she arrives promptly at 9am. Today, she reminds us, we will be visiting the Hagia Sophia before taking a boat ride on the Bosphorus. It does not take long to retrace yesterday's steps through Sultanahmet Square, past the Egyptian Obelisk, the Blue Mosque and the German Fountain, heading towards the Hagia Sophia. As we walk, Felize turns to me.

'You mentioned yesterday that you have recently undergone treatment for breast cancer. I didn't say anything at the time, but my mum had cervical cancer over twenty years ago and is still alive today. I have been thinking what she did to survive and whether it might be of benefit to you.'

As I look at her in interest, Felize continues. 'The main things I thought of are that she reduced the sugar in her diet. If she had a sugar craving, she would take some cinnamon to lessen it. She also kept – and still keeps – her body alkaline by drinking water mixed with bicarbonate of soda at least three times a week. And she kept busy. Kept moving.'

Although aware that exercise is one of the best things someone fighting breast cancer can do, I had not known cancer does not thrive in an alkaline environment, nor that cinnamon can help reduce sugar cravings. I am still thinking this over when Felize suddenly darts into a shop, emerging a moment later with a small packet, which she thrusts at me.

'Travel packets of bicarbonate of soda,' she smiles. 'You can start taking it straight away.'

Again, totally dumfounded by another demonstration of Turkish thoughtfulness and generosity, I can only stammer my inadequate thanks.

With its rich history and multiple transformations, the Hagia Sophia stands as Istanbul's most iconic landmark. Originally built in 537 CE, it was the world's largest cathedral at the time, renowned for its impressive dome that allowed light to pour in – a remarkable engineering achievement. In 1453, following the Ottoman conquest of Constantinople, the Hagia Sophia entered a new chapter: it was converted into a mosque by the reigning Sultan. During this transformation, its towering minarets were added, while its Christian mosaics were concealed.

'Islam discourages the use of icons and images, especially those depicting human and animal forms,' Felize explains as we reach the front of a long queue and enter the building. 'The focus is to remain on the worship of Allah, rather than on any physical traits.'

In 1935, under the leadership of the Republic of Türkiye, the Hagia Sophia underwent its third transformation when it was turned into a museum.

'Turning it into a museum not only preserved its historical and religious history, but allowed for both its Christian and Islamic heritage to be recognised.' Felize continues as we stand upon marble floors worn smooth by centuries of footsteps, gaze at walls adorned with angels, emperors and religious figures, and are bathed in the ethereal light filtering through the massive dome 56 metres above us.

'But in 2020, it was turned back into a mosque – yet another transformation,' Felize says mournfully. 'And not only did it again lose half of its identity, the Christian half, but it lost its protection. Now so many people come to pray each day that it is being damaged, and the queues to enter are so long.'

Just as Felize finishes saying these words, the Call to Prayer, an Islamic tradition recited five times per day to invite Muslims to prayer, echoes out, and standing in this 1,500-year-old building, watching the worshippers, a tingle of awe runs through my body.

'I agree with you. It is a shame this building is being damaged and over-visited, but I have to say, standing in such an ancient place, seeing so many devotees still come to pray, listening to a chant dating back to seventh-century Prophet Mohammad – it is pretty awe-inspiring. Pretty special. I am so glad we have got to visit here.'

'Yes,' Darryl interrupts flippantly. 'Who knows if visitors will be allowed in if it has another transformation?'

'It is a special place,' Felize laughs in reply. 'I just hate seeing it deteriorate. But now – are you hungry? We have time to get something to eat before our cruise on the Bosphorus.'

'I am,' Darryl replies. 'Can we get another of those spinach *pide*?'

Sitting in another of Istanbul's many welcoming cafés a short time later, munching through a steaming hot spinach and feta *pide*, Darryl shifts the mood by raising a disconcerting topic.

'I was researching Istanbul last night on my iPad and I learnt it is located on one of the most active and dangerous fault lines in the world.'

'It is,' Felize replies. 'People talk about California's San Andreas Fault, but Istanbul's is just as active.'

'Experts predict a very high probability of a major earthquake here within the next few decades,' Darryl continues. 'Doesn't that worry you?'

'Well, a bit,' Felize admits. 'But there is nothing I can do about it. I have to continue living, so it is best just not to think about it.'

'Did you say an earthquake within the next few decades?' I ask, remembering last year's devasting quake in southern Türkiye that caused untold damage and killed over 1,300 people.

'Yes. Istanbul is actually overdue for a major earthquake,' he replies.

Not really familiar with earthquakes – they are rare in Australia – Darryl's findings are unsettling. So much so that, over the course of our travels through Türkiye, the likelihood of one occurring will occasionally pop into my mind – marring an otherwise carefree moment. But today, ignorant of this impending angst, I simply finish my *pide* before cheerfully declaring, 'Well, the sooner we get on the water, the better. I would rather be on a boat than on land amongst concrete buildings if an earthquake hits.'

Used to Australia's strict laws regarding water safety, our upcoming cruise upon the Bosphorus is something of an eye-opener for the both of us. Taking a little over ninety minutes and showcasing landmarks from both the European and Asian sides of the city, we sit on the upper deck of a large cruiser – no safety rails, no life vests in sight – and watch in amusement the antics of our ship and all the others around us.

'There don't seem to be any rules about staying to the left or right. Or about speed,' I eventually observe. 'Every boat just seems to go flat out in any direction they like.'

'Do they ever have accidents?' Darryl asks Felize.

'Of course,' she replies, looking puzzled by the question.

Felize has been not only a wonderful guide but a compassionate companion, and it is with genuine gratitude that we farewell her when we return to land. Seeing Istanbul through her eyes, and hearing her insights on my cancer journey, will stay with us forever.

As usual, we have pre-organised a tip, and as usual, deciding the amount was difficult. Handing the envelope to her, aware that she wakes early each day to travel in from the outer suburbs, aware that I will forever after try to keep my body alkaline, I wish it had been much more. Felize, if you ever read this, I am sorry.

Since we return to Istanbul in ten days and have an early start tomorrow, the afternoon is a leisurely one. Collecting our laundry, we pack our bags and check our onward train tickets. We revisit the Grand Bazaar for fun, but not wishing to add more to our suitcases we leave empty-handed. Dinner is another dish of vegetables in a nearby restaurant, followed by another stroll through the beautiful nighttime Sultanahmet Square.

Lying in bed, listening to the day's final Call to Prayer, I cannot help hoping that the rest of Türkiye we are about to see will be as good as Istanbul.

It is 5.30am on the last day of May. We have pre-organised breakfasts packs and, collecting them from reception, we make our way outside to our waiting transfer. With the sun not due to rise for another hour, our district of Istanbul is bathed in muted darkness, still snoozing.

It takes around forty minutes to reach Sogutlucesme train station, the departure point for our high-speed train to Ankara, Türkiye's capital. Part of the journey involves traversing the Eurasia Tunnel, a 5.4-kilometre road tunnel under the Bosphorus Strait, connecting the European and Asian sides of Istanbul. Realising we are travelling under the sea with only a thin layer of concrete for protection, Darryl's earlier comments about the almost certain possibility of an earthquake slip unbidden into my thoughts. It is a relief to re-emerge above ground – and even more so to arrive at the station with plenty of time to spare.

'It's another hour or so before our train leaves,' I say, glancing at my watch. 'Let's find a café somewhere and grab a coffee.'

While there are no cafés handy, there are some stalls selling the thick Turkish coffee we have come to love, along with several *simit* vans offering their wares. Purchasing from both, we settle onto some handy stools and bide our time just people watching.

At some stage, we do investigate our breakfast packs, but finding they contain sandwiches with meat we have to discard them. The accompanying water, juice and apples we keep for later.

Just like when travelling on some of the fast trains in Europe, accessing our high-speed vessel involves navigating security and a passport check before being allowed to board. Here, we locate our comfortable business class seats, stow our bags on the rack above our heads and settle in, excited to see what countryside the upcoming four-hour journey will bring.

Surprisingly, it takes over ninety minutes to leave Istanbul's urban sprawl behind. Speeding eastward, we pass through suburbs of modern high-rise buildings, busy industrial zones, populated residential areas and pockets of green spaces. Around the same time an attendant hands us a complimentary and unexpected breakfast box containing a cheese roll, orange juice, a small cake and coffee, the view outside our window transitions into farmland, rolling hills and tunnels.

Reaching Eskişehir, our halfway point, we make our first stop. Being a university city, the train soon fills with chattering students. From here, the changing scenery goes into overdrive until, at one point, I cannot help exclaiming loudly to Darryl, 'I am loving this journey. In the past hour or so, my view has gone from industrial buildings to cows grazing to grapevines growing. We have passed huge rivers and brand-new highways. Sometimes the land outside has been green and lush, other times barren, rocky hills. Now, for the past hundreds of kilometres, it's been fields of crops. I had no idea Türkiye's scenery would be so varied.'

'I've noticed the fields of crops,' Darryl replies. 'I've been wondering what's in them.'

Pulling out my phone, a quick Google search reveals that, depending on the season, these fields could contain sunflowers, wheat, barley, corn, beet or a host of different fruit and vegetables.

'Most of the food grown is for domestic consumption and livestock,' I continue. 'But what's becoming a problem is water or irrigation. While some of the water for these crops comes from rivers and dams, a lot comes from underground water basins. And these underground water basins – especially around this Anatolian region – are being overused. The water levels have been dropping by one metre per year.'

'What does that mean?' Darryl asks.

'Sinkholes, saltwater intrusion, undrinkable water,' I reply, continuing to read. 'The government is trying to raise water consumption awareness and is building new dams and reservoirs. Hopefully, these measures work.'

Eventually, twenty minutes ahead of schedule, we glide into Ankara's enormous glass, concrete and steel station. Alighting from our train, we are surprised to find ourselves in what looks more like a shopping centre than a train station – and even more surprised to see signage displaying our hotel.

'According to Google Maps, our hotel should be a six-minute walk in that direction,' I point out to Darryl. 'But look. It's right here. It's actually part of the train station.'

Delighted at this convenience, we quickly discover it come with a drawback.

'Is there anything to see near here? Well, there is the shopping centre, but apart from that, not much else,' our receptionist apologises as she hands us our room key. 'You could get a taxi and head further into the city – it's about a twenty-minute journey. Or you could visit Ankara Castle. That's popular with tourists.'

Not-really keen on having to take a taxi anywhere, we instead spend the afternoon exploring the attached shopping centre. A small supermarket provides some water and, in the early evening, a restaurant provides a tasty vegetarian burger.

We are only overnighting in Ankara because of train scheduling, so the following morning finds us eager to continue our journey. Today, we will be travelling to the town of Göreme, located in the well-known Cappadocia region. Unlike yesterday's clean, sleek, high-speed bullet, today's train, the Güney Kurtalan Express, is filthy and old. A slow-service train commencing in Ankara and servicing the east of Türkiye, it has a twenty-seven-hour journey ahead of it. Fortunately, we only need it for six.

This time, we find ourselves winding downwards through incredibly stark rocky hills, with large, empty highways visible in the distance. Later, the acres of cultivated fields start up again, and this yield, Google advises, will be lavender. Trying to picture what this vast area would look like coloured purple, and again thinking of the declining water table, the hours while away. Eventually, we pull into tiny Yenifakili station, our alighting point.

'Are you sure we get off here? No one else has.'

'Apparently Yenifakali is closer to Göreme than Kayseri, where most will get off the train,' I reply. 'Look, there's someone. He could be our driver.'

Although he speaks very little English, the man I have pointed out to Darryl is indeed our driver, and he quickly ushers us into his waiting car. Within minutes of departing the negligible station, we find ourselves travelling a narrow, potholed road, Cappadocia's alien landscape visible in the distance.

CHAPTER 24

Not Ballooning in Cappadocia

Around sixty million years ago, a geological accident occurred, thanks to the perfect mix of volcanic action, erosion and climate. The result of this accident – and time – is the Cappadocian region of Türkiye: an otherworldly province whose unique landscape is found nowhere else.

To explain a little further: around six million years after the dinosaurs vanished, massive volcanic eruptions covered this region in thick layers of a soft volcanic rock called tuff. Over time (millions of years), wind, rain, floods and temperature fluctuations eroded this tuff, carving out valleys, canyons, caves and fairy chimneys – tall, thin rock spires. In some places, erosion-resistant basalt rock formed on top of the tuff, resulting in mushroom-shaped fairy chimneys.

Discovered by our very early ancestors, these naturally carved chimneys were further hollowed and made liveable. Later civilisations adapted even more so, building underground cities, monasteries and churches inside the rock formations. Today, so stunning and unique is this area that it has been declared a UNESCO World Heritage site and attracts millions of visitors from around the world each year.

Naturally, we had heard of Cappadocia and seen pictures. Just a few months earlier, *Travel Guides*, an Australian television program, had even filmed here. But nothing of what we had seen beforehand prepared us for the sheer magnificence that began opening up before us as our car travelled deeper into the Cappadocian landscape, edging closer to Göreme, the region's central town.

'I didn't realise how vast and surreal this place would be,' I murmur eventually. 'So beautiful. Mile upon mile of pastel-toned hills. Crazy cave houses. It's like we are on another planet. Absolutely spectacular.'

'When I thought of Cappadocia,' Darryl replies, 'I just thought of hot-air balloons. I didn't realise it would like this. Namibia was like the moon, but you're right – this could be another planet.'

Due to its ideal weather conditions and special landscape, Cappadocia has become the ideal location for hot-air ballooning. So popular and predominant is this pastime here, I am not surprised Darryl has mentioned it.

'I'm looking forward to seeing the balloons, but I think it's going to mean an early wake-up.'

'I don't mind waking early,' he replies. 'But I'm not keen on going up in one – I'm not even sure I would be able to get into the basket.'

'I have no intention of going up in one,' I laugh. 'The havoc my Verzenio plays on my stomach each morning – I couldn't trust myself anyway.'

'So, we are agreed,' Darryl laughs. 'We will probably be the only ones who visit Cappadocia and don't have a hot-air balloon ride.'

'Too bad,' I laugh in return. 'I just consider myself fortunate that I have managed to visit here. And that I'm able to appreciate this incredible area.'

It takes around ninety minutes to journey from Yenifakali train station to Göreme, the tourism capital of this district and our home for the next few days. Alighting at the Royal Stone Houses – Göreme, we note that it appears to be located right on the outer edge of town. Further ahead, in the distance, we can just see the beginning of a row of shops and restaurants, along with a cluster of hotels built within those unique stone chimneys.

Pushing aside the thought that maybe we should have paid the extra to stay in a fairy chimney, I focus instead on the room we have just entered. It is large and spacious, with a good-sized bathroom – but it is on the ground floor. As I inspect it further, I note the bedhead rests against a wall.

'See the wall our bedhead is pushed up against?' I point to Darryl. 'On the other side of that wall is the stairwell. I hope it won't be a problem.'

By early evening, feeling hungry, we go in search of dinner. As noted earlier, most of Göreme seems to straddle one long uphill road, with cafés, restaurants, shops and tourism offices beckoning to visitors. Scattered throughout, and more densely clustered on the outskirts, are the distinctive fairy chimneys. Looming over the town is a flat-topped, beige-coloured, ragged stone hill that looks like the perfect viewing platform. It really is a unique-looking place, and with the temperature hovering in the mid-twenties, if feels good to be exploring here – great to be alive.

'*Testi* kebab! *Testi* kebab with accompaniments and dessert!' a tout sings out to us. '*Testi* kebab – traditional claypot cooking.'

Having noticed this dish before – where meat, vegetables and spices are sealed within a clay pot and slow-cooked – his pitch catches our attention.

'Is there a vegetarian option?' we call back.

'Yes, yes! *Testi* kebab without meat. Come, sit upstairs. Great view!'

From past travels, we have learned not to automatically dismiss touts, some of our best experiences have come from following them, so we soon find ourselves seated in a large, open-walled restaurant offering beautiful panoramic views. As we watch our waiter crack open our clay pots, spilling their fragrant vegetable contents, the surrounding mystical landscape glows golden-orange as the sun gently sets. It is one of those truly memorable moments.

Later that night, we experience a couple more memorable moments. Hot-air balloon flights in Cappadocia take off just before sunrise, when the temperature is cooler and the air calmer. With sunrise occurring around 5am, it means passengers are collected and transported to their lift-off locations by 3am.

At 2.30am, we are both woken by the sound of doors slamming and footsteps clumping loudly down wooden steps. So loud and so close do the footsteps seem to our heads that sleep is impossible until the last aeronaut has descended.

Then, at 5am, it all starts back up again – only this time, knowing the balloons are about to appear, it is the spectators who wake us. Too tired to bother joining them, I just grumble to myself and try to get back to sleep. I'll take a look tomorrow morning.

'What are our plans for today?' It is 8am and we are sitting in our hotel's breakfast room, picking at our plates of pastries, salad and fruit. We have been sitting like this, mute, for the past half hour, too tired to speak. With the infusion of a second cup of Turkish coffee, however, we are starting to awaken.

'We have a guide arriving at nine,' I reply. 'I have no idea where we are going or what we are seeing but it is going to take all day, whatever it is. I'm not really expecting much.'

Interestingly, these words prove so incorrect, so off the mark, that I will never make such an assumption again.

Finishing our breakfast, we make our way to the hotel's entrance, where we find our guide already waiting for us – and, surprisingly, he has a driver with him.

'Good morning. My name is Emir and this is Asaf, your driver. Are you ready? Shall we go?'

Happy at not having to trudge anywhere on foot, we return greetings and get into the car.

'We do not have far to go for our first stop,' Emir smiles as we leave Göreme behind. 'About four kilometres.'

With seemingly little traffic on the roads in this region, the journey does not take long, and soon we are pulling into the car park of an enclosed valley. Multiple footpaths crisscross the area, winding past lone or clustered fairy chimneys – many of which feature double, even triple, rock caps.

'This is Pasabag – Monk's Valley, or Valley of Priests,' Emir explains as we pass through the visitors' entrance. 'The chimneys here are some of the best examples in the area, and so the site has been enclosed to preserve them. It is called Monk's Valley because, from the fourth to the tenth century, monks sought out this place, seeking solitude. Many of the chimneys have chapels carved within them.'

It is still early in terms of tourist hours, meaning we are currently the only visitors wandering the site. Having the freedom to walk undisturbed in the cool morning air, with a beautiful blue sky above, to examine each unique spire, to peek into chimney caves unheeded, allows us to fully appreciate nature's idiosyncrasies, and to reflect on how fortunate it is that this area has been protected.

'Thank you for that,' I say to Emir as we prepare to get back into the car. 'Such a rocky, alien landscape, yet filled with crazy sculpted rock living spaces. It was beautiful.'

'It was special,' Darryl agrees. 'What's next?'

'What do you know about ceramics?' Emir laughs.

Arriving at the town of Avanos a short time later, descending below ground into a treasure-filled cavern, and receiving a lesson on pottery making, it quickly becomes clear how little we do know about ceramics.

'Part of what makes ceramics so durable is their composition,' we are told. 'Avanos pottery contains up to eighty per cent quartz, making it exceptionally hard. You will find pieces from here in both the Blue Mosque and Topkapi Place. Would you like to purchase something? You will have no problem taking it back to Australia.'

'How much would a plate that size cost?' Darryl asks, pointing to a small saucer-sized dish designed to be hung on the wall.

'Something like that would be around 1,500 dollars.'

As much as we would have loved a memento, the pieces are beautiful and the place unique, their prices make it easy to say no.

Apart from hot-air ballooning, there was one other attraction in this area that I had heard about before our arrival. Years ago, I watched a documentary on underground cities and learned of a place called Kaymakli, an ancient subterranean complex built somewhere between 200–700 BCE, and used over centuries as a refuge during Muslim raids, Mongolian incursions and Ottoman persecution.

Extending eight levels deep and capable of sheltering five thousand people for extended periods, I remember being captivated by the animated reconstructions, steep tunnels, narrow shafts, cramped living quarters, marvelling that entire communities had once lived underground.

Truth be told, I had forgotten that Kaymakli was in this region. The documentary was a distance memory. But as Emir begins explaining our next destination, the recollection comes rushing back.

'It is one of the largest and deepest of Cappadocia's underground cities,' he says. 'Its tunnels are steeper and narrower than most others. While it goes down eight levels, only four are open to visitors.'

'How steep exactly?' Darryl asks. 'I may have trouble – I can't bend much.'

Arriving at a barren knoll, we enter a large chamber cut into the hillside, its sloping floor falling away to darkness – and quickly discover just how steep and confined these shafts truly are. While Darryl is able to descend with difficulty to the second level, the rest of the cramped, dark floors are beyond his physical capabilities.

'You keep going,' he tells me. 'I'll wait on the surface.'

Reluctant for a couple of reasons, I return with Darryl – and it is only when we are once again within view of sunlight that I explain why.

'I usually love exploring caves,' I confess. 'But all I could think about was Türkiye's earthquake risk. What it would be liked trapped down there if there was one? It would be horrendous. I hope you haven't ruined caves for me forever,' I add, only half-joking.

Having really only expected to explore the town of Göreme by foot, our explorations of the wider Cappadocia region have been amazing so far. Even lunch, a vegetable *gozleme*, a crispy, golden Turkish flatbread stuffed with a variety of fillings and grilled, proves unforgettable. Eaten at a rustic open-air café high on a hilltop, the views of the surrounding moonscape are breathtaking.

'That's Pigeon Valley, and over there is Pigeon Town,' Emir explains, pointing to a rugged valley etched with thousands of small carved pigeon houses. 'Locals have been farming the droppings here for centuries, using them as fertiliser.'

'And that over there?' I ask, pointing toward a spectacular-looking rock fortress. 'Is it man-made or what?'

'That's Uchisar Castle,' Emir replies. 'It is a natural rock fortress, but it's been hollowed out with tunnels, rooms and staircases. It is the highest point in Cappadocia and has been a perfect lookout point since ancient times. So, if you have finished your lunch, we have one more stop: the Göreme Open-Air Museum.'

It is mid-afternoon, and the day has warmed considerably when we arrive at Zelve Ören Yeri, also known as the Göreme Open-Air Museum. Clambering out of the car, a quick glance at my phone reveals the temperature is hovering in the mid-thirties – the hottest day of our adventure yet, and a portent of the temperatures to come.

While looking for the museum's entrance, Emir provides a rundown on what we are about to see and explore.

'This is one of Cappadocia's most important historical and cultural sites,' he begins. 'Now UNESCO-listed, there are over a dozen cave churches and monasteries here, carved out by monks who lived in isolation. Many of these churches still display their original and well-preserved frescoes.'

'How old would that make them?' I ask.

'It was early Christian monks who created this, so some of them date back to the tenth to twelfth centuries.'

With its unique blend of startling natural beauty, religious history and ancient artwork, the museum is well worth a visit. We spend some time here, admiring still-vibrant wall-paintings, poking through the monks' dining halls, kitchens and sleeping quarters, and appreciating the dramatic landscape. Eventually, however, the long day and heat wears us down, and all we want to do is return to the comfort of our hotel.

'I will not see you again,' Emir tells us as we thank him a short time later. 'But Asaf will return in two days to drive you to Konya. Tomorrow, you are free to explore Göreme.'

CHAPTER 25

Traversing the Konya Plains

Suffice to say, it is several hours before we venture out again. Googling vegetarian restaurants nearby, the results reveal an Italian restaurant specialising in meat-free meals, and so, in the early evening, with the sun slipping gently over the horizon, we go in search of it. It turns out to be on the rooftop of a hotel, and sitting there, enjoying dishes like blistered green peppers, garlic-rubbed tomatoes and pumpkin-tahini balls, we watch the alien landscape slowly fade and the town's lights flicker to life.

At 5am the following morning, after a far less disrupted sleep, we wake and climb the steps to our rooftop balcony to watch the sky fill with hot-air balloons. Although it is a well-filmed sight, seeing it in person, dawn breaking, hundreds of colourful balloons rising above an otherworldly landscape – takes my breath away. It is a picture so stunning, so surreal, that even though I am not in one of those balloons, I still count it as a Bucket List moment.

After yesterday's full schedule, today is quieter. The temperature again climbs into the mid-thirties, and a hot wind springs up, coating the town in a layer of red dust. The conditions do not lend themselves to doing much, and so, after uploading a new blog post, I join Darryl, who has remained relaxing on the roof.

In the late afternoon, we manage another short walk through the town but skip eating at a restaurant, happy to snack on items picked up from a tiny supermarket.

'This is one of those days I have been unsure about,' I say to Darryl the following morning. We have had breakfast, checked out of our room, and are currently waiting in reception for Asaf and our new guide. Today, we will be journeying by car across the Konya Plains.

'Why?' Darryl asks.

'Apparently, it normally takes three hours to drive to Konya, but according to our itinerary, it is going to take us eight.'

As we are coming to expect, today's guide, Ahmet, proves to be another lovely, well-informed man. As we leave the town of Göreme behind, he points towards some stray hot-air balloons floating high above us.

'Those are probably students training to become hot-air balloon pilots, or pilots in training,' he explains. 'Flying balloons in Cappadocia requires specialised training. It is tightly regulated by the government.'

'How many balloons go up each day?' Darryl asks.

'There are over two hundred in total, but only 180 are allowed to fly each morning,' Ahmet answers. 'They go up in two groups of ninety.'

A little further on, Ahmet gestures again – this time to acres of eroded, pale-coloured land.

'These fields have been mined for pumice. It is becoming a big problem near Göreme. Farmers are losing their agriculture land to pumice companies.'

'We travelled here mostly by train,' I reply. 'And while we saw hundreds of kilometres of crops and small farms, we hardly saw any farmhouses. Why is that?'

'Türkiye does not have farmhouses in the same way,' Ahmet explains. 'Here, people live in villages and go out to their farms each day.'

'After Konya, we are catching the overnight train to Izmir,' I add.

'Ah, then you will see many poppy fields as you travel from Konya,' he nods.

'Poppy fields?' I exclaim.

'Yes, we grow poppies here in Türkiye,' Ahmet says. 'It is very tightly controlled. The oil is sent to the government to be used for medicinal purposes.'

'We'll keep an eye out for them,' Darryl laughs.

It takes us a little over ninety minutes to reach the first of today's destinations: the Ihlara Valley, a breathtaking canyon famous for its lush greenery, ancient cave churches and snaking river. Stepping from the car at the edge of a plunging 150-metre-deep green, leafy gorge, it is remarkable how stark the contrast is to arid Göreme. Behind us, caves pockmark the soft volcanic cliff face, while far across the valley, more caves and crumbling ruins are visible.

'These days, the Ihlara Valley is one of Türkiye's most popular hiking destinations,' Ahmet explains. 'But once, many people lived here in these caverns – and many of these caves were churches. Some of the churches date back to the seventh century. The people were only moved from here in the 1950s and 1960s.'

'That recent?' we exclaim. 'Where did they go?'

'The government built new houses for them in some of the nearby villages. Not everyone left, though. Some refused.'

'Why did they have to leave?' Darryl asks.

'Many of the caverns and churches were crumbling and no longer considered safe. They were also moved to protect the area – to preserve the churches and the frescoes they contain,' Ahmet replies.

Back in the car, and it's only when we once again find ourselves traversing open, empty plains that I realise just how unique, how verdant, how out of place the Ihlara Valley looked compared to the surrounding landscape.

'Yes, the Konya plateau is one of the driest regions in Türkiye,' Ahmet says when I point this out. 'It is known for its dry climate and rich agriculture lands. The Ihlara Valley is our hidden gem. We have another gem not far from here. It is not on your itinerary, but I think you should see it.'

Intrigued by his words, it is with some curiosity that we emerge from the car a short time later. We are at the edge of a grassy hill, and while a small wooden structure is visible in the distance, the rest of the area is nothing but empty grasslands.

'This is Aşikli Höyük,' Ahmet explains somewhat proudly. 'It is one of the earliest known villages in the world. It dates back to 8,200 BCE – so it is around ten thousand years old.'

'Seriously?' I exclaim.

'Yes. Ten thousand years old. Archaeologists have discovered that people lived here permanently. They grew crops such as wheat and barley. They hunted wild animals like sheep and goats. They have even found evidence of medical practice here – a female skull was found with a hole surgically cut into it, and signs of healing, meaning she survived the procedure. It is the earliest known brain surgery.'

Exploring the site, stepping into the wooden structure that protects what remains of the village housing, and reading about the huge nearby midden (prehistoric human habitation site marked by a mound of refuse) which has provided critical insight into life here, my feelings are almost indescribable. To know I am walking where people once lived, ate and slept, over ten thousand years ago, feels nearly unbelievable. It is something I will never forget.

This time, as we continue along the virtually empty highway, the surrounding plains begin to fill with emerging crops – wheat, sugar beet and flowers, Ahmet tells us. In the distance, a beautiful snow-capped volcano rises against the sky: Mount Hasan.

Looking at the fields stretching to an invisible horizon, the conversation turns once again to water.

'Once, you only needed to go down sixty metres to find water for these crops,' Ahmet sighs ruefully. 'Now it is over two hundred metres. It is going to become a big problem.'

Midway through today's journey, we arrive at the town of Aksaray and pull up in front of a towering structure with thick stone walls and small, high windows. Smooth, bleached pavers lead to a grand 13-metre-high white marble gate adorned with intricate geometric patterns and Arabic inscriptions.

Opening my car door, the heat hits me, but I am too intrigued to notice. And when Ahmet begins to speak, my interest only deepens.

'This is the Sultanhani Caravanserai, a major stopping point on the Silk Road,' he says – and those words capture my full attention. Anything to do with the Silk Road, the network of trade routes that connected China to the Mediterranean, always does.

'It was built in 1229 and is the largest and best-preserved *caravanserai* (inn) in Türkiye. Visitors and traders came here to rest, the massive stone walls protecting them from bandits. Here they found shelter, food and hospitality.'

Passing through the monumental entrance, a vast courtyard opens before us.

'This area is where stories and knowledge were exchanged, camels rested, and exotic goods displayed.' Ahmet continues.

'And this,' he adds, leading us into a massive, dimly lit hall, 'is where, in winter, merchants and animals sought warmth. Today, only the pigeons use it.'

Stepping further into the cool space, trying to imagine it once alive with flickering firelight, the scent of spices and the buzz of trade, I do not immediately notice Darryl flinch beside me.

'It is a great building – and I love how cool it is in here after the heat outside,' he says, brushing something imaginary from his shoulder. 'But I just missed receiving a gift from one of those pigeons. I think I'll wait outside.'

Laughing at Darryl's near miss, Ahmet and I both accompany him back out into the sunlight, where Ahmet points towards a nearby rest stop.

'Are you hungry? It is after lunch, and this would be a good time and place to rest – to have something to eat.'

The facility Ahmet is pointing to, with its cheerful café and large souvenir shop, looks ideal. Sitting and enjoying a toasted sandwich, our conversation ebbs and flows, initially touching on how things have changed in Türkiye over the past ten to fifteen years.

'Partly as a result of disruptions caused by Covid, but mainly due to President Erdogan's economic policies, inflation has gone from around eight per cent in 2010 to forty-seven per cent today (2024). In 2010, when they first started printing the two-hundred-lire note, it was worth 135 US dollars. Today, it is worth six dollars,' Ahmet laments.

The conversation then shifts to more recent times – and more personal anecdotes.

'Because of Türkiye's close relationship with Russia, the West has become more biased towards us. I have a daughter who lives and works in England. For two years, I have been trying to get a visa to visit her, but I keep getting refused. She has just had a baby, but still I am not allowed to go. I have my own home in Türkiye. I have money in the bank. There is no risk of me staying in England – I can prove my home is here – but still the answer is no.'

Used to being able to travel almost anywhere in the world, Ahmet's story is a sad surprise – but we can't let it overshadow the day. Instead, helpless to do anything, we push the conversation aside in favour of some reviving Turkish coffees before continuing our journey.

Now on the final stretch, the seeded plains and occasional towns flash by as we reach speeds of 130 kilometres per hour on near-empty highways.

Fifty minutes shy of Konya, Ahmet announces a detour – and while I want to object (I have had enough of car travel), I refrain. Arriving at Çatalhöyük a short time later, I am I glad I did.

'Çatalhöyük,' Ahmet explains, 'dates to around 7,500 BCE – so about nine thousand years ago. It is a little younger than Aşikli Höyük, but this settlement was much larger. It was discovered by James Mellaart, a British archaeologist, in 1958. So far, eighteen layers of buildings have been uncovered, and more are expected.'

Touring what turns out to be a large, well-preserved site, with one of the most interactive, high-tech museums I have ever encountered, we learn more.

'The homes here were often accessed via ladders through the roof, with no streets between them,' I read from one of the displays. 'The dead were often buried beneath the floor.'

'Çatalhöyük is one of the first known examples of urbanisation,' Darryl reads from another. 'The people were agriculturalists, growing crops like wheat and barley. They also hunted and gathered.'

'They also painted murals, created sculptures and made ceramics,' I exclaim. 'Many of the walls had paintings of animals and abstract art. It's incredible. I had no idea we were so advanced so long ago. I think I date everything back to Jesus – two thousand years ago – but this is seven thousand years older. I really am going to have to change my way of thinking.'

At around 5.30pm, eight and a half hours since we departed Göreme, our car finally enters the sprawling city of Konya and pulls up on a dusty street in front of an even dustier hotel. Here, we warmly thank both Ahmet and our driver, Asad, knowing that after a quick meal, they will be making the long return journey back to their homes in Cappadocia. Their guidance and expertise have turned a long, tiring day into one of our most rewarding and informative yet.

CHAPTER 26

The Overnight Train to Izmir

While the foyer of our hotel, the Hotel Mesnevi, with its large expanse of cool marble flooring and inviting hanging glass lights, looks good, the same cannot be said of our room. Dirty and old, with a broken blind, twin single beds and dripping shower, it is by far the worst accommodation we have encountered on this adventure so far. Despite our fatigue, we have no desire to spend time in it and so go in search of something to eat.

Stepping back onto the warm Konya streets, we soon discover our hotel does have one redeeming feature: it is within a short walk of many of Konya's main attractions.

Dating back to the third millennium BCE, Konya is one of Türkiye's oldest cities. Reaching its heyday during the twelfth and thirteenth centuries, it was once one of the wealthiest and most intellectual cities in the world. Now a thriving metropolis of 2.3 million people, with strong religious influences and a growing economy based on industry, agriculture and tourism, it is also the final resting place of Rumi. The famous thirteenth-century Persian poet and inspiration for the Mevlevi (Whirling Dervishes) Sufi order, lived and worked here, and his tomb, located in the Mevlana Museum, attracts thousands of visitors annually.

We're not bothered with visiting any attractions today, it is too late and we have plenty of time tomorrow, so we wander aimlessly. It doesn't take long to notice that Konya is much more conservative than any of the places we have visited in Türkiye so far.

'I'm feeling a little self-conscious wearing shorts,' I eventually mention to Darryl. 'Have you noticed that many of the women here wear hijabs, and quite a few are in full burkas?'

'Yes,' he replies. 'And fewer men are in Western clothes. And how about the number of mosques! Get ready to hear the Call to Prayer.'

'The street stalls are different too,' I add. 'Less souvenirs for tourists, more food items. They seem to love sweet stuff. I keep seeing biscuits and that weird white-looking candy.' Rectangular in shape and similar in texture to nougat, we later discover the highly popular Mevlana candy is especially associated with Konya and is offered to visitors as a symbol of hospitality.

With our simple toasted sandwich lunch at the Sultanhani Caravanserai feeling like a long time ago, we eventually turn our attention away from sightseeing and instead focus on finding somewhere to eat. Perusing some of the menus on display, it quickly becomes apparent that Konya doesn't see many vegetarians. The offerings are heavily meat-oriented and we grow more disheartened the longer we search. It is only through another display of Turkish hospitality that we find anything at all.

A tout, seeing us about to walk away from his displayed menu, asks what we are looking for. Explaining that we are vegetarian and struggling to find a restaurant with suitable meals, he waves us to a nearby table.

'No problem,' he laughs. 'You sit, and I will get the chef to make you a vegetable dish. We also have bread and salad. Will that do?'

Thanking him profusely, we gratefully sit, and before long find ourselves partaking in enormous bowls of juicy white-bean and vegetable stew. Accompanied by a fresh salad and copious quantities of crusty bread, it is exactly what we need, and we depart promising to return.

Although almost 9pm, it is still warm as we make our way back to our room. Not far from our hotel, we find a stall groaning with delicious-looking fruit, manned by a generous vendor. He speaks no English, but simply offers us multiple samples of his stock to try. When we settle on purchasing some succulent cherries and plump bananas, the lack of a common language is no barrier – he simply holds up notes in his currency to show how much we need to pay.

'What are you doing?' It is 4.30am, and I have just been woken by the day's first Call to Prayer. In the bed next to me, Darryl is holding up his phone.

'I'm recording the Call,' he replies. 'It woke me up and has been going for ages, so I decided to record it. I'll play it later for the kids – let them hear how noisy it gets here in the early hours.'

While it is frustrating to have been woken so early by the incantation, there is something special about lying there, listening to it. We do not hear it in our part of Australia. Hearing it means we must be journeying somewhere – we must be in another country, creating another adventure.

Continuing our catalogue of room faults, that morning we find the television does not work, the water pressure in the leaking shower is terrible, and the air-conditioner is useless. Grateful that we have only the one night here, tonight we will be sleeping on a train on our way to our next destination, we shower as best as we can, repack and make our way to the breakfast room. Here, surprisingly, our choices are varied and plentiful, fuelling us well for the day ahead.

'It's so hot,' I complain. 'My phone says it's 35 degrees. I need to sit for a while.'

We have just spent the past four hours pounding the scorching streets of Konya. At the Mevlana Museum, we read about Rumi's teachings and stood before his sarcophagus, alongside those of many of his family members. Nearby, we marvelled at the Selimiye Mosque, admiring its Ottoman architecture – but it was ablutions fountain that held our attention. Crafted from intricately etched marble and topped with a domed roof, the fountain was in constant use, with people jostling for a chance to access its cleansing waters

We explored the Bedesten Bazaar, sniffing spices but, more importantly, purchasing packets of pumpkin seeds and Medjool dates – snacks for tonight's train journey. But best of all was the Underground Market, where I discovered that leather goods in Konya are far cheaper than in Istanbul.

'I noticed a leather jacket just like this at the Arasta Bazaar in Istanbul,' I cry to Darryl, holding up a beautiful soft cream creation. 'It cost six hundred euros, nearly a thousand Australian dollars. I've bargained this down to two hundred dollars!'

'I didn't know you were after a jacket,' Darryl replies, giving me a puzzled and slightly exasperated look.

'I didn't want to tell you,' I reply meekly. 'But this is even better than I was hoping to find.'

Now, hot and exhausted, the thrill of my purchase behind me, all I want to do is sit and escape the heat.

'Let's go back to the restaurant we had dinner at last night,' Darryl suggests. 'We promised we would. It's probably a good idea to have something substantial before we catch tonight's train.'

Our friendly waiter from yesterday is again on duty, delighted to welcome us back. Rushing into the kitchen to speak with the chef, he soon presents us with large bowls of vegetable stew, this time with lentils – a slight variation on yesterday. And when we ask for a Turkish coffee at the end of our meal, we are surprised to see him dart across the street to a nearby café, returning with tiny cups of the rich, aromatic beverage.

'I don't think they make Turkish coffee here,' Darryl mutters to me quietly.

'He didn't say anything,' I softly reply. 'He just went and found us some. Another example of amazing Turkish hospitality.'

There are still a few hours left before our 7pm train departure, but the city is dusty, hot and airless. Loath to spend more time outside, we instead seek refuge in the air-conditioned comfort of our hotel foyer.

At 5.45pm, we ask for a taxi and can only stare at the dilapidated vehicle that arrives. Travelling to the train station, it becomes apparent why the vehicle looks so battered – our driver barely knows how to drive. With tyres screeching as we round bends and roundabouts completely ignored, the climax comes when we very nearly hit the back of a car that has stopped for a pedestrian. Suffice to say, it is a relief to arrive at the station.

'Are you sure this is the right platform?' Darryl asks.

'That's what we were told,' I reply.

It is 6.30pm, half an hour before our train's departure, and we are standing on a platform looking at an empty train. There is absolutely no one else around. Starting to panic slightly – we are meant to be leaving in thirty minutes – it is a relief when, twenty minutes before departure, guards and passengers begin to arrive and we are allowed to board.

This train's exterior looks much cleaner than the one that brought us into Türkiye, and when we locate our sleeper cabin, the interior is better too. It doesn't have the same layer of grime, the bedding looks fresher, and the complimentary items in the fridge are refreshingly cold. With another hour or so of daylight left, we pull out our pumpkin seeds and dates and settle in, hoping to spot some of the promised poppy fields. Unfortunately, whether it is the wrong time of day or simply too dark, the flowers elude us.

At 7.40am, after a night often disrupted by newly boarding passengers, we arrive at the city of Izmir. We are not staying here; instead, we have onward train tickets departing at 12.30pm. With the temperature already in the low thirties, we are not looking forward to a five-hour wait on Izmir's hot platforms.

'There is an earlier train,' I mention to Darryl, checking my phone. 'Maybe we can buy tickets for that.'

Locating the station's ticket counter, it takes some miming and a bit of help from Google Translate, but eventually, we manage to secure two new tickets.

When catching a train in a foreign country, where you cannot speak the language or understand the announcements, we always worry that we might miss our stop. Over time, we have learnt to always have the train timetable available on our phone. Whether it is a photograph or a live website version, it means that as it gets closer to our destination arrival time, we can start checking station names.

Today is no different. With an expected arrival time of 11am, we start noting the stops from 10am, checking that they correlate with the timetable.

I am not sure why, but today the system is working perfectly – until it isn't.

'Selçuk,' I idly read the name of the station we have just arrived at. 'SELCUK!' I yell to Darryl, completely panicked. 'This is our stop – quick, get off!'

What ensures next is complete, heart-stopping mayhem. It is not easy to suddenly gather all your belongings, pull bags from the overhead luggage racks, and find a walking stick. By the time we have managed it, new passengers have already started boarding, blocking the aisle. Looking at each other in shocked horror, it would be a nightmare if we missed this stop, Darryl starts pushing through the crowd in one direction, and I the other. Reaching the door, I watch in shock as it locks shut in front of me. No amount of pulling at the handle will open it. Horrified, aghast and resigned to having to make new plans, I am stunned when the door suddenly reopens and I can tumble out onto the platform.

'I got to the door just as it was closing,' Darryl gasps. 'I stuck my walking stick out, so it had to re-open. Then my bag fell onto the platform and a guard started yelling at me to remove my stick from the doorway – but I kept yelling back at him, telling him you were still on the train so they had to re-open the other doors.'

It has been our closest near-miss ever, and our hearts are still pounding as we gather up our bags, pull out my phone and work out how best to locate our new accommodation.

CHAPTER 27

Touring Ancient Ephesus

Best known as the gateway to the ancient city of Ephesus, one of the largest and most well-preserved ancient cities in the world, Selçuk, with its mix of historic charm and modern convenience, is a popular stop for travellers. Compact, with a population of almost forty thousand, the town is surrounded by rolling hills, olive groves and the ruins of ancient structures. It even has a fortress – Selçuk Castle – which stands guard over it.

'It's hot. We could try and find a taxi,' I say, still scrolling my phone. 'Or we could walk. Our hotel looks to be about fifteen minutes on foot.'

'Let's walk,' is Darryl's predictable reply.

With its steeply cobbled footpaths, captivating ruins and fascinating shops, it takes closer to thirty minutes before we arrive at the Nilya Hotel. Pushing open the solid wooden doors that guard its entrance, we find ourselves in a grassy courtyard laced with ancient pavers, with heavy grapevines hanging from an overhead pergola. It is cool, beautiful and exactly what we need after our harrowing morning. We are shortly presented with a large room furnished with Turkish antiques by lovely hosts, and it feels a shame we are only staying for one night.

'How are you feeling?' Darryl asks after a reviving shower. 'I'm hungry. Should we go and look for some lunch?'

'We have a guide arriving at two to show us Ephesus and the local museum. We have enough time to duck back into town and find something to eat if you want.'

Slowly retracing our steps from earlier, this time we pay even more attention to the cluster of ruins located close to the town centre. A large sign is on display and, reading it, we learn that this was the location of the Temple of Artemis, one of the Seven Wonders of the Ancient World.

'What was the Temple of Artemis?' Darryl asks.

'No idea,' I reply. 'But it must have been pretty important to be considered a Wonder of the World.'

With the town centre consisting of one main street lined with shops, cafés and restaurants, with smaller streets branching off into residential areas, it doesn't take us long to find a suitable place for lunch. Our large spinach *pide* should provide plenty of energy for the tour ahead.

At 2pm, back at our hotel, our guide arrives: a scruffy-looking gentleman, in his late sixties.

'Hello,' he greets us. 'My name is Yelshin. You know, a bit like Boris. You were meant to have another guide, but he has a foot disease and was unable to come.'

As visions of foot diseases and former Russian presidents flash through my thoughts, Yelshin continues. 'And I only have a motorbike, so if you want to visit Ephesus, you must walk – it will take about forty minutes. Or you can pay for a taxi. But it is very hot today. Thirty-six degrees, I think. Maybe you would like to see the Ephesus

Museum first? It is air-conditioned. It is not far from the train station. And we can get a chai there. But you will have to pay.'

While I can only look at Yelshin mutely, startled into silence, Darryl is having a hard time trying not to laugh.

'Yes,' I eventually agree. 'It is hot today, too hot to walk for forty minutes, so we'll have to get a taxi. And yes, it would be good to visit the museum first. I actually thought that was part of the tour package.'

'Was it?' Yelshin replies, looking surprised.

Retracing our steps yet again, this time a large osprey sitting in its nest atop a tall pole captures our attention, then a sign featuring a large boomerang.

'The Boomerang Guest House,' Darryl reads aloud.

'Yes,' Yelshin nods knowingly. 'Selçuk used to see lots of Australian backpackers – here to visit Ephesus or on their way to Gallipoli. Not so many these days.'

It takes about an hour to stroll Ephesus Museum. One of Türkiye's most prominent, it showcases a vast collection of archaeological finds excavated from the ancient city, as well as other nearby sites.

While I appreciate seeing its famous statues of Artemis (goddess of the hunt and the moon) and Nike (goddess of victory), and deeply admire the ancient everyday items on display such as pottery, glassware and coins, it is talking with Yelshin over his promised cup of chai that entertains me the most.

Sitting on little stools in the museum's slightly rustic café, sipping scalding-hot cups of what turns out to be black tea, we listen as Yelshin reminisces about his adventures as a guide, his life in Selçuk, his daughter's slightly dim husband, and about Ephesus.

'It was founded in 1,000 BCE and was once one of the most powerful cities in the world,' he tells us. 'Back then, it was located close to the sea, but now the harbour has filled with silt, and the sea is much further away. Being near the sea allowed goods, ideas and people to move around freely. Ephesus became a very wealthy city, especially after it became part of the Roman Empire. And St John – after Jesus died, he travelled to Ephesus. He lived and practised here. Later, he started writing his Gospel and eventually died here. The Virgin Mary also lived here. And Cleopatra and Mark Antony – they visited too. And Herostratus…'

Trying to stem the flow of words, Darryl jumps in with a question.

'What was the Temple of Artemis, and what was so important about it that it became one of the Seven Wonders of the Ancient World?'

'Its size, mainly,' Yelshin promptly replies. 'It was one of the largest, most impressive temples in the world when it was built. And it was important because it was both a place of worship to the Greek goddess Artemis, who had many followers, as well as a major centre of trade. The temple attracted traders, craftsmen and travellers, from all over to Ephesus.'

'What about Hero someone?' I ask. 'You just mentioned him.'

'Herostratus. He burnt down the original Temple of Artemis just so his name would be remembered forever. Even though the city officials banned anyone from mentioning his name, it didn't work.'

With our cups of chai long finished and the day's baking temperature diminishing slightly, we head to a nearby taxi rank in search of a ride to Ephesus. After listening to Yelshin's stories and hearing his obvious enthusiasm for the place, we are both eager for our visit. As it turns out, we were right to be excited.

Alighting from the taxi at the top of a gently sloping hill, we are greeted by the gleaming cream-stoned ruins of one of the most well-preserved ancient cities I have ever visited. Stone-paved streets, worn smooth by centuries of footsteps, beckon and, heeding their call, our slow descent takes us past towering columns and crumbling archways – hints of just how grand this place once was.

Arriving at the Library of Celsus, with its marble facade, imposing statues and towering pillars, the sense of grandeur is only reinforced, compelling us to stop for a few social media photos. Continuing onward, we duly note what remains of the Temple of Artemis before one of Ephesus' most impressive sights reveals itself: the magnificent Roman Theatre, an enormous amphitheatre carved into the hillside, and capable of holding 25,000 spectators.

A large chattering tour group has just beaten us to its entrance, so we do not linger, instead moving on to the Terrace Houses. Here, we gain insight into the daily lives of the wealthy who once lived in Ephesus – their mosaic floors, frescoed walls, and even plumbed bathrooms.

Finally, not far from the exit, we reach the ancient Agora. Like many other agoras we have visited, there is not much left of this one, just a few scattered stones and fallen columns, but it is still possible to discern its square layout, to envision the once-bustling marketplace where merchants sold goods and philosophers gathered to discuss important matters.

All in all, this educational tour of ancient Ephesus, under the guidance of such an odd-ball host, has been one of the most enjoyable to date. But as we leave the ancient sight, it appears Yelshin hasn't finished with us yet.

'We'll get a bus back,' he excitedly announces, guiding us towards a waiting crowd. 'Here it is!' he crows as a packed, standing-room-only minivan pulls up. 'All good?' he enquires cheerfully as our vehicle careers its way home, with us hanging on grimly.

CHAPTER 28

From Pamukkale to Istanbul

With our train departing at 8am, we are up early the following morning. Having skipped dinner the night before, we are very appreciative of the enormous breakfast of yoghurt, cheese, fruit and toast our host has prepared for us, and we devour it quickly before making our way back to Selçuk Station.

While only a three-hour journey, this morning's train, is our busiest yet, full of tourists, students and little old ladies clad in black, clutching multiple bags. We have noticed these ladies on previous journeys, often filling the first-class carriages, and so we sit back, waiting. Sure enough, about an hour into our journey, a guard comes through, asking to check passengers' tickets. Each little old lady, when presenting their ticket, is met with a scowl from the guard and instructed to move.

'You have to admire them,' I laugh. 'They know their ticket isn't for first class, but they try to get away with it anyway.'

After yesterday's near miss, we are even more vigilant with our station-checking this morning. Not even the man walking the train selling pretzels from a basket balanced on his head, nor the lad selling potato chips from a bucket, can distract us.

Arriving at our destination, Goncali Station, we are again the only passengers to alight – making it very easy for our waiting driver to identify us.

It is a short drive to tonight's accommodation, the Venus Hotel in the village of Pamukkale. Passing olive groves, vineyards and cotton farms, the area looks to have a peaceful, rural charm, with gentle hills and winding country roads leading to small villages. Alighting in front of a large, sprawling brick and glass complex, two stories high and surrounded by greenery, we soon realise this is our most modern Turkish accommodation to date. With lifts, a large swimming pool, and full of Asian and American tourists, it feels completely different from the off-the-beaten-track places we have been staying at. We are not sure if we like it, but with a guide organised to collect us a little after noon, we simply dump our bags and push any concerns aside as we head back to reception.

As in Selçuk, our guide, Hakan, turns out to be another odd-ball character. After making us wait while he polishes off his tea and sandwich, he calmly announces he has no car.

'But I have organised one of the hotel staff to drive us,' he says earnestly. 'For just 250 lira.'

With no other options, and accepting that 250 lire is only around eleven Australian dollars, we just shrug our shoulders and climb into a dilapidated vehicle, manned by what looks like a pubescent teenager.

Today's upcoming tour is to one of Türkiye's most breathtaking natural wonders: the turquoise pools and white travertine terraces that cascade down the hillside behind the small village of Pamukkale. Stunning to look at, I had first become aware of this site years ago while flipping through a travel brochure on Türkiye – and knew immediately we had to visit.

It is a very short journey to the summit, where the beauty begins. With instructions to collect us later, our ride departs and we make our way through some heavily manned gates. Ahead of us are some ruins, and as we walk towards them, Hakan begins to explain.

'This is Hierapolis, the ancient spa city founded by the Romans in the second century BCE. It was famous for its hot springs, which were believed to have healing properties. Wealthy Romans would come to bathe and relax in the warm waters. Today, along with Pamukkale, it is UNESCO World Heritage listed.'

Guiding us deeper into the weathered rubble, Hakan points out a remarkably well-preserved theatre built into the hillside, a large necropolis dotted with sarcophagi, and a steaming pool where tourists are bathing.

'This is Cleopatra's Pool,' Hakan tells us. 'You can swim here if you wish. The waters are warm and healing, and if you look closely, you can see fallen ancient columns that you can swim among.'

'No thanks, Hakan. These ruins are great, but what we are really here to see, and would like to know more about – are the white terraces,' I say, gesturing toward them. 'Since we left Australia, we have seen a lot of ruins, but nothing like these terraces.'

'Ah, the calcium terraces,' Hakan replies. 'What would you like to know?'

'Well, what are they and how are they made?'

'They are natural travertine – a type of limestone – created by mineral-rich thermal waters,' Hakan explains. 'The water here is warm and heavy with calcium carbonate. Over thousands of years, as the warm water flowed over the cliffs and cooled, the calcium carbonate solidified, forming these white terraces and natural pools. Pamukkale means "cotton castle" in Turkish, because the terraces look like cotton clouds. You can swim in some of the pools if you wish.'

'We won't swim,' I reply. 'But I would like to take my shoes off and walk through one.'

A short time later, Darryl, whose injuries prevent him from joining me, asks, 'How was it?'

'Terrible,' I moan. 'It looks beautiful, like soft snow dotted with turquoise pools, but it is so deceiving. One step in and I nearly slipped – it's incredibly slippery. The next step, I realised how sharp the floor is – like walking on broken cutlery. It was also packed with hobbling tourists, and we kept trying not to slip into each other.'

Back in the car, as we make our way back to our accommodation, I take one last backward glance at the stunning, alabaster landscape with its shimmering pools – so vivid against the surrounding hills and deep blue sky. Some places, I think to myself, are best admired from a distance, rather than experienced up close.

Although we may not like sharing our hotel with so many other tourists, we do appreciate its facilities. That night, we make use of its poolside restaurant and order a three-course set vegetarian dinner. With the temperature still in the mid-thirties and the dying sun casting a warm glow over our garden setting, it feels surreal knowing our journey through Türkiye is almost over.

'India soon,' I comment to Darryl, dipping into the hummus on my mezze plate. 'I have received all our train tickets, I am just waiting on driver confirmations and pick-up times.'

'We still have a few more days back in Istanbul,' Darryl reminds me, finishing his lentil soup. 'What time do we get back there tomorrow?'

'Late,' I reply over my baked eggplant.' Around 11pm. It's going to be a long travel day.'

And it is.

Commencing at 9.30am, our first long, slow train journey, between Denizli and Eskişehir, onboard the inaptly named Pamukkale Express, takes nine hours. As I sit and gaze at the passing scenery, grape and fruit plantations, ancient ruins, salt plains, stone walls, shepherds tending their sheep, cows, goats, and even those elusive poppy fields, thoughts flitter through my mind.

What will happen when the water basin runs dry? How much do all these Roman sites contribute to the Turkish economy? Why are Turkish people so hospitable and generous?

Eventually, I give up on my questioning, and just relax. I watch as the train empties and fills, and as we pass through different weather zones – first hot and sunny, then wet, cold and windy. A man opposite us offers steaming hot cups of tea from his thermos, then later a chocolate bar. Someone else offers water – more examples of Turkish thoughtfulness.

Finally arriving at Eskişehir Station, we step into chaos. Trains have been cancelled, others delayed. Our high-speed train to Istanbul is still running, but no one can tell us when. Most Türkiye train stations, we have discovered, do not have central noticeboards advising which platform your train departs from – it is up to you to work it out.

Whiling away time at a station café, we explain our situation to our waiter: that we cannot understand the announcements, they are all in Turkish, and we have no idea when or which platform our train will be departing from.

'No problem,' he replies. 'You have your coffee and sandwich, and I will listen out for you. I will let you know.'

Which he does.

This train – the high-speed express – is the same one we caught from Istanbul to Ankara all those days ago, only in reverse. With night having fallen, there is nothing to see from the windows, and so the journey is spent reading or relaxing. Just like last time, a complimentary meal arrives, but having eaten not long before, we stow it away for later.

At 11.30pm, thirty minutes behind schedule, we arrive in Istanbul. Though it is late, the station is buzzing with people, but our driver, the same one who dropped us, easily locates us. Driving back to the

Saba Hotel, we again pass beneath the waters of the Bosphorus – the feeling is just as eerie, just as uncomfortable, as that first time.

Like the station, the area around our hotel is still teeming with life when, a little after 1am, our driver waves us farewell. Entering the familiar building, we secure our key, we have been upgraded apparently, and make our way to our room. It is located on the fourth floor, with a balcony overlooking the Blue Mosque, so, despite the late hour, we sit and gaze for a while, struck once again by how incredible Sultanahmet Square looks at night: the illuminated mosque, the soft murmur of late-night wanderers, the air still holding the warmth of the day. But, tired after our long day of travel, we eventually shower and head to bed.

CHAPTER 29

Farewell Türkiye

'Our final day in Türkiye. Is there anything in particular you wanted to do?'

Despite last night's late arrival, we are up early and keen to embrace our final day in Istanbul. We have hand-washed our T-shirts, socks and underwear, who knows when we will get another chance, and they are drying on our balcony. Tomorrow's plane tickets have been closely checked. We are now enjoying breakfast in the hotel's rooftop dining area, but this time, due to the days getting warmer, the heat has forced us to remain inside.

'There is one last thing I want to do,' I answer Darryl. 'Something from the Bucket List.'

'Oh?' Darryl asks.

'Visit a Turkish hammam,' I reply. 'Have a traditional steam bath.'

'No,' Darryl quickly responds. 'I've seen what they do to you in those places – how hard they scrub.'

'It'll be fine,' I laugh. 'Just tell them not to brush so hard.'

An integral part of Turkish and Ottoman culture for centuries, a Turkish hammam is a traditional steam bath, similar to a sauna but with an emphasis on deep cleansing. Istanbul is full of places offering the service, so it is not difficult to secure a booking for later in the day.

'We get picked up at four,' I advise Darryl, shutting off my phone. 'Any ideas of what to do before then?'

'Let's just wander,' he replies. 'Maybe head back to the harbour.'

A definition of the word 'wander' is to walk or move in a leisurely or aimless way – something we have become quite skilled at during our travels. And over the following hours, that is exactly what we do.

Already familiar with Sultanahmet Square, we soon leave it behind and head towards a nearby garden. A sign on its ornate stone entrance advises that we are about to enter Gülhane Park – once part of the outer gardens of Topkapi Palace and now one of Istanbul's oldest and most beautiful places to stroll.

Ambling along its tree-lined pathways, sitting on convenient benches in the peaceful gardens, people-watching, and observing colourful birds drink from gurgling fountains, we find it the perfect way to escape the city's heat and hustle. The park slopes gently downward and, emerging from its lower gates, we find ourselves overlooking the Bosphorus, with a tiny island and tower directly in front of us.

'It is called the Maiden's Tower,' I read after a quick Google search. 'Legend has it that it was built by an Ottoman sultan to protect his daughter. An oracle predicted she would die from a snake bite on her eighteenth birthday, so he built this tower to isolate her.'

'And?' Darryl prompts.

'She died anyway,' I continue reading. 'A basket of fruit was sent to the tower on her birthday, and inside was a venomous snake that bit her.'

Continuing with our explorations, we follow the line of the Bosphorus and eventually find our way blocked by a large open-air café. It looks fresh and inviting, and with its incredible view of the busy waterway, we are easily enticed inside.

'I'll have an apple tea, please.' Despite, or perhaps because of, its sweet flavour, I have come to really enjoy this traditional symbol of Turkish hospitality and now find myself ordering it whenever I can.

'It may be the last time I can order it,' I explain to Darryl. 'Which is a shame. I've never seen it sold anywhere else in the world.'

Still wandering, we eventually find ourselves back at the wharf where we departed on our cruise with Felize. Recollections of her nonchalant acceptance of boat accidents here make us laugh once again.

Having been reminded of Felize, my thoughts drift to the delicious spinach *pide* she ordered in a café near Sultanahmet Square. We have enjoyed many *pide* throughout our travels in Türkiye, but that first one is still the best yet – and so, for lunch, we return to that little eatery.

Eventually, our meandering brings us back to our hotel, and here we rest until, at 4pm, a golf cart arrives to transport us to our hammam.

'Long steam or short?'

We have just been warmly welcomed, asked to remove all our clothes and handed a *peshtemal*, a traditional cotton towel, to wrap ourselves in. Now, we are being guided towards a warm, steamy room designed to open our pores and prepare our skin for what comes next. We quickly realise that 'long or short steam' refers to how much time we can bear to withstand the intense heat.

'Short steam,' I answer at exactly the same moment Darryl replies, 'Long.'

Laughing, we compromise. After a medium amount of time, we exit the humid room, our skin dripping moisture and glowing.

'Sauna now,' an attendant instructs, guiding us into a suffocatingly hot chamber. 'To take away your tension. Relax your muscles.'

'Sauna finished. Through here, please. Lie down.'

We are led into a slick, sodden chamber, the air heavy with moisture, and lie prone, side by side, on a hard, heated marble platform. Having removed my towel, I am stark naked. Darryl, I notice, has left his towel modestly in place. Water gushes from a continuously flowing tap, suds foam in an enormous cauldron, and the steam is so thick that it is almost impenetrable. Two attendants wait, ready to begin.

'It's okay?' one of them asks as she starts scrubbing my body with a special mitt called a *kese*. This vigorous scrubbing removes dead skin cells, leaving the skin smooth and renewed.

'Yes, it's fine,' I reply.

Alongside me, Darryl is so completely covered in thick, fragrant soap suds that I cannot see him. The suds, which contain olive oil, are massaged deeply into our skin, cleansing it.

'Please wait here and relax. I will bring you a tea.'

Our suds have been splashed away with warm water, taking any lingering dead skin with them. Now wrapped in fresh towels, we recline on loungers in a fresh, cooling room. Sipping our tea – and yes, it is apple – I ask Darryl what he thought of the experience.

'I wasn't looking forward to it at all,' he admits. 'But actually, it was quite nice. And you?'

'I was a little worried about my arm,' I reply. 'Having had lymph nodes removed, there's always the risk of lymphoedema, and they usually advise avoiding saunas. But this was something I really wanted to do. A hammam is something everyone who comes to Türkiye should try. So, I just blocked out my worries and thoroughly enjoyed the whole thing. I would definitely do it again.'

It is dinner time when our golf buggy drops us back at the Saba Hotel. Aware that India is about to introduce a complete change of menu options, we feast on a large vegetable and bean casserole in a nearby restaurant, and Darryl enjoys a final piece of Turkish delight. Returning to our room, we fold our washing, ready our bags and check our passports. Lying in bed, the excitement of onward travel starting to build, I can only laugh when a familiar noise draws my attention. It is the Call to Prayer, echoing from both the Blue Mosque and the Hagia Sophia. It is so appropriate, such a joyful reminder of the amazing time we have had in Türkiye, that I fall asleep very happy.

It takes over an hour to drive from our district of Istanbul to the international airport. On our arrival, we are confronted by an enormous glass and concrete structure, and it takes some time to find our check-in counter. While we wait in line, a Qatar Airways staff member is scrutinising onward visas. Noting our India visas, he frowns.

'That is a confirmation of visa only. It is not an actual visa.'

Slightly alarmed, I check quickly through my emails and thankfully locate the correct paperwork.

Traversing airport security is always problematic for Darryl, and today is no different. Passing through the full-body scanners, the metal in his body sets them screaming, and he is forced to empty his pockets, remove his shoes and belt, and re-enter the machine. Of course, they scream again. I don't get off lightly, either. Handing in my backpack for X-ray, I realise too late that it contains two soft cases, each with a metal knife, spoon and fork – our usual travel cutlery. Normally I pack them in our checked-in luggage, but today I forgot, and so the knives and forks are promptly confiscated.

Finally, we board our flight – and here we receive a nice surprise. We were told at check-in that we had been upgraded to premium economy, but we had not realised how good an upgrade it actually was. We had not realised how much bigger the seats were, how convenient the reclining footrests, or how much more the seatbacks inclined. Suffice to say, we are very appreciative – and arrive in Doha, our midway point, wondering how we will ever cope with normal economy again.

At Doha airport, we have thirty minutes to dash from Gate 8 in Terminal E to Gate 53 in Terminal C. Frustratingly, this time is further reduced when security stops Darryl and insists on slowly swabbing him. It is when they turn to me that I really start to panic.

'Our plane boards in twenty minutes,' I plead. 'We have to go.'

Surprisingly, they wave us through and, thankfully, an inter-terminal train has just arrived. Scrambling aboard, we hold our breath as we glide through the incredibly large airport and finally reach our gate.

'That was intense,' Darryl says, as we sink into our regular economy seats.

'It was,' I reply. 'And what's worse, we didn't even get to stop at any of the duty-free shops, nor look at any of the shops selling gold. Did you see how many there were?'

It takes around six hours to fly from Doha to Delhi, so it is nearly 2am when our flight touches down. At this time of morning, exiting the airport is relatively straightforward, the only hiccup occurring when choosing a customs counter. The type of visa you hold – sticker or electronic – dictates which counter you must approach. It takes a little while to work this out, find our luggage and then locate the exit doors.

Now comes the big test. Will someone be waiting for us on the other side?

CHAPTER 30

Hello, Crazy India

Dealing with a local travel agency, rather than a domestic or international conglomerate, does mean it can be slightly worrisome when first arriving in a country. You are trusting they have done as you requested, whether it be booking your train tickets, securing your guides or helping with accommodation. You have paid them your money. Now you have arrived and are about to make your first point of contact. If this fails, then you are in trouble.

It is closing in on 3am when we step into the waiting area of Delhi airport and, even at this obscene hour, the large hall is swarming with people. It immediately brings back frightening recollections of our arrival into Beijing in 2019, where the arrivals area was equally busy and it took a long, anxious time to locate our waiting driver.

Today, however, all concerns are quickly banished and tension dispelled when we spot a gentleman holding a large sign bearing my name.

Approaching him, it becomes apparent that he does not speak any English, but it doesn't matter. Grabbing Darryl's suitcase, he motions for us to follow and guides us through the exit doors and into the airport car park.

The minute we pass through those doors, the hot, humid air of Delhi hits us.

'It's three o'clock in the morning and still thirty degrees,' I say to Darryl, glancing at my phone.

'It doesn't surprise me,' he replies. 'When I think of India, I think of heat.'

It takes only twenty-five minutes to reach our hotel, the Metropolitan Hotel and Spa, and although the scenes through our car window are not unexpected, they are still eye-opening and confronting.

To see so many people sleeping out in the open, on footpaths, benches and kerbsides, is disturbing. It's even more so when you notice the young children; and no one has more than a thin cloth to lie on.

Arriving at our hotel, we are transported back to Asia in the post-Bali bombing era, when your car boots were checked and vehicles' undersides scanned for explosives. Even our luggage is put through security scanners – something we will need to do at every hotel in India.

At this hour, reception do not really want to know us. They simply hand us our key, provide the wi-fi code and wave us towards a concierge. He, in turn, shows us to our room – a large, tired space with a distinctive musty smell.

'I knew India was going to be intense,' I say, glancing around. 'That it would be hot, the travel harder than usual. And I knew that at the end of each day we would want to return to a really nice, cool hotel room with amenities on hand. So, I splurged and booked five-star hotels. It was lucky I did, because it looks like an Indian five-star hotel isn't quite the same as an Australian one. Although, after seeing all those people sleeping out in the open, I really shouldn't be complaining.'

After yesterday's long travel day, it is mid-morning when we awaken. Locating the breakfast room and scrutinising what's on offer, I turn to Darryl.

'It's interesting how each country we have visited has had such different breakfasts. In Greece it was very continental – yoghurt, fruit, pastries. In Türkiye, much more savoury – cucumber, salads, cheese, sometimes even a slice of cake. And now India – look at this. Heaps of curries, dahl, *roti* and *lassis*. I just hope I can find something my stomach will tolerate.'

'I'm happy,' he replies, helping himself to a large dish of curry. Clearly, his stomach has no issues.

Also helping myself to a variety of dishes, I soon realise that eating in India may be difficult for me. Since finishing chemotherapy, I have been unable to tolerate anything spicy, and the Verzenio I am still taking causes nausea and diarrhoea at the slightest provocation.

'I think I will stick with toast and coffee,' I say to Darryl, pushing aside my plate.

We have nothing planned for this first day in India. It is meant to be a rest day, so we treat it as such – and it is not until mid-afternoon that, keen to stretch our legs, we re-emerge from our room. Although slightly apprehensive of what we might encounter beyond the safety of our hotel gates, we know we need some exercise. Aware that there is a large shopping area, Connaught Place, about a fifteen-minute walk away, we decide to head there.

Stepping from our accommodation, within seconds we find ourselves swarmed – much like ants descending on a dropped treat.

'You want tuk-tuk? You want guide? Where you going? I take you?'

To be so hassled so quickly is not only disconcerting but also deeply frustrating. Determined not to give up so easily, we shake off the first group and continue onward. Our hotel is on a tree-lined road, and the amount of greenery in such a large city is surprising. Little do we know then, but inner Delhi is full of parks and gardens.

Before long, another group approaches and the pestering starts again. This time, it is so intense that when a tuk-tuk driver ask for the third time if we would like a lift, we just nod and climb into the seat behind him.

'I take you to shopping emporium,' he tells us.

'No. Connaught Place,' we reply.

'Connaught Place not safe for tourists before 6pm, when the police come to guard,' he argues. 'Shopping emporium much better – safe. Five floors. Many shops.'

We never do find out if he was telling the truth, more likely he wasn't and we were just gullible tourists, but we decide to do as he suggests.

'Okay, shopping emporium,' we agree.

It takes around ten minutes to reach our destination. Sitting in our tuk-tuk, dodging and weaving through India's mad, intense traffic, closing our eyes at the near-misses, it is both terrifying and exhilarating.

'The emporium has lost two floors,' Darryl tells me a short time later. Accompanied by a retinue of attendants we cannot shake, we are wandering a building full of small outlets, wondering what we are doing here.

'We were told it had five floors of shops – but there are only three.'

Despite the missing levels, it still takes some time before we manage to flee, our entourage continuously pressing items upon us.

'You want linen pants? We make. How about jewellery? We have gold. Spices. Incense. Painting.'

On and on they go, and it is exhausting. Finally, we find the exit and make our escape.

'How was it? Good? Where to now?'

It is the tuk-tuk driver who brought us here – lying in wait.

'I've had enough,' I laugh. 'This is too much.'

'It is,' Darryl agrees. 'Let's just go back to the hotel. We are too easy a target. Too easy to hassle.'

'It's a shame,' I mourn. 'We usually enjoy wandering new cities. I'm not sure if that is going to be possible in Delhi.'

CHAPTER 31

Exploring Delhi

After a tame dinner of vegetables and noodles eaten in our hotel's restaurant, followed by a welcome full night's sleep, we are up early the next morning, keen to meet our guide. His name is Sandhi, and he arrives a little after eight, accompanied by the same driver who collected us the night before.

'Welcome to Delhi,' he greets us. 'My notes say we have a full day of city sightseeing ahead: Humayun's Tomb, Qutub Minar, Jama Masjid Mosque, the Red Fort, Lotus Temple and a rickshaw ride through Chandni Chowk. I am not sure if we will manage all of it in one day.'

'It won't matter,' Darryl replies.

'It won't,' I agree. 'Whatever you show us will be great.'

'Let's start with Humayun's Tomb and go from there,' Sandhi says. 'I will try to show you everything, but it may not be possible.'

Already liking Sandhi's upfront honesty, our admiration for him grows as, navigating the intense Delhi roads, his conversation regularly includes interesting and insightful details about his city.

'We have twenty million cars in Delhi and eighty million tuk-tuks… The population of inner Delhi is twenty million, but if you include the outer suburbs, it rises to 34 million people… Sixty-five per cent of the population is under the age of thirty-five… We have an 86 per cent literacy rate… There are 1,300 mosques… Delhi actually consists of seven different cities, built by different rulers over the centuries… Around 1,000 BCE, Delhi was a hilly place but the soil was used to build everything, so it is now flat… It is currently holiday time – many people have left the city and gone to Shimla or the Himalayas, where it is cooler.'

'The temperature is meant to reach 44 degrees today,' I say, stemming the flow of conversation. 'I don't think I have ever experienced heat that intense.'

'You are going to Agra?' Sandhi asks. 'It will be hotter there.'

Considered the inspiration for the Taj Mahal, Humayun was a Mughal emperor (the Mughals ruled India from 1526 to 1857), and his tomb is a magnificent red sandstone mausoleum with white marble domes. Built in 1570, it is notable as the first garden tomb on the Indian subcontinent, and the first structure to use red sandstone on such a grand scale. (This is interesting, as throughout our adventures in India we will encounter many more impressive red sandstone edifices).

Surrounded by *Charbagh*, a symmetrical Persian-style garden layout divided into four parts by water channels or walkways, we navigate this expanse to reach the mausoleum.

'I'm surprised by the size of these gardens,' I remark after some walking. 'Considering it's in the middle of a city.'

"The area around our hotel is surrounded by parks and trees,' Darryl adds. 'And some of the areas we passed through on our way here looked green too. I wasn't expecting that of Delhi.'

'Central Delhi *is* green,' Sandhi confirms. 'Twenty-five years ago, in the 1990s, pollution was terrible and getting worse – as was congestion. So, the government moved all industry to the outer suburbs.'

'Delhi. Green and full of trees!' I laugh. 'That's what happens when you travel – your expectations are completely challenged. I remember thinking Moscow would be miserable and full of grey concrete buildings. Instead, it was the complete opposite – bright and fun, with so many buildings in happy pastel colours.'

'And remember Beijing?' Darryl agrees. 'Also surprisingly green. Some of our Western countries have a lot to learn. Even Australia.'

'It is interesting what you say, what you have experienced on your travels,' Sandhi muses. 'There is a saying, you know: "Travel is the best karma of your life", because it teaches you not to believe everything you think.'

Although it is still relatively early – just 10am – my watch is already showing a temperature of 43 degrees. After stepping into the mausoleum and seeing a rather unremarkable tomb, it is a relief to return to our air-conditioned car, gulp down the chilled water provided, and continue on to our next stop: Qutub Minar.

'I mentioned earlier that Delhi consists of seven historical cities,' Sandhi says, as we enter beneath a large arched gateway and find ourselves in a sprawling courtyard. Directly ahead stands an intricately carved structure, seventy-three metres tall, made from red sandstone and marble.

'This area is Lal Kot, built in the eighth to ninth century, then expanded in the twelfth. It is considered the first of Delhi's seven cities – and that 824-year-old tower is known as Qutub Minar. It is the tallest brick minaret in the world. If you look closely at the carvings throughout this complex, you will notice many of them have been defaced.'

'Defaced? Why?' Darryl asks.

'Much of this complex was constructed by Muslims using materials from demolished Hindu temples. Islamic tradition discourages the depiction of living beings, especially humans and animals, as they believe it leads to idolatry. Removing them symbolised the shift in power from Hinduism to Islam in India. What it gives us today is a great example of Hindu-Islamic architecture.'

'We learnt something similar when visiting the Hagia Sophia,' I reply. 'Its Christian mosaics were covered when it was converted into a mosque.'

While it is too hot to comfortably explore the entirety of this place, some areas are patioed, offering much-needed shade. With worn stone floors and golden-stone roofs supported by intricately carved columns, these shaded spots are eagerly sought after. As we wander through the area, happily snapping photos and chatting with Sandhi, we are approached by an elderly Indian couple and their middle-aged children.

'They would like to have their photo taken with you,' Sandhi explains after a rapid conversation. 'This does happen in India – foreigners are often approached for photographs.'

'It happens in China as well,' I laugh. 'We would be happy to pose – but can we get one with them too? Could you take it using my phone? After all the photos we have posed for with strangers, I think it's time we got one as well.'

Driving to the next place on our itinerary, what we see through the car windows begins to guide our conversation. Spotting some large official-looking buildings, Sandhi points them out.

'Those buildings are part of the Central Vista Redevelopment Project – an initiative of Modi's. Most of the parliament and government offices in Delhi have been moved here. They are currently building accommodation for the parliamentarians. Eventually, all government officials will be housed in one complex. It will help with both costs and security.'

'What are your thoughts on Modi?' I ask, referring to Narendra Modi, India's fourteenth Prime Minister. 'By all accounts, he has been good for your country.'

'His reforms have done a lot for India,' Sandhi agrees. 'Since he was elected in 2014, the economy has grown significantly, and we have seen much social progress and innovation.'

'What are some of his reforms?' Darryl asks.

'Make in India. Digital India. GST and healthcare,' Sandhi replies promptly. 'Also reforms to clean up cities and rural areas, empower women, improve sanitation and reduce our reliance on fossil fuels. I could go on – but look, India Gate. We will not be visiting, but we can stop quickly for a photo.'

Not too dissimilar to the Arc de Triomphe in Paris, India Gate is a majestic arched sandstone structure built as a tribute to the Indian soldiers who lost their lives during World War I. As proposed, we stop briefly for the obligatory photo before Sandhi hurries us back into the car.

'Chandni Chowk next. I have organised a rickshaw for you.'

'I am not getting into a rickshaw,' Darryl hisses to me a short time later, as we scramble from the car into a tightly congested square. Surrounded by sharp, haphazard dwellings, three stories high and built from an assortment of junky-looking materials, the square also accommodates drying laundry, fruit stalls, a couple of young goats and several dilapidated man-powered rickshaws.

'Why?' I hiss back. 'You have to.'

'I do not. I can't think of anything more dangerous than sitting in the back of a rickshaw, relying on a man peddling us through Indian traffic.'

'No, it is fine,' Sandhi laughs, overhearing us. 'The rickshaw drivers know what they are doing. They have been riding these bikes all their lives, and you won't be travelling on main roads – just through this old part of Delhi.'

It takes a little more convincing, but eventually Darryl agrees to join me in the back of a rickshaw. Powered by a bony, toothless man clad in jeans, I worry our combined weight will be too much for him – but I needn't have. With Sandhi in his own rickshaw, our scrawny driver easily manages to take us on a tour we will never forget. It's an absolute highlight of our adventure.

Designed in the 17th century, Chandni Chowk is one of the oldest and busiest markets in Delhi. Its streets are tiny, narrow lanes crowded with everything – from overflowing stalls and shops selling spices, textiles, jewellery, incense and saris, to people, dogs and baby goats. It is congested, noisy, chaotic, vibrant, aromatic, diverse, traditional – and timeless.

It is dirty in places. Smelly in others. Power lines hang low above, and air-conditioning units drip from buildings overhead. It is wonderful.

Chandni Chowk is also broken into sections, each selling specific items – silver jewellery in one, wedding fabrics in another, electrical items in a third. It is when we reach an area containing many food stalls that Sandhi has us alight our rickshaw.

'Come, we will return to our rickshaws later – but first, we go through here on foot. Have you tried *parathas*? It is a type of flatbread that has been fried. I will take you to the best *paratha* place in Delhi. They also have very good *lassi* – an Indian yoghurt drink.'

'I am not going to eat or drink anything,' Darryl hisses at me again.

'Come on. I trust Sandhi,' I reply. 'He won't let us have anything that will make us sick.'

Fighting our way through tiny, pungent alleyways, pushed and jostled from all sides, we eventually enter a place packed tight with diners. Here, we manage to secure small stools and watch as men fry dough in ghee-laden pans, then stuff it with a variety of fillings. Our *paratha* – filled with potatoes and spices – looks crunchy and good, so much so that even Darryl manages a taste. He still refuses the *lassi*, though. As I swallow the last of the delicious, creamy drink – flavoured with cardamon and mango – I turn to Sandhi.

'What's with all the baby goats? I keep seeing them. Not adult goats, just small ones.'

'It is coming up to Eid al-Adha, or Bakrid,' Sandhi explains. 'It is the Muslim festival of sacrifice, commemorating Ibrahim's willingness to sacrifice his son in obedience to God. Muslims will sacrifice an animal, like a goat or sheep. The goats you see have been born for this purpose – to be sacrificed.'

It is a rather unsettling topic of conversation, so we are relieved when Sandhi changes it by suggesting a visit to the nearby spice bazaar.

'The spice bazaar in Chandni Chowk is Asia's largest wholesale spice market,' he tells us. 'It has been running since the seventeenth century, and many of the shops have been operated by the same families for generations. You will know when we are close – your nose will start tingling.'

Not really believing him, it comes as a surprise when, not long after, our noses do start tingling, then actively itching, and our eyes begin to stream. It is painful and annoying, more so when I start coughing – we haven't even entered the actual spice market yet. With thoughts of what germs might be floating around here, I am not the only one barking away, I turn to Sandhi.

'I can't go in there. I can barely breathe out here.'

'I don't think I can either,' Darryl agrees. 'It's pretty powerful.'

'And I keep thinking of Covid,' I add. 'Is there somewhere else where we can look at, maybe purchase, some spices? Just… not inside the actual market?'

'I do know a place,' Sandhi replies, looking slightly bemused. 'And it is not far.'

Following Sandhi through a narrow alley, where men recline on the cool tiled floors of their shops, waiting for customers, we soon arrive at the place he has in mind. It is a veritable spice emporium, with prices a fraction of what we would pay in Australia. Knowing how tough it is to bring food items into the country, I am happy to find some tea and turmeric packaged to withstand even our strictest customs officers. It is not apple tea, unfortunately – but mango will do.

Back in our rickshaws, Sandhi advises that before we leave Chandni Chowk, we must visit the Jama Masjid Mosque. Built between 1650 and 1656 from red sandstone and white marble, it is one of India's largest and most famous mosques. Alighting in front of a dull redstone building crowned by three grand domes and flanked by two towering minarets, we immediately notice the steep rise of steps leading to its arched entrance.

Normally, we would be happy to tackle an incline such as this – but today, with the temperature now reaching 44 degrees, we are hot, tired and aware that we have seen quite a few mosques lately.

Explaining to Sandhi that a glimpse of its exterior is enough, our rikshaw soon has us back to the car – and our tour through one of Delhi's most memorable and incredible places comes to an end.

CHAPTER 32

Journeying to Jaipur

'Can I offer a suggestion?'

We have just departed Chandni Chowk, Delhi's largest market, and are back in the car, giving immense thanks for its efficient air-conditioning. With the outside temperature now at 45 degrees, it would be unbearable without it.

'Your itinerary has us visiting Delhi's Red Fort. If you are continuing on to Agra, then I know you will be visiting the Red Fort there – it's one of the best and most important in India. I suggest that instead of visiting this Red Fort, we visit Raj Ghat instead. Raj Ghat is Mahatma Gandhi's memorial, and after spending today with you both, it is a place I think you will appreciate.'

Listening to Sandhi offer this suggestion, I smile softly. It is this ability to flex and adapt, to have guides who make suggestions based on our interactions, that makes an individual tour so much more preferable than a large group excursion.

'I love the idea,' I exclaim. 'Especially as I think we are also visiting another fort in Jaipur.'

Mahatma Gandhi was an Indian lawyer and a prominent leader in the Indian independence movement against British rule. Best known for his philosophy of non-violent resistance – or *satyagraha* – he used it to lead India to independence in 1947. Assassinated in 1948 by a Hindu nationalist, Gandhi's methods of peaceful protests inspired movements worldwide, and his legacy continues to influence civil rights and freedom movements today.

With that said, what actually comes to mind when I think of Gandhi are the white cotton robes he wore, and his little round spectacles.

'See the stencil on that garbage bin?' Sandhi asks.

We are currently walking through some serene and beautiful gardens. Designed to reflect the simplicity and tranquillity that Gandhi himself embraced, they are meticulously landscaped with lush green lawns, neatly trimmed hedges and a variety of trees and flowering plants.

'It is the logo for Narendra Modi's national campaign to promote cleanliness, waste management and sanitation across India. When people see this stencil of Gandhi's little round glasses on a garbage bin, it encourages them to dispose of waste properly.'

We see this stencil on many more garbage bins during our travels through India over the next few weeks – and every time we do so, its simple, easy-to-understand message remains powerfully clear.

'We remove our shoes here. But you can leave your socks on.'

We are approaching a black marble platform, one end of which holds an eternal flame symbolising Gandhi's lasting legacy. The other end is adorned with decorative marigolds, symbolising purity and devotion.

Doing as Sandhi says, we leave our shoes with an attendant and step onto a stone footpath leading to the dais. Immediately, the heat from the burning-hot path sears through our thin socks into our soles of our feet, making us hop and stagger in pain. Some wet mats have been laid in places, to which we quickly and gratefully hobble, and it is only with dampened socks that we are able to continue.

'We won't linger,' Sandhi apologises. 'But visitors are expected to walk around the memorial, maintaining a respectful silence.'

While happy to comply, even pausing for a few moments to reflect on this remarkable man, we are not sorry to escape the burning pathway, reclaim our shoes and return to the shelter of our car. Before we depart the park, however, Sandhi draws our attention to a long row of trees, some with a placard in front.

'These trees have been planted by world leaders and other notable dignitaries,' he tells us. 'Queen Elizabeth II planted a tree here, as did Ho Chi Minh and Yasser Arafat.'

'Any Australians?' Darryl asks.

'Your Prime Minister, Mr Albanese, came here in 2023, but he did not plant a tree. Mr Keating and Mr Whitlam both have.'

It is after 5pm by the time we arrive back at our accommodation. Although we have not managed to see everything on our itinerary, we will be returning to Delhi in a few weeks, and Sandhi has assured us he will again be our guide. Tonight, knowing we have a 4am wake-up ahead of us, we quickly eat in the hotel's dining room, repack our bags and settle down to rest.

At 4.30am, laden with two bulky breakfast boxes provided by the hotel, we are met by our now-familiar driver and a friendly new guide. We are not touring anywhere today; this guide has been provided simply to help us board our train. This level of assistance is a new experience for us – and does make us feel somewhat special.

Arriving at the ridiculously inadequate train station car park, a pot-holed area jam-packed with people, tuk-tuks, touts and cows, parking is impossible, and the noise is incredible. Deciding our breakfast packs are just too cumbersome to travel with, we offer them to our grateful driver before accompanying our guide out of the car. He leaves us queuing in the line for security while he grabs a platform ticket, but soon returns to escort us into the station.

Inside, we get our first taste of what a train station in India looks and feels like: platforms stretching for hundreds of metres, crowded with people lying on bare tile floors or wooden benches – sleeping, talking, waiting. Luggage, boxes, bags, belongings everywhere. Hot. Humid. Pungent.

As the trains in this country are longer than normal (hence the lengthy platforms), it is important to find exactly where your carriage will stop. Waiting at one end of the platform with your carriage at the other would be a grave mistake. Indicated by small electronic signs, we follow our guide to our carriage location with difficulty – and are grateful to have him.

Surprisingly, our train arrives on time and when it stops, the station mayhem steps up to a whole new level, with passengers swarming to board before those disembarking have even had time to exit. Experienced with this behaviour, our guide simply barges his way through, using my suitcase as a battering ram – and again, we are grateful to have him. He leaves us once he has located our seats, and we settle in for our upcoming journey to Jaipur.

It is an incredibly eye-opening journey and takes around four hours. Sitting in a row of three, the man next to me is frantic. His phone has been pickpocketed at the station in Delhi, and he cannot stop fretting. His wife and family, in the aisle behind, are also visibly upset.

'He says it was an iPhone,' I murmur to Darryl. 'I would think it cost him a fortune. No wonder they are all so distressed.'

Although I don't have a window seat, I still have a good view of the passing scenery – and what I see enthrals me. I see mountains of garbage; cows and donkeys. I see men defecating and naked men showering. I see people sleeping anywhere and kids playing cricket. I see brown, flat cultivated fields and sharp, rocky hills.

Halfway into our journey, some young kids in the seats adjacent start playing music – and so the remainder of our journey is spent looking out the window while trying to drown out endless verses of 'Old MacDonald Had a Farm' and 'Wheels on the Bus'.

Before our guide in Delhi departed, he took a photo of us, and it has been forwarded to our new escorts. It means that when we alight from the train in Jaipur, they should be able to readily identify us. Stepping from the train onto the Jaipur platform, it appears the photo recognition has worked. Two men come running towards us, shouting out greetings and brandishing garlands of flowers.

'Welcome. Welcome to Jaipur! This is for you,' says one of the men as he wraps a string of golden-orange marigolds around our necks.

'And this is for you also,' says the other man as he plops a vibrant, turban-style hat onto our heads.

It is by far the most embarrassing – and outrageous – welcome we have ever experienced, with people staring at us from all directions. It takes a few moments before our initial shock evaporates.

'I feel like a celebrity,' Darryl eventually laughs, once we have reached the anonymity of our car. 'We are never going to forget this.'

'No, we won't,' I grin. 'But you know what? We are in Jaipur, India – a place we never thought we would visit. So let's just embrace it. Forget about ever being embarrassed.'

CHAPTER 33

Having Fun in Rajasthan

When I was less than a year old, my parents bundled me into the back of a motorhome and drove from England to India. In India, one of the areas they spent time in was Rajasthan, a place known for its colourful cities, desert landscape and rich culture.

The time they spent here heavily influenced their view of the world, later leading them to drop their conservative way of life and, instead, become hippies. Needless to say, conversations about Rajasthan featured heavily while I was growing up, which is why I am so happy to be arriving today at Jaipur, Rajasthan's capital.

It doesn't take long to reach our hotel, the ITC Rajputana. Stepping into its chandeliered, marble-lined foyer, there is no doubt that this is a five-star hotel equal to any Australia has to offer – a view reconfirmed later when we learn that Shane Warne and Brett Lee both stayed here.

With a tour of the city organised for the afternoon, there is just time to quickly peruse our room, it may be the nicest we have had so far, grab a bite to eat in one of the hotel's cafés, and return to reception. Here, we find a new guide waiting for us – a flamboyant, rather conceited gentleman who, in time, will prove to be one of our best guides ever.

'Welcome to Jaipur, I am Gee-Gee,' he announces as he shakes our hand. 'You have me for a quick tour of the city this afternoon, then all day tomorrow. If you are ready, we will get going.'

In ancient through to medieval times (2,500 BCE–1,700 CE), India was divided into multiple kingdoms ruled by powerful dynasties such as the Gupta, Maurya and Mughal Empires. During the 1600–1700s, the British, through a mix of military conquest, political manoeuvring and economic exploitation, gradually took control of India, splitting it into provinces and princely states (states ruled by a local monarch or ruler, such as a maharaja).

In 1947, India regained its independence, reshaping its boundaries based on language. Today, India consists of twenty-eight states, defined by language, culture and administration, and eight union territories, which are centrally governed. Rajasthan, the state we are currently visiting, is the largest of the states.

'And Jaipur is Rajasthan's capital,' Gee-Gee explains as we settle into our air-conditioned car. 'Founded in 1727, it was one of India's first planned cities, laid out using ancient Hindu architectural principles. In 1876, all of the buildings were painted pink to welcome the Prince of Wales, who later became King Edward VII.'

'Why pink?' I ask as, entering Jaipur's old town, I spy multiple pale pink sandstone buildings adorned with arched windows, overhanging balconies and wooden doors.

'Pink is the colour of hospitality,' Gee-Gee replies. 'And over time, the colour became a hallmark of the city's identity – which is why it remains pink today.'

As Gee-Gee mentioned, this afternoon's tour of Jaipur is not a long one. We spend it mainly confined within the imposing pink sandstone walls of Jaipur's Old City, and we come away having gained some valuable insights.

Namely, that the streets are narrow and bustling, the choking traffic noisy and chaotic. Sharing our road with cows, rickshaws, tuk-tuks and horse-drawn carts, we pass pink low-rise buildings where monkeys swing from roofs and balconies, and shrines where small crowds gather. Exiting our car at some point and continuing on foot, we pass vendors sitting on concrete footpaths, selling their wares, and a snake charmer who, for a fee, allows us to photograph his rattlesnake.

At sunset, as the sky turns a golden-pink hue to complement the surrounding buildings, we stop in front of a five-storey palace with 953 small windows.

'Hawa Mahal, or the Palace of Winds,' Gee-Gee tells us. 'Built in 1799 by a maharaja to allow royal women to observe street life without being seen. They would sit behind these small windows, which also allowed cool breezes to pass through – hence the name.'

Night has truly fallen by the time we return to our hotel. Passing through its foyer, a sign in front of a darkened bar advertises mezze plates and cocktails – something completely at odds with what we have experienced of India so far. Very much liking the sound of both, we find comfortable lounges and, over bowls of olives, dips and breads, let reminders of the day dictate our conversation.

'I haven't mentioned it yet,' I comment as a waiter places a furtive margarita in front of me, 'but I came to India wanting to see cows wandering the streets freely – I probably didn't really believe that they did. Seeing them do just that – it's incredible. I love it.'

Due to their religious significance in Hinduism, government protections, lack of strict animal control and bans on slaughtering cows, they can wander freely in many Indian states, including urban areas.

'You haven't had to mention it,' Darryl laughs. 'Every time we pass one, you yell and point it out. It's nice that it's a bit cooler here than

Delhi. Only 38 degrees today. Who would have thought there would be a day we considered 38 degrees bearable?'

'Gee-Gee's a bit of a character,' I say, changing the subject. 'Very knowledgeable – I'm looking forward to tomorrow's tour and what we will learn. But maybe a little full of himself.'

'I didn't like the way he only acknowledged you,' Darryl replies, a little indignantly. 'He didn't really include me in the conversation. And what's with the French? Why did he keep breaking out into French?'

'No idea,' I laugh. 'We have a big day of sightseeing tomorrow – it's going to be interesting.'

As with each of the places we will be staying in India, breakfast is included, and this morning, sitting and enjoying an extensive buffet breakfast in an enormous dining area, our attention is caught when we hear the people at the table next to us speak. Their accents easily identify them as Australian, and it isn't long before we strike up a conversation.

It turns out they are from the Gold Coast, less than twenty minutes from where we sometimes live, and flew into India just the day before. Laughing at how small the world is becoming, that you can travel so far from home yet meet someone who lives virtually around the corner from you, we wish them well with their travels.

Gee-Gee is waiting when we finish with breakfast and return to reception. Quickly bundling us into a car, he outlines the day ahead as we once again find ourselves driving the chaotic Jaipur roads, fighting tuk-tuks, rickshaws, pedestrians and cows for right of way.

'You mentioned yesterday you like to see a place at street level – to get out of the car and just walk. I thought we would do that first. Get out at Jaipur Old City and walk the streets.'

'That would be great,' I reply eagerly. 'Hopefully I'll be able to get some good footage.'

I haven't mentioned it before, but at many of the places we have visited on this adventure, I have made small videos of where we went, what we saw and what we did. Around a minute long, they have been well received on social media, and I have enjoyed making them. This offer from Gee-Gee – to walk amongst the Jaipur locals – should provide the perfect opportunity to create a new one.

'After our walk, we will visit Amber Fort. You are meant to ride an elephant up to the fort, but I don't agree with people riding elephants. What do you think? Do you want to ride the poor elephant, or should we do what's best and drive?'

Slightly surprised and bemused, it is not often a guide makes his feelings on a subject so obvious, it takes a moment for either of us to reply. Eventually, however, conceding that Gee-Gee may have a point, Darryl answers.

'We probably will not want to ride one. But it would be nice to see an elephant. Can we just drive past them?'

'Sure. We have more activities planned for this afternoon, but we can discuss those later.'

'I did want to see a stepwell as well,' I add. 'Apparently Jaipur has a good one.'

Mostly unique to India, stepwells are structures used to store and conserve water. Their distinctive design features symmetrical steps leading to a water reservoir, allowing easy access even when water levels fluctuate. Visiting one has been on my to-do list ever since seeing one in the movie *The Best Exotic Marigold Hotel*.

'Yes. The Panna Meena Kund is not far from Amber Fort,' Gee-Gee answers. 'We can stop on the way. It doesn't get many visitors, so it won't be crowded.'

It is still relatively early when we alight from our car, but the streets of Jaipur Old City are fully awake. Stumbling along the misshapen paved footpaths, there is so much to see that I soon have enough footage for many videos. While the bustling markets and shrines, where devotees line up to pray, are captivating, it is the skilled artisans practising centuries-old industries that make the best viewing. Watching craftsmen hammering away at brassware, polishing and cutting gemstones, weaving carpets, shaping resin bangles over open flames, and creating hand- and block-printed fabrics is fascinating.

An advantage of having a driver is that once we have finished strolling, there is no need to retrace our steps back to the car – it comes to us. This is particularly welcome this morning because, along with a rise in temperature – we are back into the mid-thirties – the awakening day has brought a sharp increase in begging.

Although we knew this would be the case wherever we travelled in India, it is still disconcerting to be confronted by both the poverty and the numbers of beggars. The sight of lean young women with undernourished children at their feet and babies on their hips is particularly difficult. While we could offer something, doing so often attracts many others.

'It is best to just smile and politely shake your head,' Gee-Gee tells us as we climb back into our car – trying not to be affected by the huge eyes of the children looking beseechingly at us, or by the mothers knocking imploringly at our windows.

'Look – cows!' I point to Darryl a short time later, trying to get the image of what we have just left out of my mind.

'How come the cows always look so healthy?' Darryl asks Gee-Gee. 'What do they eat?'

'Grass is often donated,' he replies. 'And people leave food out for them. The first *roti* of the day is for the cows. It is left outside your door, while the last *roti* of the day is put out for the dogs.'

A *roti* is a traditional Indian flatbread made from wholewheat flour, water and maybe a little salt. Soft, thin and served with curries, vegetables or dahl, it is one of the few foods I am currently able to tolerate.

It takes less than thirty minutes to drive from Jaipur's Old City to Amber Fort. Along the way, we pass some enormous elephants, and watching them navigate the chaotic city traffic, looking so resigned, so out of place, makes our decision not to ride one feel like it was the right one.

Before reaching Amber Fort, we make a slight detour down a narrow, untidy gravel road. Coming to a standstill, we exit our car and follow Gee-Gee over a pile of rubble and through some wire gates.

'Panna Meena stepwell!' I cry excitedly, spotting the striking rectangular structure with its descending steps leading to a pool of green water. 'Can I walk to the bottom?'

'No.'

Unseen by me, a guard is lounging deep in the shade of a nearby gate house. He has heard my question and answered it.

'No. It is strictly forbidden,' he further emphasises.

While it is a shame, it would have been good to have explored this area more fully, to rest, maybe take a photo on the mesmerising steps, we make do with viewing it from above and appreciate the chance to visit such an intriguing structure.

'Stepwells were not only places to store water,' Gee-Gee tells us as we make our way back to the car, 'but places where people would gather and rest. Now, are you ready for Amber Fort?'

CHAPTER 34

The Train to Ranthambore

India is home to hundreds of forts, each with its own rich history and unique architectural style. Built by various dynasties – including the Mughals and the British – they served as defensive strongholds, royal residences and trade centres. Local resources often dictated their colour and design. The Red Fort in Delhi, which we skipped, was built from red sandstone; today's Amber Fort is considered white, constructed mainly from white marble.

Perched high on the ridgeline of a rugged, sparsely vegetated hill, our first sighting of this extensive and majestic garrison from the valley below is impressive enough that we stop the car just to take some photos.

'It is one of India's most famous and splendid forts,' Gee-Gee tells us as we take in the imposing multi-tiered structure, admiring the weathered sandstone walls, the massive bastions and watchtowers standing so proudly against the landscape and the cows cooling themselves in the river that flows through the space between us.

'They have even made some Bollywood movies here,' he adds proudly, as we climb back into the car.

Entering the fort's main entrance, it becomes clear that the building is not only massive but artistic as well – with elaborate carvings, vibrant frescoes, delicate latticework, and an area completely covered in tiny mirrors.

'This is Mirror Palace, the most famous part of the fort,' Gee-Gee says, as we watch the tiny glass mirrors reflect and scatter the day's beaming sunlight.

'If you stand just here and look at the mirrored wall, I will take a photo. You will love the result.'

It is not the first time Gee-Gee has spoken like this but, used to him by now, we do as he says. The resulting photograph, our reflections bounced across thousands of tiny, mirrored pieces, is, we have to begrudgingly admit, artistic.

'I think I like this part of the fort the best.'

After ascending a steeply sloping ramp, cursing its lack of cover and the 36-degree heat, we have just reached an upper tier. Standing on one of the fort's walls, and gazing out over its vast paved courtyard and the striking surrounding countryside, Darryl has just voiced my thoughts.

Our panoramic view, stretching for miles, is breathtaking. It even includes glimpses of another fort, which is perfectly blended with the stony landscape and slightly more elevated than Amber Fort.

'That is Jaigarh Fort,' Gee-Gee tells us. 'It is connected to this one by some secret tunnels, which were used during wars – but no longer.'

Somehow, I never really equated India with war, a place of firepower, forts and conflict – which has made today's visit all the more thought-provoking.

Back in the car, Gee-Gee reveals a little more of today's itinerary. Our next stop will be the shoreline of Man Sagar Lake, where we will be able to view Jal Mahal, a stunning palace that appears to float in its centre.

While I knew of the Lake Palace in Udaipur, featured in the James Bond movie *Octopussy* and seen on posters the world over, I was unaware Jaipur had one too. It is currently closed, unfortunately, meaning we cannot visit, but it is still fascinating to admire it from afar. To contemplate how, in the eighteenth-century, they were able to construct a building where four of its five stories are submerged.

Disappointingly, we can't linger long. We cannot even discuss our contemplations, for this area of the shoreline is home to many beggars, and they quickly surround us, seeking charity. They follow us back to the car and encircle it, knocking repeatedly at the windows, their eyes imploring. It is actually quite devastating to witness – and it takes a while to shake off the encounter.

Before lunch, which will be eaten at an obscure restaurant hidden inside the Jaipur City Palace, we make a quick stop at the Jantar Mantar observatory. An eighteenth-century astronomical observatory designed to study celestial bodies and track time, the place astounds us. The fact that people could build such massive stone instruments to accurately calculate time, predict eclipses, track stars and determine altitudes nearly three hundred years ago is incredible. The fact that it is located in India makes it even more amazing to me.

I don't want to sound judgemental, but I hadn't associated India with ancient scientific advancement. Today's visit has taught me a valuable lesson.

Located in the heart of Jaipur, the City Palace, a beautiful blend of Rajasthani, Mughal and European styles, with its spacious courtyards and elaborate gardens, keeps us entertained for the rest of the afternoon. While its central section is still a royal residence for the current Maharaja's family and is thus off limits, the rest is open to the public – including the aforementioned restaurant, a place Gee-Gee assures us only guides really know about.

'We try to keep it secret,' he laughs over a late lunch of club sandwiches and mango lassis.

'As we were walking through the palace to this restaurant,' I frown, 'I noticed a large group of school kids sitting in a pavilion, drawing and painting. What was that about?'

'Much of the City Palace has been set aside for local artists and industry,' Gee-Gee explains. 'They were students selected from various schools to learn the art of Rajasthani miniature painting. Later, we will visit another part of the palace set up for local craftsmen to sell their wares.'

'How about the gates into the palace?' Darryl exclaims. 'They impressed me. Especially the spikes – what where they for?'

'The spikes were to protect against elephant attacks,' Gee-Gee laughs. 'Something we don't have to worry about these days.'

After lunch, we take our time exploring the different areas of this huge complex. While the museum is interesting, and spying men erecting convoluted scaffolding made from bamboo is entertaining, it is the hall given over to the craftsmen that we find the most rewarding. Wandering through this area, we observe artisans using blocks to hand-print intricate designs onto fabric. We see craftsmen intricately inlaying jewellery with coloured enamel, and others carving elaborate designs onto wood, then inlaying them with metal pieces to create stunning patterns.

We spy stone carvers, marble workers, pottery artisans and more. It is an incredible space – more so when Gee-Gee reminds us of its purpose.

'Many of these crafts are in danger of being lost,' he says. 'Whether due to industrialisation, lack of support or simply the changing tastes of younger generations, India risks losing these skills entirely. Here, they are being preserved – and younger artisans are being trained.'

Departing the City Palace concludes our tour of Jaipur with Gee-Gee. In his uniquely cocky way, he has provided a thoughtful, comprehensive and entertaining look at a fascinating city – giving us experiences, like being swamped by beggars or photographing rattlesnakes, that we will never forget.

We are not sorry to be returning to our hotel – the temperature has just reached 39 degrees, and there is no place we would rather be. Entering its air-conditioned comfort, that little darkened bar once again beckons, and so dinner becomes another selection of mezze plates, accompanied by a margarita.

Despite the numbing effects of my drink, sleep doesn't come easily that night – and I can't tell whether it is the two-and-a-half-hour time difference between Türkiye and India, or the sensory overload from everything we have seen, smelled and experienced over the past few days. Whatever the cause, I wake the next morning feeling slightly woolly-headed – but no less eager to move on to our next destination.

Jaipur train station is by far the busiest station we have ever encountered. Waiting passengers, loaded down with string-wrapped parcels, bulging suitcases and wide-eyed children, crowd the hot, dirty platform. There are bodies everywhere, standing, sitting or lying .

Our train is late, and we spend the time idling in a filthy but less crowded waiting room, grateful that we are able to do so. Some are not so lucky. As our train finally pulls into the station, with people spilling from windows and doorways, I begin counting the passing carriages. Fascinated by the variety of classes, and their differing conditions, I stop counting after thirty.

When booking our train tickets with My Flight Trip, we had been told which class we would be travelling in. Today's journey is a short one – just over two hours – and we will be in a third-class air-conditioned sleeper.

'What does that mean?' Darryl had asked.

'No idea,' I had replied.

Boarding the train, we discover that it means sharing a small compartment with four others. Converting into six bunk-style beds – two wide and three high – today the four lower beds have been stowed to allow us to sit. The two upper bunks, high above our heads, are occupied by two sleeping ladies.

While it is somewhat cramped, given we all have at least one bag each, it does allow us to interact freely. All our companions are Indian citizens, in fact, I haven't seen another Westerner all morning, and all speak excellent English and are happy to chat.

One, we learn, works for Goldman Sachs, and he explains a bit about the Indian pension scheme. It is voluntary and can be accessed from the age of fifty-eight.

'Or if you haven't worked in six months,' he adds.

Two others are university students, both studying to be dentists. They happily talk about the Australians who travel to India each year to have their teeth worked on.

'Visiting the dentist must be very expensive in Australia – we get so many of you.'

The fourth makes us laugh when he answers his phone, scowls, then quickly hangs up. It was someone cold-calling him – from India.

'We get those phone calls all the time in Australia,' I grin. 'I can't believe you get them here too.'

Often our chatter is interrupted by hawkers peddling food items like *samosa* and *pakora*, or drinks like *chai* and *lassi*. We don't think much of it until one of our companions decides to make a purchase. Accepting his chai, he pulls out his phone, opens an app and scans the hawkers QR code to pay.

Noting our surprise, how does a hawker have access to such technology?, he explains.

'The app is called the Unified Payments Interface or UPI. It is India's real-time payment system. It's revolutionised digital payments here – cashless transactions are now easy, even in small places.'

'I suppose we shouldn't really be surprised,' Darryl comments. 'India is one of the most progressive countries, technology-wise. But it *is* incredible to know you can buy almost anything, anywhere, just using your phone. Australia is so far behind.'

Travelling in a southerly direction, further from the cooling Himalayas, and the earth outside is baked dry. Cows, sheep and goats roam, struggling to find anything to eat in the dusty brown soil.

'Everything looks dry and dead now,' someone tells us, 'because it is summer. Wait until winter – this will all be green then.'

A little before our 12.30pm arrival time, two of our fellow travellers remind us to start getting ready to disembark. Earlier, we had explained our near-miss in Türkiye, and they had promised this would not happen today.

'We use an app called Where is My Train,' one of them says as we gather our bags. 'It tells you everything you need to know about your train journey. Try and download it when you can.'

CHAPTER 35

Searching for (Elusive) Tigers

Unlike the stations in Delhi or Jaipur, Ranthambore has a much more rural look and feel. The platform we alight on is long, crumbling and weed-choked. Pavers are broken and it is not easy wheeling our bags. A driver is waiting for us, and as we follow him from the station, we pass a number of grazing cows, which add to the rustic vibe.

It doesn't take long to reach our accommodation, the Sawai Madhopur Lodge, and driving through its ornate gates, noting the long, low building, the rolling green lawns complete with scurrying squirrels, and the chauffeured golf buggies, I immediately feel as if I could be on safari. Which, in a way, we are.

Six months ago, I had never heard of Ranthambore. When our Indian leg first made it onto the itinerary, my research focused on the more popular destinations: Agra for the Taj Mahal, Delhi and Jaipur. And although it wasn't as easily accessible by train, I also insisted we include Varanasi to see the Ganges. It was My Flight Trip who suggested we stop at Ranthambore.

'It is one of India's most famous wildlife reserves,' I had read in an email from one of their consultants. 'Its national park was once a royal hunting ground but is now a protected Bengal tiger reserve. It is one of the best places to see tigers in the wild.'

Immediately captivated by the thought of seeing, and hopefully photographing, a tiger in its natural, untamed habitat, a stop in Ranthambore was easily added to our travel route.

What this means is that, never having heard of this place and not really having had time to research it much, we have no idea what to expect. To find ourselves today alighting from our vehicle in front of a former hunting lodge, where, our driver has just nonchalantly informed us, Queen Elizabeth once stayed, is unexpected and incredibly thrilling.

'This is exactly how I imagined it would look and feel when one went on safari,' I chatter excitedly to Darryl as smartly dressed porters collect our luggage.

'It is a bit like something you would see in a movie,' he replies with a grin.

It doesn't take long to obtain our room key, after which a golf buggy transports us to our accommodation. Entering through heavy wooden doors, we find the interior dark and cool, with outside temperature hovering around 39 degrees, this is much appreciated, but its decor somewhat lacking.

'I don't think they have done any refurbishments since Queen Elizabeth visited sixty years ago,' says Darryl wryly, noting the lumpy brown furniture, the faded lampshades and the old-style paintings.

'It's a good size anyway,' I reply. 'And we are only here for two nights.'

With all meals included in our accommodation, we head to the dining room in the early afternoon in search of a late lunch. Strolling the lush lawns and wide, sweeping paths, we spy cheeky monkeys cavorting in the trees overhead, squirrels chasing each other and multiple varieties of colourful birdlife. Add in the stifling heat, and it definitely feels like India.

'So... Tigers tomorrow?' Darryl asks a short while later as he dips a chunk of crispy *roti* into his dish of creamy vegetable curry.

'Yes,' I grin, then add, slightly glumly, 'But because they are most active in the morning, we need to leave early. So – a 4.30am wake-up.'

Full from our late lunch, and knowing we have an early start ahead, we spend the rest of the day hibernating in our darkened room. Every now and then, the power cuts out and our showers are only lukewarm – but both add to the safari atmosphere. Night falls early in this part of India, but the temperature does not seem to notice. By dinner time, it is still in the mid-thirties – too hot for us to feel like eating. With no television in the room, we watch a few episodes of *Clarkson's Farm* on my laptop before calling it a day.

It is still dark when, at 4.45am, we make our way back to reception. Here we find an array of cakes, biscuits, tea, and coffee waiting for us. This is early breakfast – full breakfast will be available on our return from hunting tigers. Along with food, there is also a waiting jeep, into which we clamber, nourished for our upcoming adventure.

Our destination this morning is Ranthambore National Park, a good forty-minute drive along long, narrow roads filled with other tourist-packed jeeps. With the temperature already in the high thirties, and a smouldering golden orb rising on the horizon, it is clear the heat will only intensify. Sparse, thorny bushes, wandering cows, and a mix of urban dwellings give way to denser vegetation and rocky hills the further we travel.

At the park's entrance, we stop, and three others, of Asian descent, join us in our jeep. Chattering excitedly as they settle in, we grin; despite appearances, their accents unmistakably stamp them as Australian.

'It's true what they say,' I can't help commenting. 'No matter where in the world you travel, you will always find an Aussie.'

Along with our fellow Australians, a guide climbs in and takes the seat beside our driver and, as our vehicle leaves the bitumen road behind, he turns to us.

'Welcome to Ranthambore National Park. It is going to be a hot and dusty morning – let's hope we see a tiger.'

Once a private game reserve for the rich and royal, Ranthambore National Park is a five-hundred-square-kilometre wilderness tucked within ancient mountain ranges and surrounded by serene bodies of water. Its terrain is a mix of dense, dry tropical forest, open bushland, rugged cliffs and rocky hills. Alongside Bengal tigers, the park is also home to a huge variety of wildlife – including leopards, wild boar, hyenas, jackals, sloth bears, buffalos, crocodiles, monkeys and mongoose.

'There is no guarantee we will see a tiger,' our guide continues. 'There are only seventy-five in the entire park. And only twenty per cent of the park – about one-fifth – is open to tourists. So maybe we have a chance of seeing fifteen tigers. But tigers are solitary animals and can roam up to 15 square kilometres a day. So, you can see how hard you need to look, and how lucky you need to be to spot one.'

'I hope we are one of the lucky ones,' I whisper to Darryl. 'It's so hot, humid and dusty this morning – I would hate to have to come back this afternoon.'

What I haven't mentioned yet is that, knowing how difficult it is to spot a tiger in the wild, most visitors are advised to book two safaris. Should we fail this morning, or should we wish to repeat the experience, a second excursion has been scheduled for later today.

What I hadn't expected was the incredible heat and relentless dust. Knowing both will be worse by afternoon, there is no way I want to repeat this. If I am going to see a tiger, it needs to be this morning.

'Although only twenty per cent of the park is open to visitors, that's still a large territory,' our guide interrupts my whispering. 'So, we have divided it into ten zones. Today, we will be searching in Zone Five. Other jeeps will be covering the remaining zones.'

'Let's hope Zone Five is the lucky one!' one of our companions whoops.

It takes three hours to explore Zone Five. Three hard, hot hours, driving on dusty, potholed tracks in stifling forty-degree heat. Three hours of swirling grit in temperatures that raise an itchy rash on my arms. Three hours where the breeze never comes, and the jeep's bone-crunching jolting never stops.

Three hours of searching in vain, but three incredible hours nonetheless, spotting animals, some we have never seen before, under conditions we have never experienced before.

'Look — a buffalo!' someone cries.

'And look at all the spotted antelopes,' replies another.

'There's a wild boar,' Darryl adds.

'And a mongoose!' I reply. 'I've never seen a mongoose.'

'There's a peacock in that tree, a crocodile in the water below, and a hyena drinking next to it,' says our guide.

Although we are reluctant to stop searching, eventually we return to the park's entrance, where we admit our failure to one of the attendants.

'That is unfortunate,' he replies. 'Zones one, two, three, four and ten – they were the lucky ones today.'

Because of our daybreak start, it is still relatively early – just a little after 10am – when we arrive back at the lodge. As promised, a large breakfast is waiting for us. Afterwards, we retreat to our room. With outside's suffocating temperature, a good portion of the day is spent handwashing laundry and relaxing.

'What do you think about this afternoon's excursion? Are you up for it? If so, we need to start getting ready,' Darryl says.

'I'm not up for it,' I reply. 'My watch is reading 45 degrees. It's just too hot for me. I can't even contemplate jolting around in the dust and heat for another five hours.'

'I am up for it,' Darryl says. 'I really want to see a tiger, now that we are here.'

'Go for it,' I laugh. 'I'm happy to just relax, read my book, maybe do a blog.'

And that is exactly what I do, during the time it takes Darryl to return to and explore Ranthambore National Park. To ride in his own private jeep (the three other Australians also opted out), to enjoy his very own personal guide, and to spy not one, but two beautiful Bengal tigers, roaming separately and freely in their natural habitat.

CHAPTER 36

Agra and the Stunning Taj Mahal

Today's two-hour train journey from Ranthambore to Bharatpur, where a driver will meet us for a transfer to Agra, is one of our shorter ones. Being short, however, doesn't make it any less interesting. Sitting in air-conditioned chair class, we watch in fascination as merchants walk the aisles, peddling their wares. Carried in nothing more than plastic trays, cardboard boxes or battered buckets, the items they are selling include ice-creams, hot pizzas, water, burgers, chips, sandwiches, lassis, samosas and chai.

Outside the train, our view is just as captivating. Like our journey two days ago, most of the landscape is bare, dry and brown. Some fields still hold remnants of crops, but these are in the process of being cleared. What makes this especially intriguing is that, instead of machinery, fire is being used – and it is women who are wielding the flames. In fact, in all the countries we have travelled through recently, in nearly every instance where I have seen someone working the land, it has been a female.

As we edge closer to our destination, the usual angst returns, and we wonder which station we need to alight. But this time, we have help. As suggested, I have researched and downloaded the app Where is My Train, and so far, it is working brilliantly. Not only does it list every train station on our entire route, it also tells us exactly how many minutes we are ahead or behind schedule. Currently, we are five stations shy of Bharatpur and running ten minutes late. While we have travelled on many trains around the world, never have we had such a helpful app to assist us. India's technological advancement has surprised us again.

As we have come to expect, there is a guide waiting when we alight from the train at around 10am. Although it is still relatively early, the day's heat is already intense. Glancing at my watch, I note the temperature: 44 degrees. This may become our hottest day yet.

'Welcome, my name is Esh,' he says as we gratefully sink into a cool waiting car. 'It will take about fifty minutes to reach Agra, and we have one stop along the way – Fatehpur Sikri.'

'What's that?' Darryl asks.

'Fatehpur Sikri is a sixteenth-century city built by the Mughals,' Esh replies. 'It was abandoned due to water shortages. Today, it is a UNESCO World Heritage site, famous for its Mughal architecture.'

'What else is planned for today?' I ask.

'This afternoon, you visit Agra Fort. Tomorrow, the Taj Mahal.'

'I'm happy to skip Fatehpur Sikri,' I say to Darryl. 'It's nearly 45 degrees. I'm not that keen on walking around an abandoned city in this heat. How about you?'

'I agree. Let's save our energy for Agra Fort this afternoon.'

While Esh seems happy with the change of plan, I suspect he also has no desire to pound hot pavements, it does leave him in a bit of a predicament.

'I cannot drop you at your hotel before noon,' he muses. 'We will make a quick visit to a marble inlay factory instead.'

Despite our protests, no amount of persuasion convinces him to just take us straight to our hotel and so, eventually, we find ourselves in a warehouse, listening as someone explains the intricate art of marble inlay – a lesson that will prove invaluable when we visit the Taj Mahal tomorrow.

'Marble inlay is one of the most striking features of the Taj Mahal, perfected during the Mughal era,' we learn. 'The process involves designing, carving, shaping stones, and polishing. The entire mausoleum is adorned with elaborate inlay work using semi-precious stones like lapis lazuli, jade, turquoise and onyx.'

'That was actually quite interesting,' I say to Darryl once the visit concludes. 'How time-consuming it must be – drawing a design onto a piece of marble, chiselling it out, then insetting tiny pre-shaped pieces of semi-precious stones.'

'And tedious,' he replies. 'It'll be interesting seeing the ultimate example.'

Having delayed our arrival, Esh is now happy to take us to our accommodation – the Taj Hotel and Convention Centre. Dropping us at its heavily secured entrance, he departs, promising to return at five.

'It should be a little bit cooler by then. Better for exploring Agra Fort.'

The historic city of Agra, with a population of just 2.3 million, is relatively small by Indian standards. These days, tourism, handicrafts and manufacturing drive its economy, but during the Mughal era, it was the bustling capital of the empire – until the seat of power was moved to Delhi. And while nearly everyone the world over has heard of Agra's centrepiece, the Taj Mahal, it was only when we decided to visit India that we learnt of Agra Fort.

'Agra Fort, also known as the Red Fort of Agra, is one of the most significant historical monuments in India,' I had read to Darryl from my computer screen. 'It was the main residence of the Mughal emperors.'

'Another old building,' he had replied, laughing.

It is right on five when Esh returns to take us to this 'old building'. We have spent the intervening hours appreciating the opulence of our hotel – its vast dining room provided a satisfying lunch, the rooftop pool area offered mesmerising, albeit hazy, views over the entire city, and our spacious, cool room has been a welcome retreat.

But stepping out from the hotel foyer, any serenity we have gained is immediately lost when the 46-degree heat hits us like a slap to the face. Never have we experienced anything like it.

'It feels like I'm in an oven,' I gasp. 'Didn't you say it would be cooler this afternoon?'

'We are nearing the monsoon season,' Esh replies. 'Soon, the afternoon rains will cool things down. Today, we have to put up with the heat. It may be a little cooler at the fort.'

Although located just three kilometres from our hotel, it takes a little over twenty minutes to reach our destination – our way is clogged with rickshaws, motorbikes, cows and pedestrians. At one point along the route, we glimpse a cluster of grand colonial-era buildings.

'These were built by the British when they ruled India,' Esh explains. 'After independence, many were abandoned. These days, the government gives them to people who can afford to restore them.'

Not long after this, when the road starts to widen and the urban chaos begins to dwindle, a stark red sandstone structure begins to dominate our view. Looking like something constructed from reddish-brown Lego blocks – only on an enormous scale – it is both formidable and beautiful.

'And you called that "just another old building",' I laugh at Darryl. 'Look at it. It's incredible. And gorgeous.'

Set on 94 acres (38 hectares) and surrounded by twenty-metre walls, it takes us two hours to explore what turns out to be the most impressive fort we have ever seen. The conditions are awful, a breeze has sprung up, but instead of offering relief, it blasts us with hot air, turning the oven into a convection oven, yet what we see and learn is amazing.

'Seventy-five per cent of the Fort is still used by the military,' Esh tells us. 'The British Army once used it as a base, too… Agra Fort has many underground tunnels… The famous Kohinoor Diamond was once kept here… And this room – this is where the emperor who built the Taj Mahal was imprisoned by his own son during a struggle for power. It faces the Taj Mahal, so he spent the last years of his life looking upon it.'

Though obscured by distance and dust stirred up by the hot, dry air, the outline of a building famous the world over is visible as Esh speaks. It is our first glimpse of the Taj Mahal – a true Bucket List moment.

'We visit there tomorrow,' I say. 'But could you tell us more about it now? It would be nice to have some context beforehand.'

'The Taj Mahal is a mausoleum commissioned by the Mughal emperor Shah Jahan in memory of his beloved wife, Mumtaz Mahal,' Esh explains. 'She was heavily pregnant with their fourteenth child when he convinced her to accompany him on a military campaign. Without access to medical supplies, she died during labour. Overcome with guilt and grief, he vowed to build the most magnificent mausoleum in her memory. Construction began in 1632 and took twenty-two years to complete. Tomorrow, you will see why.'

Night is falling by the time we begin our return journey to the hotel. As we travel, small droplets of water hit the windscreen – only to quickly evaporate.

'Good,' Esh says, nodding approvingly. 'The monsoon season is nearly here.'

The following morning is another ridiculous 4.30am wake-up. Last night, over an early room-service dinner, we had received a message advising that the best time to visit the Taj Mahal was around 5am, before the heat and crowds. Although slightly surprised that a government-run site would be open so early, we readily agreed. If yesterday's heat was anything to go by, we were more than happy to trade a few hours of sleep for some early-morning cool.

Esh is in a chatty mood this morning, and, as we travel, he shares some interesting facts.

'Shortly we will leave the car and transfer to an electric buggy that will drop us closer to the entrance,' he explains. 'Since 2021, all fuel-powered vehicles have been banned from travelling within five hundred metres of the monument.'

'Why were they banned?' Darryl asks.

'To protect the Taj Mahal from the effects of pollution,' Esh replies. 'For decades, the air quality was damaging and discolouring the marble. In 2018, the Indian Supreme Court stepped in and ordered the government to act. That's when they created this fuel-free zone and relocated or shut down nearby factories that were contributing to the damage.'

'I suppose when you have one of the world's most iconic landmarks – one of the Seven Wonders of the World – in your city, you want to preserve it,' I muse.

'It also gets a clay face mask every ten years,' Esh adds.

'A face mask?' I echo.

'Yes. The Taj Mahal is built of white marble inlaid with gemstones. Over time, pollution and weather turn the marble yellow. So, every decade or so, a layer of natural clay is applied, left to dry, then washed off with distilled water. What's left is a clean white surface.'

Starting to appreciate just how special, and fiercely protected, this building is to the Indian people, it is still dark when, as promised, an electric buggy conveys us to the Taj Mahal's entrance. Here, while Darryl and I are kept amused by a large group of frolicking monkeys, Esh purchases our tickets before leading us towards what is known as the Great Gate.

As we pass through this arched entrance, our timing could not be more perfect. The sun has just risen, illuminating spectacularly the white marble monument in front of us. Being so early in the day, the crowd is minimal, meaning nothing is obstructing our view of the glowing white structure, its plump domes and elegant minarets. Stepping forward, and a rectangular body of water – the reflecting pool – captures and throws the monument's image back at us. All in all, it has to be one of the most exciting and memorable moments of my life.

'Remember yesterday, at the factory, where you saw how difficult it was – the skill required to create inlay marble?'

After posing for the obligatory photo on the Princess Diana seat, we have made our way past the glassy reflection pond, climbed some stairs, donned protective shoe coverings, and are preparing to enter the Taj Mahal.

'Look at this facade, the elaborate decorations – all inlaid marble,' Esh continues, making a sweeping motion with his hand towards the outer walls of the monument.

Realising that he's drawing our attention to entire marble panels where designs have been carefully chiselled out and inlaid with fine pieces of gemstones, we can only stare. What we had previously thought of as just a famous white building is, in reality, an exquisite piece of fine art – the craftsmanship is incredible.

'That's why it took twenty-two years,' Darryl says suddenly, remembering what were told yesterday.

'That is why it took twenty-two years,' Esh repeats solemnly.

While its exterior is rightly recognised as one of the most beautiful buildings in the world, inside, the Taj Mahal is rather disappointing: dimly lit, restrained, empty. Two beautifully decorated tombs are on display, but they are purely symbolic – the real tombs of Shah Jahan and Mumtaz Mahal lie in a lower crypt not open to the public.

Before our tour ends, there is time to inspect some nearby buildings, a mosque and guesthouse that mirror each other in design, and to take many photos. While the photos don't really do the place justice, I am hoping one of them will become the cover for this book.

It is still midmorning when we return to our hotel. The early wake-ups, India's suffocating heat and my medication have begun to take a toll. I am still covered in a prickly rash and constantly feel nauseous and fatigued. Knowing that we have only one week left of this incredible adventure, I decide to stop taking my Verzenio until we are home again. We have some big days ahead of us, and I need energy and a settled stomach to handle them.

Over a light lunch in our hotel's dining room, where, surprisingly, we bump into the three Australians who searched for tigers in Ranthambore with us, I mention my decision to Darryl.

'It's a worry, discontinuing such an important medication, even temporarily, but I think it's a good idea,' he replies. 'Tonight is going to be pretty hectic – you need to feel well.'

Happy with my decision, I can't help but smile wryly at Darryl's choice of word for the next leg of our journey – the leg we have both been dreading: the overnight train journey to Varanasi.

'Hectic' is probably the mildest way of describing it.

CHAPTER 37

Surviving the Overnight Train to Varanasi

The temperature is still 45 degrees when, at 6.30pm, we find ourselves waiting with the masses at Agra train station. Around us, the sweltering platforms are strewn with resting bodies and jumbled luggage, and when a last-minute platform change for our train is announced, the resulting stampede sends our anxiety levels skyrocketing. Our turban-capped driver, however, is skilled at getting passengers onto trains, and although time hasn't allowed us to enter the correct carriage, we are nonetheless on the train.

Each second-class sleeper carriage looks much the same – a long, narrow, grubby corridor flanked by thin, swaying curtains, each one hiding a set of bunks. There are some tense minutes as we search for our assigned carriage and berths, but eventually, we find them. Under Darryl's lower bunk, there is just enough room to stow our bags, and we sit his walking stick on top, hoping it will dissuade anyone from stealing them – we didn't think to bring a lock and chain, as some suggested. On both bunks is a brown paper-bag containing a thin sheet, a ratty blanket and a small, lumpy pillow, with which we quickly make up our beds.

'Stop. Stop. We've just made them.'

Between the fast-rocking train and a cramped corridor full of constant foot traffic, it wasn't easy laying out our bedding. To have a train attendant come along and start pulling it apart is very annoying. As each newly boarding passenger gets a fresh set of linen, it is obvious he thinks our just-made beds belong to the previous travellers. He doesn't speak any English, and it is only when I quickly pull out my phone and use Google Translate to relay his mistake that he stops dismantling them.

With nowhere to sit, we have no choice but to climb into our beds. Mine is low-ceilinged, narrow and grimy, and my backpack, lying beside me, takes up a lot of space. Along with my shoes, strategically placed at the foot of my bed, it is difficult to uncoil my legs – but eventually I find a comfortable position.

Across the narrow aisle, hidden behind their own swinging curtains, is an Indian family occupying four bunks. Unlike other travellers, this family have no reservations about staying quiet – their conversation is loud and penetrating. The youngest member plays games on an iPad, and its strident beeping and pinging prevent any hope of immediate sleep. Resigned, I read a book on my phone and hope I have no need to use those carefully placed shoes. Earlier today, we had stopped drinking all liquids – if there is one thing neither of us wanted to do, it is scramble for a grungy toilet on this heavily occupied train.

For six months, this leg of our adventure has been the most talked about, anticipated and dreaded. Anticipated, because taking an overnight sleeper train in India will add invaluable experience to our train-travel repertoire. Dreaded, because it *is* an overnight sleeper train – and this *is* India. Now, to actually find myself living something we have discussed so much feels almost surreal.

Despite the cramped conditions, the strident iPad and my slowly complaining bladder, I eventually fall into a fitful sleep. Waking some time later, I realise the iPad has thankfully been silenced. The only sounds now are the burping, farting and snoring of a carriage at rest. A quick glance at my phone shows the time is 3am – ninety minutes until our scheduled arrival. To confirm this, I open the Where is my Train app and see that we are running thirty minutes ahead of schedule.

At 3.30am, I wake Darryl, and at 4am, we gather our belongings, struggle through the crowded, sleeping corridor and exit the train.

Unlike our previous arrivals in India, today there is no welcoming committee. Although we're slightly concerned, at 4am Deendayal Upadhyaya train station, our Varanasi arrival point, proves too distracting, too emotionally stirring to worry about our tardy driver.

If we had thought ourselves hardened to India's hardships, what we see and walk amidst as we leave the platform to wait at the station's entrance, proves we have some way to go. At other stations we have passed through, we have seen men and women of varying ages sleeping rough on grimy platforms. But this morning, we see so much more. We see the men and the women, but also lone kids, teenagers, toddlers, single mothers, entire families, and people with disabilities.

The most heart-wrenching vision is a naked baby lying in a crouched position, bottom in the air, beside its mother and young siblings on a ramp leading from the platform. A long stream of urine runs from the infant to the base of the incline. The sight is so unexpected, so piteous, that the image will stay with me forever.

Eventually, our driver arrives, full of apologies – he hadn't anticipated the train arriving so early. Bundling us into his car, he explains that we have a forty-five-minute drive to reach our accommodation, the Taj Ganges Hotel.

'Because it's so early, your room may not yet be ready,' he also warns.

Having arrived in one of Varanasi's outer suburbs, our initial view is of dusty streets and strolling cows, bustling markets and busy eateries. Midway between here and Varanasi's historic core, where the streets narrow and the architecture ages, we cross a bridge.

'Malviya Bridge,' our driver tells us. 'And the Ganges River.'

The River Ganges, or Ganga as it is affectionately known by the locals, is one of India's most sacred rivers. Originating in the Himalayas and emptying into the Bay of Bengal 2,500 kilometres later, it is an integral part of Indian life. Pilgrims travel to its banks to be cleansed of sin and offered salvation. Hundreds of millions of people rely on it for drinking water, agriculture and fishing. The *ghats* (steps) that line its banks here at Varanasi have been used for sacred ceremonies and cremations for over three thousand years.

Growing up with alternative parents, the Ganges has been part of my vocabulary since childhood. It was something I insisted on seeing if I ever made it to India. Today, by crossing this bridge and peering into the large expanse of brown murky water below, that dream has been realised – another Bucket List moment achieved.

'The Ganges,' I can't help crowing in excitement. 'Something I never thought I would see. I can't believe we have.'

'I agree,' Darryl replies happily. Although not quite as familiar with the Ganges as I am, it is obvious he is equally affected.

Unfortunately, when we reach the hotel our room isn't ready. Handing over our bags to be put into storage, I manage to find a restroom, where I have a quick unsatisfactory wash, after which we head to breakfast.

'I've just received a message from My Flight Trip,' I mention to Darry as I savour my coffee.

'Someone is going to arrive at seven this morning to take us to Sarnath. We will then return here and hopefully our room will be ready. Tonight, we watch a ceremony on the banks of the Ganges.'

'Ugh, so no shower for a while yet,' he grimaces. 'What's Sarnath?'

'This is Sarnath – one of the most famous, sacred and religious places in the Buddhist world,' Manish, our latest guide is explaining. 'It is where Buddha, in 528 BCE, after obtaining enlightenment, taught his first sermon – thus starting the journey of *dharma*, the path of righteous.'

It is another sweltering Indian morning, and we are currently standing in a park-like open site surrounded by ancient brick ruins and a few scattered pillars. Not far away is a massive cylindrical stone and brick structure – the Dhamek Stupa. A *stupa* is a dome-shaped Buddhist shrine used for meditation and often built to house relics, such as the ashes of monks or sacred texts. While its sheer size and weathered presence commands attention, it is a smaller, tiered monument – the Chaukhandi Stupa – that Manish directs us to.

'It is just here that Buddha met his disciples and gave his sermon.'

'Buddha stood just here,' I gasp.

Like the Ganges, Buddha was a common word in my childhood vocabulary. Throwing aside their Christian upbringings, my parents instead embraced the principles of Buddhism – live wisely, act kindly and train the mind to end suffering and seek enlightenment. While they didn't always succeed, I did grow up believing Buddha's teachings made far more sense than many other religious doctrines, which makes this morning so special. I am (maybe – how can we really be certain after 2,552 years?) standing where he once stood.

It is another of those surreal moments, this adventure seems to be providing a number of them, but my excitement soon wanes. The day is growing too hot to be standing amongst scattered brick ruins so, after a brief tour of a nearby museum, we return to our car.

As in Jaipur not so long ago, we have a bit of a situation as we approach the vehicle. A number of homeless women, clutching tiny children, begin to follow us, begging for food. Reaching our car, they stand, looking at us indignantly, knocking at the windows. Despite Manish's disapproval, their pleading becomes too much for me. I have a bottle of water and some nuts in my backpack. Grabbing them, I thrust them at the nearest women, unable to look her in the eye – it feels so little, and I am thankful when we can finally drive away.

CHAPTER 38

Life Near the Ganges

Thankfully, when we return to the hotel our room is ready, and my hot, cleansing shower is one of the most welcome and satisfying I have ever had. Knowing we will be heading out again that evening, much of the day is spent relaxing – though we do call into the hotel café for a samosa and coffee. At five, Manish returns, and little do we realise, but he is about to give us one of the most incredible experiences of our lives.

'Every evening in Varanasi,' he explains as we climb into a car, 'a Hindu ritual is held on the banks of the Ganges River. It is called the Aarti ceremony, and it is a devotional offering of fire, light and prayer – to the river.'

'An offering to the river?' I ask.

'Yes,' Manish replies. 'Ganga is considered a goddess in Hinduism.'

'How long does it last?' Darryl asks.

'It lasts for forty-five minutes, but to secure a good position, one needs to be there one-and-a-half to two hours beforehand. If we leave now, we will have time to walk through the old town area and along the Ganges, where we will pass several *ghats*.'

Like many cities, Varanasi has two distinct areas: the Old City, located on the western bank of the Ganges, and the New City, which sprawls beyond. Our driver leaves us shortly after we enter the older district. Exiting the car, we find ourselves in a dense maze of dirty, narrow alleys. Knotted powerlines, like tangled balls of wool, swing overhead, while the walls of ancient buildings rise high on either side – some crumbing with age. Terrified we may lose Manish in the crowded, twisting streets, we stick close behind, constantly dodging motorbikes, cows and hand-pulled carts. As we edge closer to the river, tiny shops and stalls line the way, and the air is filled with the scent of incense, spices and, occasionally, cow dung.

'This is incredible,' I eventually say to Darry, struggling to make myself heard over the constant honking of scooters, ringing of temple bells, and the calls of shopkeepers urging us to buy. 'It's what I imagined India to be, really. Chaotic. Crowded. Crazy.'

'Don't forget loud,' Darryl adds. "And how old is this place? How many years has this been like this?'

'Varanasi Old Town is over three thousand years old,' Manish replies. 'It is one of the oldest continuously inhabited cities in the world. It has been a centre for religion and trade for thousands of years. Pilgrims, traders and residents have kept it crowded for centuries – and these days, tourists make it even more so.'

Eventually, one of the tight lanes we are following leads us to the water's edge, and here we pause. While it was an exciting moment this morning to glimpse the Ganges for the first time, now we are actually standing on its bank. The river is much wider than I expected, its opposing, crowded sandy shore visible in the far distance.

'The water levels are low at the moment,' Manish tells us. 'That's why you can see the far shore so clearly. Come the monsoon, this will be a raging body of water.'

Along with people swimming or cleansing themselves in the coffee-coloured liquid, many vessels line the Ganges' edge. Mostly wooden rowing or motorised boats, they are there to ferry tourists – or serve as floating seating for tonight's Aarti performance.

'I was told to find you a boat for tonight's show,' Manish says as we begin walking again. 'But they become very crowded and very uncomfortable. I have a better place – above the crowds, where you will be able to see much more. Maybe even have something to drink or eat.'

'That sounds fine with me,' I reply. 'We have an early-morning boat ride organised for tomorrow, anyway.'

'And I'm not sure I would be comfortable sitting on one for so long, watching a performance,' Darryl adds.

It takes around forty minutes to make our way along the crowded foreshore to the rooftop perch Manish has in mind – a chaotic, fascinating stretch of time, passing kids playing cricket and holy men praying, alongside wandering goats and vendors selling incense. Past several *ghats* where people are bathing, and through crowds of young girls with their faces painted blue.

'They paint themselves blue to represent the goddess Shiva,' Manish explains.

Edging closer to our destination, the raised platforms where tonight's performance will be held, the crowds swell, the incense thickens, and the sound of ringing bells intensifies. Just when we start to worry about losing Manish in the heaving, sweating crowd, he turns and begins leading us up a number of narrow, twisting stairwells. After what feels like an age, we finally emerge at a tiny café, on whose rooftop chairs have been placed. Settling down with a cool bottle of water and taking in the vista below, I know we couldn't be in a better position. Containing tens of thousands of people spilling from land to water, billowing smoke from burning ghee lamps, and millions of marigolds strewn across rectangular beds – it is a vision we will never forget. More so, when, just after sunset, priests in saffron robes appear and begin synchronised rituals with brass lamps, the sound of conch shells fill the air, and the chanting of mantras (repetitive sacred phrases) begins.

'Don't lose Manish now.'

It is hours later, after ten. The incredible, mesmerising spectacle is over and, along with fifty thousand or more other bodies, we are surging the Old Town streets, heading for our car. Merchants block our way, still pressing for business, eateries are full, and beggars are plentiful. One man, dragging himself on his stomach along the filthy Varanasi street, is particularly moving to see.

'No fear,' Darryl replies. 'I'm looking forward to bed. It's been a big day.'

'And it's another 4am wake-up tomorrow,' I remind him.

If we didn't have such an anticipated venture planned for this morning, I would be cursing yet another of these crazy early starts. It is 4.45am, and we are back in Varanasi Old Town. Yesterday, we walked the banks of the Ganges, heading north. This morning, we are approaching it from the opposite direction – our objective: to secure a boat on which we will greet the yet-to-awaken sun.

Already, at this darkened hour, pilgrims are cleansing themselves in the Ganges waters, kids are splashing happily, and others are enjoying a morning dip. *Sadhus* (holy men) sit near the lapping edge, chanting softly. Dogs roam and distant temple bells sound now and then. Unlike yesterday, this morning feels steady and calm – the city yet to fully awaken.

'Notice the buildings lining the bank,' Manish says partway into our walk, gesturing towards a long row of mostly sandstone structures, many with large terraces overlooking the river. 'These are *mahals* or *havelis* – palaces, built hundreds of years ago for kings, nobles and wealthy merchants. And notice that mark way up there? That's the level the water will reach when the river starts to rise.'

'But that means this entire area will all be underwater,' Darryl frowns. 'The water gets that high?'

'Yes. When the monsoon hits, many of the walkways and *ghats* will flood – but they've been designed to handle it. During this time, boating is often suspended, so it is fortunate you are here now. Next month, you may not have been able to take a ride on the Ganges.'

Typical of India, there is no convenient pontoon or jetty to access the vessel Manish eventually finds us. Instead, we have to clamber over numerous others to reach it – something Darryl finds nearly impossible. The boat is old, with flaking paint, a smoking engine and an unsmiling skipper, but it floats – and, over the next half hour, it takes us on an unforgettable ride.

Zigzagging our way along the Ganges, we see camels strolling the far bank, people releasing small floating offerings, and others washing their teeth in the river. Children swim, other boats pass by, and gulls wheel overhead. Just as the sun rises, a light shower of rain falls, but it is not enough to dampen our enjoyment. Passing some *ghats* where open fires are burning and people are tossing large lumps into the flowing water, Manish explains.

'These are the cremation *ghats* – Manikarnika and Harishchandra. This is where bodies are brought to be burnt. What's being thrown into the river are the parts that didn't burn.'

'Does everyone get cremated these days, or do they still put whole bodies into the water here?' I ask.

'Most get cremated,' Manish replies. 'But certain people – *sadhus*, pregnant women, children, and those who die from snake bite – are wrapped in cloth and set afloat instead.'

Our ride ends at Manikarnika and, stepping onto the steep stone steps that lead to higher ground, we note the smoke-blackened buildings, the multiple pyres and ash-covered ground.

'Manikarnika Ghat is one of the oldest and most sacred *ghats* in Varanasi,' Manish tells us as we walk past family members mourning or preparing their loved ones for the flames. 'And it never stops burning.'

With the smell of smouldering wood thick in the air and bodies continually arriving by bamboo stretcher, we don't linger. Instead, we head back into the Old Town maze. Being much closer to the cremation sites, the streets here are even filthier and busier than yesterday's. Many times, we have to stop and press ourselves against a wall as people wielding cartloads of wood or wandering cows pass us by. Proceeded by mourners and carried on the shoulders of family members, we always know when to move aside for a passing body.

'Would you like to stop for a chai?'

Although the hundreds of tiny shops that line the narrow lanes here are not yet open, the food and chai stalls are busy at this time of day. Sitting on tiny stools in the open, incense-scented air, holding paper cups filled with hot black tea, surrounded by dirt, noise and crowds, I cannot help marvelling at where we are.

This time next week, we will be home in Australia. Life will completely change for us. But for Manish, like the hundreds before him, and the many who will follow, it will continue on just the same.

CHAPTER 39

Back in Delhi

'Look how young those boys are. The littlest doesn't look more than a year old.'

It is early afternoon, and we are waiting at Varanasi Train Station. Amidst the usual press of bodies, bags and belongings, I have just noticed three tiny, bedraggled children, all under five, wandering around together.

'There's no adult with them,' I continue. 'Look. Someone has just bought them a bottle of lemonade.'

Startled to see such young kids fending for themselves in this overwhelming environment, we continue to watch as they squat together on the dirty platform floor, taking turns to drink from the bottle.

'Look how the older two make sure the youngest gets his fair share,' Darryl observes.

'They're making sure he gets even more,' I reply. 'Not the usual behaviour you see with kids.'

We continue to watch the trio until our train arrives, knowing the image of them will likely stay with us forever.

This one, the Varanasi to Delhi Express, is our final train journey in India and turns out to be our easiest. It takes eight hours and I spend most of it sitting comfortably in my air-conditioned chair class seat, reading my book. Every now and then, I set it aside in favour of the passing scenery – fields of crops, kids playing cricket, glimpses of the Ganges, even a peacock. And at dinner time, an attendant delivers steaming cartons of rice and tofu – a nice surprise.

Just like our initial arrival to this sprawling city, it is late when our train pulls into Delhi Station – well after eleven. Our fears that our pick-up vehicle may not be waiting are quickly put to rest when a knock at our compartment window reveals a smiling face. Our familiar driver has somehow found us before we have even stepped off the train.

This time, the sight of bodies sleeping on pavements, footpaths and roadsides does not concern us as much as we make the short journey back to the Metropolitan Hotel – either we are too tired to dwell or we are already growing immune.

Entering our room, we immediately fall into bed, exhausted after another long, extraordinary day.

Our last day in India, the final chapter of this huge, amazing adventure, finds us, in the early morning, sitting in the Metropolitan Hotel's familiar breakfast room. Drinking what has become my staple morning drink, a mango lassi, and eating one final *masala dosa*, we run through what's been planned for the day.

'I mentioned to Sandhi before we left Delhi last week that I wanted to get some clothes made. So that's first on the agenda.'

'Clothes made?' Darryl replies looking a bit startled.

'Yes. Like I did in Vietnam. It's possible to get measured up this morning and have the items delivered to your hotel that night. I'm after a few linen pants and tops.'

'Sounds great,' Darryl replies, unenthusiastically. 'Shopping. Then what?'

'There are a few more places Sandhi wants to show us,' I laugh. 'And they don't involve shops.'

It is good to meet up with Sandhi again, and the forty-minute drive to the emporium, where my clothes will be made, passes quickly. Initially, the conversation revolves around our impressions of his country and the places we have visited since we last spoke.

'You were right to have us skip the fort here in Delhi – we've seen several since… Seeing the Taj Mahal at sunrise was pretty special… We came to the conclusion that searching for tigers is really hard work… The trains were great, even the overnighter to Varanasi… It's hard to name a favourite place – probably Varanasi.'

Once that topic is exhausted, the conversation shifts to health and feminism.

'Have you heard of Ayurveda?' Sandhi asks, when the subject of my breast cancer diagnosis comes up. 'It's India's ancient system of natural medicine, focusing on maintaining balance between the body, mind and spirit. It uses diet, herbs, massage, detox and yoga to promote health. It is widely supported by the government here in India. One of the places we will visit today sells Ayurveda products.'

'I have heard of it,' I reply. 'And after travelling throughout your country, it's something I'll look into more when we get home.'

Feminism comes into the conversation when, edging closer to our destination, a rickshaw driven by a woman passes us. Noting the surprised look on our faces, Sandhi explains.

'Earlier this year, Delhi launched an all-women fleet of rickshaw drivers. Not only is this empowering women, but many people are saying they feel much safer with a female driver.'

With the fast production of clothing so popular here, the process moves swiftly once we arrive at our first destination. I explain what I want to the onsite tailors, have my measurements taken, and chose some suitable fabrics. I have brought examples of what I want made, which makes everything even easier. Departing the outlet with promises that the items will be delivered before ten this evening, I can only trust that all will be well. Our plane home leaves at nine tomorrow morning – I don't really have a back-up option.

It doesn't take long to reach the two places Sandhi is keen for us to visit. Driving to them, we are once again reminded of the skill of Indian drivers. Delhi alone contains nearly ten per cent of the total vehicles in all of Australia, and this becomes clear as we traverse the ridiculously congested roads. With so many vehicles competing for such limited space, road rules as we know them are useless. Here, it is every man for himself.

'But they do it in such a polite and structured manner,' comments Darryl when I point this out. 'If they drove like this in Australia, it wouldn't work – we'd be hurtling abuse at them. But here, it does.'

'Here,' Sandhi laughs, 'if you cut in front of me, causing me to break, that's okay. Because, sometime soon, I will cut in front of someone else, and they will have to break. It's give and take here.'

Completely understanding Sandhi's summary, it is not long before we arrive at a large grassy parkland where, in the centre, stands a building shaped like a giant white lotus flower.

'Lotus Temple,' Sandhi tells us. 'We won't go in, but I wanted to show you – I thought you would find it interesting.'

'It looks incredible,' I reply. And with its unusual shape, glowing white marble facade and glimmering pooled gardens, it really does. 'It reminds me of the Sydney Opera House.'

'It is one of the most visited buildings in the world,' Sandhi continues. 'But what's especially unusual is that it follows the Baha'i faith. This means it is open to all religions – no one belief system dominates. Any holy book can be read here.'

Never having heard of a religion so tolerant of other beliefs, the Baha'i faith and Lotus Temple definitely arouse our curiosity. But with the temperature climbing into the high thirties, it is too hot to stand discussing religion for long.

'Our final stop in Delhi,' Sandhi tells us a short while later.

Unlike our arrival at the Lotus Temple, this next stop is at one of the largest car parks I have ever seen. After exiting our vehicle, it takes a good fifteen-minute walk to reach and enter the site through high-security gates.

'The BAPS Swaminarayan Akshardham Temple,' Sandhi continues. 'One of the largest Hindu temples in the world.'

On either side of us, decorative pillars stretch out into beautifully landscaped gardens. In front of us stands a massive sandstone structure, warm pink and creamy white in colour, with every inch of its facade covered in hand-carved motifs. Its domes and spires reach skyward. It looks ethereal. Ancient.

'The work involved in creating this,' Darryl exclaims. 'Look at all the carvings.'

'Every one of those carvings was done by hand,' Sandhi replies, 'and each tells a story from ancient Indian scripture and mythology. But what surprises most visitors is that this temple was built in 2005.'

'It's only nineteen years old,' I exclaim. 'It looks centuries older.'

Having visited many mosques, churches and temples on this journey, we keep our tour brief. Instead, we spend most of our time in the accompanying vegetarian food court drinking masala chai, then visiting the gift shop. Here, Sandhi points out the Ayurveda products he had mentioned earlier. Full of natural ingredients and a fraction of what I would pay in Australia, I am in absolute shopping heaven and leave with several items.

'Some of them are presents,' I explain to Darryl, noting his raised eyebrows. 'And the prices! These cost only a dollar each.'

'Probably lucky this is our last stop,' he replies dryly.

And it is our very last stop. Mid-afternoon, we farewell Sandhi, thanking him profusely for making our visits to Delhi so enjoyable and insightful. Late that evening, my new linen shirt, shorts and trousers are delivered to our room.

'Apart from the amount of starch and the way they have been ironed, they are perfect,' I crow to Darryl. ' Exactly what I was after.'

'Along with your bags, leather jacket, face creams – oh, and the menagerie – I'm surprised they will all fit it in your suitcase,' he replies.

'They probably won't,' I grin. 'That's why I've been dragging that fold-out bag along with me.'

CHAPTER 40

Homeward Bound

It appears India has not finished with our early-morning starts – today, our final day in the country, is another 4am unwelcome wake-up. Our driver is waiting, and as we make our way to Delhi's international airport, we notice that even at this hour, the city's heat and pollution haze are already present. Still, there is far less traffic, and what would normally be a ninety-minute journey takes just twenty-five.

With plenty of time before our flight, we check in our bags, collect our boarding passes and browse the duty-free, searching for gifts for family. Like airports everywhere, each duty-free reflects its country. Switzerland has lots of chocolate, Australia features sheep-fleece goods, and Britain sells plenty of royal paraphernalia. India, we discover, offers sweets – especially *soan papdi*, a light, flaky biscuit from gram flour, ghee and sugar.

As we still have ample time, we head to a café and, taking the first sip of my coffee, my phone rings. It is airport security – they would like to know where I am. Slightly concerned, I give them our location, after which they tell me to stay put.

'Someone will come and get you.'

Now more than slightly concerned, I quickly farewell Darryl, climb aboard a golf buggy, and – escorted by a female guard – am driven deep into the innards of the airport to an office. Here, my passport is taken, and I am told to wait. If it were not so worrisome, it would actually be quite interesting watching airport operations from the other side.

'I had to remove the portable power-bank from my luggage. Even though it has never been a problem before, Singapore Airlines does not allow them in checked baggage.'

It is twenty minutes later and I have rejoined Darryl to drink what is left of my now-cold coffee.

'I wasn't the only one – a few of us had to remove items. It was pretty scary at first, not knowing why I was being taken away.'

'It was pretty scary sitting here, wondering if you were coming back,' Darryl replies.

'Just another lesson learnt on this adventure,' I laugh.

It takes two flights to return home to Australia. And on each of them, between the meals, the dozing and the movies, my thoughts drift back through all the places we have seen, the people we have met and all the other lessons learnt along the way. Each shaping our adventure – shaping us – step by step, choice by choice.

There were lessons in resilience, reminders not to let health issues hold us back, and in adaptability – staying open to shifting plans when needed, as we did in response to the Middle East conflict and the Corinth Canal tide.

We gained environmental awareness. Hearing that lychees in Mauritius now take two months longer to grow, seeing thick Sahara dust coat parts of Greece, and driving through a region in Namibia that has not seen rain for nine years made climate change feel real.

We were taught to honour local customs and respect cultural differences – whether it was removing our shoes at the Hassan II Mosque in Casablanca, or accepting the gift of my *kalawa* in Mauritius. We learnt to embrace new experiences: me, being hypnotised; Darryl, hopping into a rickshaw in Delhi. And not to be surprised when our preconceptions are challenged – like when we discovered how technologically advanced even hawkers in India can be.

Whether in Mauritius or Morocco, Durban or Delhi, we saw the sharp edges of poverty and were reminded that global inequality should not be forgotten. And we learnt that simple moments are often the most meaningful – a walk from Loutraki to Corinth, or eating muesli under the stars, can be just as memorable as visiting ancient ruins or iconic landmarks.

Then there were the history lessons – woven through nearly every stop we made. At Delphi, once considered the centre of the ancient world, we walked the same paths as those who once sought wisdom from the Oracle of Apollo. In ancient cities like Ephesus, and at Aşikli Höyük, a place inhabited more than ten thousand years ago, we were struck by the scale and depth of what had come before. With each place, our knowledge, appreciation and respect for the past deepened immeasurably. Civilisation is older and wiser than I ever thought.

But perhaps the most valuable insights and instruction came from our encounters with people – those who made our journey meaningful. Despite the odd pickpocket warning, most of those we met were kind and generous. I will never forget Felize ducking into an Istanbul pharmacy to buy me travel bicarbonate of soda, or Sandhi, in Delhi, gently suggesting that we visit Gandhi's memorial instead of yet another historic building. Or that waiter in Nafplio who went out of his way to help us find our accommodation.

Thinking about people, I am reminded of an observation I made back in Durban – that I had once viewed the world as simply Eastern and Western, but Africa revealed another compartment. I did not find a fourth, but I will not be surprised if one comes along with future travel.

As the plane touches down in Brisbane, I turn to Darryl.

'I've been getting all deep and meaningful about what this trip has taught me... us. Resilience. Education. Compassion. That travel is less about ticking off Bucket List items and more about what you learn along the way. But what did you take from it?'

'Me?' he replies, sounding slightly startled. 'Well... apart from making sure you have access to Google – good internet – I think there is a lesson I've learnt from this journey. From travelling through all these countries. An important one.'

'Yes?' I ask, curious to hear what he has discovered that I have not already mentioned.

'That it was really all just one big shopping trip.'

AUTHOR'S NOTE

I write my adventure books with two goals in mind: to share my experiences—and to help you learn from them.

Whether it is glimpsing the ancient wonder of Petra, rattling across Mongolia on the Trans-Siberian Express, standing in silence beside the sacred Ganges in Varanasi, feeling alone while crossing the Atlantic, or navigating life after a double mastectomy—these moments shape the journey I share with you.

If you take away even one insight, one spark of inspiration or understanding, then I have succeeded. But I hope you take away many.

To learn more or follow along, visit:

⚲ https://linktr.ee/emmascattergood
🌐 http://darmatravels.com

Emma Scattergood
July 2025.

PREVIOUS BOOKS BY EMMA SCATTERGOOD

Bucket Lists & Walking Sticks: An Unexpected Adventure

A terrible accident. Forced retirement.
An excuse to pull out the bucket list!

After a motorbike accident leaves her husband with life-changing injuries, author Emma organises a worldwide adventure based on the contents of an old, laminated bucket list. It will be the journey of a lifetime—seeking health and ticking off list items: from viewing ancient Petra and treading Greece's Parthenon to traversing the Suez Canal and hunting down Doc Martin.

Taking seven months and spanning Asia and Europe, this journal, told in mouth-watering and humorous detail, will pull you headlong into the sights, life, culture and beauty of each place visited. It will make you want to follow in their footsteps.

EMMA SCATTERGOOD

Itchy Feet and Bucket Lists: A Global Adventure

I've pulled the bucket list back out.
Amongst what's left are the Trans-Siberian Express,
the Terracotta Army, the Swiss Alps and the Panama Canal.

Easy words spoken—catalyst for an unforgettable adventure across the steppes of Mongolia, the wilderness of Siberia, and Putin's Russia. Through Europe during winter and over the lonely Atlantic and Pacific Oceans.

Commencing in October 2019 and undertaken by author Emma and husband Darryl, the journey delivers lessons on a developing pandemic, Google Translate, food poisoning and train accidents. Throw in some goals, like having a rum in Barbados, a coffee in Guatemala, and guacamole in Mexico, and it might just be the cure for their (or your) itchy feet.

NEXT CHAPTER TRAVEL

My Breast Cancer Adventure: Or What Can Happen Following a Breast Cancer Diagnosis

A journey does not always involve travel.
So discovered adventurer Emma Scattergood.

In 2022, Emma was diagnosed with stage 3 invasive lobular breast cancer. Unsure what it really meant, she channelled her energy into understanding and fighting this increasingly common disease—and soon realised it was another journey worth sharing.

This insightful and often entertaining book is the result: an 18-month roller-coaster through diagnosis, double mastectomy, chemotherapy, radiation and hormone therapy. A deeply personal experience that also explores integrative approaches, infections, supplements, diet, exercise and more.

Told with honesty, humour and compassion, Emma aims to:

- Shine a light on how breast cancer is detected—and what can happen next.
- Offer guidance and reassurance to the newly diagnosed.
- Provide insight for those who have never faced it.

To broaden the picture, Emma includes stories from eleven other women—each with their own unique path and perspective on survival.

ABOUT THE AUTHOR

Emma Scattergood is the author of several adventure memoirs and the voice behind darmatravels.com. A cancer survivor, she writes candidly about the unpredictability of both travel and life, blending honesty, resilience, and humour. When not on the road, she enjoys playing lawn bowls and planning her next journey.

www.ingramcontent.com/pod-product-compliance
Lightning Source LLC
Chambersburg PA
CBHW022040290426
44109CB00014B/925